DERBYSHIRE
Unusual & Quirky

Andrew Beardmore

HALSGROVE

First published in Great Britain in 2014
Reprinted 2017
Copyright © Andrew Beardmore 2014

British Library Cataloguing-in-Publication Data
A CIP record for this title is available from the British Library

ISBN 978 0 85704 237 8

HALSGROVE
Halsgrove House,
Ryelands Business Park,
Bagley Road, Wellington, Somerset TA21 9PZ
Tel: 01823 653777 Fax: 01823 216796
email: sales@halsgrove.com
website: www.halsgrove.com

Printed and bound in India by Parksons Graphics

Derbyshire – Unusual and Quirky

Welcome to *Derbyshire – Unusual and Quirky*, a book that calls to mind that classic series of travel books called *The King's England*, written in the 1930s by Stapleford-born Arthur Mee, since each volume in Mee's series was suffixed with *"There have been many books on <insert county>, but never one like this…"* Well the very same tag line could be applied to this book, as some of its elements are certainly unique. Having said that, the book still has plenty to offer in terms of conventional reference, but it delivers this in a lateral and humorous format never seen before.

Essentially, then, the book is comprised of two main sections which are called *Conventional Derbyshire* and *Quirky Derbyshire*. The *Conventional Derbyshire* section is immediately preceded by county maps along with key facts and figures relating to the county – such as county town, population, highest point, key industries and famous sons and daughters. The facts are then followed by a history of the Derbyshire *area* from Stone Age Britain to 11th century Norman Britain – by which time Derbyshire, along with most of England's counties had been officially formed – after which the last one thousand years of county history is covered, bringing us up-to-date and into the 21st century. Nevertheless, in keeping with the title of the book, *Conventional Derbyshire* also has a number of small, but appropriately historical "Quirk Alerts" interspersed, too; like an anecdote called "Splat-Nav" showing up in the 13th century chapter, all the way up to 21st century nods towards *I'm A Celebrity* and Muggles!

So, thus far into the book we have covered the facts, figures, maps and history of Derbyshire. However, it is at this point that the *Conventional* section ends and the *Quirky* section begins…and it is here that we realistically begin to earn the *"…but never one like this…"* tag line. For although the *Quirky Derbyshire* section delivers some "seen it before" place-name origins and historic trivia, it does so via several twists. For starters, it doesn't cover place-name etymology like most traditional reference books do, and it certainly doesn't focus on the more well-known county places, either – although don't assume they'll all be missed out; that rather depends, as we'll see shortly.

As for the reason for this apparent "stick a pin in a map" approach, this is because the history and trivia snippets in this section of the book are driven by a quirky poem, called a Shire-Ode. Told in rhyming verse, the Shire-Ode portrays the eccentric nature of imaginary inhabitants of Derbyshire. But as an extra twist, the poem contains dozens of place-names found within the historic county, each subtly (and some not so subtly) woven into the tale – and it is these place-names upon which the *Quirky Derbyshire* section focuses. Firstly, the places have their location pin-pointed via

two maps: one which outlines the modern ceremonial county of Derbyshire and the other the historic county. A series of chapters then follow in (largely) alphabetical order for each place featured in the Shire-Ode – and it is here that the strangest and most interesting facts and features about each place are explored, with facts including place-name status, population, earliest recording, place-name derivation, and famous sons and daughters, and feature topics ranging from both straight and unusual history to some quite bizarre happenings…plus a lot more in between, too! As a result, you get a random almanac of places that would never ordinarily appear together – along with photographs taken to prove that these bizarrely-named places really do exist!

So, feel free to commence your obscure Derbyshire fact-digging; to read about some very famous people and their Derbyshire exploits, to read about ancient battles and, quite frankly, some ridiculous legends, too…but to hopefully have a little chuckle along the way. For example, find out which Derbyshire village commemorates a soldier who served during both Culloden (1746) and Trafalgar (1805), which one runs a Grand National at over 1,000 feet and which one can justifiably claim to be Derbyshire's Gretna Green. Or discover who lives in a place called The Gutter, which village was named after bare knuckle fist-fighting, or which place-name means "wood frequented by wolves". Learn in which village a famous wag claimed that *"Every man was his own architect,"* or from which Derbyshire village you can see *eight* other counties. Then there's another Derbyshire village that saw the establishment of the first ever king of England, another whose mill doubled as television's Colditz Castle and another which breeds Harry Potter's owls. Or if it's bizarre that you want, find out which village contains an award-winning urinal, which town is home to the World Head Balancing Champion and which village is home to both The Gremlins and Naked Racing.

Alternatively, check out the quirky Shire-Ode, called *Brad and Mel*, that drives the idiosyncratic *Quirky Derbyshire* section and learn how Mel becomes a cook of national repute, but poor Brad becomes a recluse, devoted to his trees whilst becoming increasingly afflicted by the need to include Derbyshire place-names in his every-day speech! And if you'd like to hear *Brad And Mel* in song format, as recently heard on BBC Radio Derby, then go to this website ->

www.andybeardmore.com

Anyway, that's the introduction completed. As you have probably gathered by now, this book is indeed "unusual and quirky"… so it's time to prime the quirkometer and pull up a pew at St Strangeways – oh, and did I mention crinkle-crankle walls, Britain's most haunted pub, a woman who lived in a bacon box…

Contents

Derbyshire Facts and Figures

County Status:	Ceremonial county and (smaller) non-metropolitan county (i.e. minus Derby)
County Town:	Pre-1958: Derby
	Post-1958: Matlock
County Pop'n:	1,010,600
County Pop'n. Rank:	19th out of 48
Cities:	Derby
Largest City:	Derby
City Pop'n:	229,407
City Pop'n Rank:	19th English; 22nd UK
City Status:	Unitary Authority
National Park:	Peak District
Other Areas:	Pennine Way, Derbyshire Dales, National Forest
County Area:	2,625km²/1,014 sq. miles
County Area Rank:	21st out of 48
Highest Point:	Kinder Scout (637m/2,087ft)
Largest Lake:	Ladybower Res. (200.4 ha)
Highest Lake:	Lightwood Res. (363m,1190ft)
Longest River:	Derwent (106km/66 miles)
Football Clubs:	Derby County (Championship), Chesterfield (League 2), Alfreton Town (Conference), Buxton, Matlock Town, Ilkeston Town (Northern Premier League)
Rugby Union:	Derby RFC, Matlock RFC, Ilkeston RUFC (All Midlands 1 East)
Industries (Present):	Aero-engine, Agriculture, Banking, Bottled Water, Car Manufacturing, Chocolate, Engineering, Internet Banking, Quarrying, Railway, Retail, Services
Industries (Past):	Boiler, Coal, Iron, Lead, Machine Tool, Millstone, Textile, Wool
Famous People:	**CHS:** Vivienne Westwood *(born in the Tintwistle part of today's north-west Derbyshire which until 1974 was part of Cheshire);* **DER:** William Abney, Alan Bates, Catherine Booth, James Brindley, Tim Brooke-Taylor, Sir John Chandos, Sir Francis Chantrey, John Clifford, Lloyd Cole, Thomas Cook, Sir John Coke, Ross Davenport, Fred Davis, Joe Davis, Sir Anthony Fitzherbert, John Flamsteed, Thomas Greatorex, Henry Garnet, Judith Hann, Elizabeth Hardwick, Alison Hargreaves, John Hobson, Geoff Hoon, William Howitt, John Hurt, William Hutton, Arthur Keily, Donna Kellogg, Judy Leden, Thomas Linacre, Robert Lindsay, Arthur Lowe, John Lowe, Ellen MacArthur, William Newton, Jack O'Connell, Benjamin Outram, Sir James Outram, John Powys, Theodore Powys, Samuel Richardson, William Roache, Richard Roberts, Robert Robinson, Anna Seward, George Simpson, Dennis Skinner, George Sorocold, Herbert Spencer, Elizabeth Spriggs, Constance Spry, Robert Stevenson, Jedediah Strutt, Gwen Taylor, Dave Lee Travis, George Turner, Alison Uttley, Barnes Wallis, John Wetton, Joseph Wright, Kelli Young

Derbyshire Maps

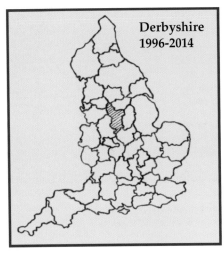

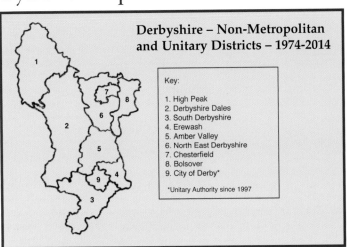

Conventional Derbyshire

Prehistory

The county of Derbyshire dates from the 11th century, and was formed towards the end of the protracted conflict between Anglo-Saxon and Viking that took place between the 9th and 11th centuries. The town of Derby, however, is much older than the shire it lends its name to, and dates from Roman times when the camp of *Derventio* was established there. But we'll come to that shortly, for the history of the *area* of Derbyshire, goes back much further than that.

It is thought that permanent occupation of Derbyshire occurred sometime during the Upper Palaeolithic period (c.40,000-10,000 BC) when hunter gatherers roamed the hilly tundra. The most startling evidence of occupation can be found at Creswell Crags, a limestone gorge on Derbyshire's north-eastern border with Nottinghamshire and close to the village of Creswell. The cliffs of the ravine contain several caves in which flint tools have been found from a number of different cultures and which therefore suggest the caves were seasonally occupied throughout the Upper Palaeolithic period as well as the Mesolithic (c.10,000-4,500 BC) and Neolithic (c.4,500-2,000 BC) periods, too. Other specific items found at Creswell Crags during excavations in the 1870s include a bone engraved with a horse's head which was found at Robin Hood Cave in 1876, a human figure engraved on a rib bone which was found at Pin Hole Cave, plus other worked bone items. These excavations, plus further excavations in the 1920s, also revealed the remains of a wide variety of prehistoric animals and other animals now extinct in Britain such as artic fox, bear, bison, hippopotamus, hyena, mammoth, reindeer, wild horse and woolly rhinoceros.

As for those engraved artefacts at Creswell, they were widely known throughout the 20th century as being the earliest known art in Britain. But then in 2003, these objects were surpassed when engravings and bas-reliefs were found on the walls and ceilings of some of the caves, and thus became Britain's first and, to date, only case of Stone Age *cave* art. The engravings were mostly found in the entrance chamber to the cave known as Church Hole and are comprised of around 90 representations of Ice Age animal such as bear, bird, bison, deer and horse. In terms of dating the artwork, scientists and archaeologists used the age of the thin layers of calcium carbonate flowstone that overlay some of the engravings to date them to somewhere between 13,000-15,000 years ago.

Of course, it wasn't just Creswell Crags that were occupied during the Stone Age; caves were also occu-pied at nearby Whitwell, plus at Lathkill Dale, Earl Sterndale, Sheldon Moor and in the Dove and Manifold valleys, too. Meanwhile excavations in 1922 at Harborough Rocks near to Brassington also turned up the animal bones of bison, hyena, red deer, reindeer, wild boar, wild horses and woolly rhinoceros, with the animals dating from the end of the last Ice Age. Harborough Rocks was also the site of a later Neolithic passage grave.

Further Derbyshire Neolithic evidence has been found in the form of pieces of pottery, flint arrowheads, polished stone axes, scrapers and knives, plus house floors, hearths and storage pits. In fact, one 1980s exca-vation of a Neolithic site (c.3500 BC) just west of Buxton provided the best-preserved evidence for timber-framed structures with central hearths so far discov-ered in early Neolithic Britain. And indeed the lion's share of Derbyshire's Neolithic evidence can be found nearby in the White Peak, the carboniferous limestone plateau that lies between the Rivers Dove and Derwent, and which therefore wasn't so thickly wooded and didn't require such arduous clearing. Hundreds of axe-

Creswell Crags in north-eastern Derbyshire, site of priceless ancient archaeological finds, plus the location of the only British Stone Age cave art.

These caves at Harborough Rocks in central Derbyshire were also occupied during the Palaeolithic period.

heads have been found across the area, plus human bones in caves and rock shelters at Dovedale, Dowel Dale, Hartle Dale, Lathkill Dale and Ravensdale. That said, other key axe finds have come from all other parts of the county, including at Cubley, Doveridge and Sudbury in the west, Belper and Duffield in the centre, Heanor and Sawley in the east, and at Derby, Etwall, Chellaston and Spondon in the south. Meanwhile, even further south in what would then have been the heavily-wooded middle Trent valley between Willington and Shardlow, evidence of scattered Neolithic dwellings and pottery pieces have been found, too.

It is likely that the Neolithic dwellers of Derbyshire were more farmers than hunter-gatherers, although this transition would have taken several generations to complete. These people also left much evidence in their area in the form of megalithic monuments and communal burial mounds or chambered barrows. The latter are fairly prevalent in Derbyshire, although all of them are confined to the White Peak area, plus they also tend to be suffixed with the place-name element "low", deriving from the Old English word *hlāw* meaning "tumulus, mound or hill". For example, Tideslow is a high point above Tideswell that includes the largest Neolithic *mound* in the Peak District, while the largest burial *ground* is to be found at Minning Low. Located at

an elevated point above today's High Peak Trail between Pikehall and Longcliffe, Minning Low was extended over time and eventually consisted of at least four chambers which were entered through low, stone-lined passages. Meanwhile, Green Low lies just to the north-east of Minning Low and its chamber is aligned with the rising sun at the winter solstice, while Ringham Low (just north of Lathkill Dale) consists of six chambers. The latter was also found to contain Neolithic bones, flints and pottery, as was the two-chambered burial site known as Five Wells that is situated at 1,400ft on Taddington Moor between Bakewell and Buxton and which is the highest in Britain.

Most of the burial mounds just discussed date throughout the Neolithic period, but the henges didn't appear until the late Neolithic/early Bronze Age periods. Derbyshire has numerous fine examples, none better than Arbor Low, which dates from around 2,500 BC and lies on a remote plateau 3 miles west of Youlgreave at an altitude of 1,225ft above sea level. Today, all of the stones lie on the ground, but they probably once stood upright with an inner and outer circle, and numbered around 40. The stones range from 5ft.3in to 6ft 10in tall while the monoliths at the circle's two entrances were between 8ft 6in to 9ft 6in high. Surrounding the stones is an oval earthen bank with an interior ditch that delivers a stunning profile when

The remote Minning Low Hill is the site of the largest Neolithic burial ground in Derbyshire.

Excavations of Minning Low in the 1970s revealed mounds of stone containing at least four burial chambers, such as the one above.

Quirk Alert: Classical Concession

Surrounding the summit of Minning Low are three concentric circles of stone wall, hedge and tree, while within are a dozen or more beeches along with the various stones that formed the Neolithic burial chambers. As you might expect of such an ancient place, Minning Low has a wonderful sense of peace, which is enhanced by its remoteness and by the wind whispering through the trees. It is also likely that Minning Low was more than just a Neolithic burial site and was also a focal point or seasonal gathering place for Stone Age tribes...and you can actually "feel" this when you sit there and contemplate. But if you want to check it out for yourself, don't put it off for too long. The place was inaccessible to the public for many years, but a concessionary path has been opened by the landowner to last exactly ten years between 31st January 2007 and 31st January 2017. However, if you can't make it in person, plug the keywords "youtube" and "minning low" into your search engine and enjoy the five minute video that results, accompanied by Gerald Finzi's Prelude Op.25. As someone comments: "one can feel the breath of Time" – although the surprise interlopers at the end sort of steal the show!

Arbor Low henge dates from c.2500 BC and sits at an altitude of 1,225ft on this remote plateau near Youlgreave. Today, all of the stones lie on the ground but were almost certainly once upright, forming an inner and outer circle.

The Nine Ladies stone circle on Stanton Moor, so-named as it was traditionally believed to depict nine ladies turned to stone for dancing on a Sunday.

viewed from above (see www.webaviation.co.uk for some fine examples). Across the fields to the south-west lies Gib Hill, a 16ft mound that started as a long barrow built of clay, but in the Bronze Age was converted into a round barrow. A similar arrangement in terms of size and design was built at the Bull Ring near Dove Holes, but none of the stones survive today.

The British Bronze Age is estimated to have fallen roughly between 2,100 and 700 BC, and the discovery of Bronze Age beakers and urns in the White Peak has been fairly common. Meanwhile over 500 round and unchambered Bronze Age round barrows have also been found – as well as Bronze Age re-use of Neolithic chambered barrows such as those at Bee Low (near Youlgreave) and Glebe Low (Great Longstone). Again, the lion's share of the round barrows are in the White Peak, but many more lie on the gritstone moors of the upper Derwent such as Crow Chin on Stanage Edge just north of Hathersage and Lord's Seat on Rushup Edge just south-west of Edale, while evidence of still more can be found in the Trent valley in the south of the county.

As for Derbyshire's numerous stone circles, most date from around 2,000 BC (i.e. Bronze Age rather than the Late Neolithic period) and range from 15 to 100 feet in diameter. Unlike the burial mounds, though, many are found in gritstone territory, like at Abney, Bamford Moor, Beeley Moor, the Eastern Moors, Eyam and Stanton Moor. The configurations differ across the county, but the most typical consists of a ring of upright stones, no more than two or three feet high, set in a circle on the inner edge of a bank, with one or sometimes two entrances and perhaps a single stone standing beyond.

The largest stone circle in the Peak District is at Wet Withens on Eyam Moor and consisted of 16 or 18 stones, of which 10 still remain…but you'll have a job corroborating that fact as firstly, the area is extremely remote being 500 metres from the nearest path or track, and secondly, it is largely overgrown with heather and tall grasses! Meanwhile, the most famous Derbyshire stone circle, is the Nine Ladies on Stanton Moor – a misnomer, in fact, as a *tenth* stone has been found since the site was originally named in the late 18th century, plus potentially an *eleventh* filling the remaining gap.

By the late Bronze Age, the building and usage of stone circles and burial chambers had fallen out of favour, and as Derbyshire entered the Iron Age (c.700 BC), extensive settlements and hill-forts began to appear. By around 300 BC, the move from bronze to iron tools was complete and Derbyshire evidence of iron-smelting from this period has been discovered on the Burbage Brook near Hathersage and elsewhere in northern Derbyshire. Recent excavations have also revealed large settlements along the middle Trent valley, while Derbyshire's Iron Age hill-forts range from small enclosures perhaps designed merely to protect stock, right up to the magnificent defensive fort built around Mam Tor in the High Peak. Mam Tor had in fact already been heavily populated during the Bronze Age, with more than one hundred platforms cut

Quirk Alert: A Fiddle and a Flute

The Nine Ladies stone circle is so-named as it was believed to represent nine ladies turned to stone for dancing on a Sunday…while 40 metres away is the solitary King Stone, deemed to be the ladies' fiddler! The site is yet another ancient Derbyshire place that is so atmospheric it simply has to be experienced first-hand. But once again, if you can't make it in person, why not this time listen to the song called 'Nine Ladies' at www.andybeardmore.com. It's a slight variation on the turning to stone theme, and I "tried" to make it suitably atmospheric – and hence the flute rather than a fiddle. Apologies in advance for the singing!

Mam Tor. The "Shivering Mountain" was home to an impressive Iron Age fort with ramparts encircling the entire hilltop.

Fin Cop in Monsal Dale was also the site of an Iron Age hillfort and was defined by a double rampart on its two accessible sides.

into the hillside, some of which supported circular houses. However, the ramparts that are clearly visible today are deemed to be of Iron Age origin. They consist of a single, stone-revetted rampart, with a ditch and counterscarp bank which follows the contours of the hill – although further landslips on the eastern side of the notorious "Shivering Mountain" have destroyed whatever defences were erected there. There are also two clearly defined entrances, with the main one to the south-west and a smaller one to the north-east. From above, you can clearly see where the ramparts double-back on themselves at these entrances to form narrow passages. Meanwhile, another Derbyshire Iron Age hillfort is Fin Cop, which is located 4 miles north-west of Bakewell and was defined by a double rampart on its two accessible sides. Then there is Castle Naze which is located on Combs Moss roughly halfway between Buxton and Chapel-en-le-Frith and which was much smaller and triangular with the one accessible side defended by a deep ditch and double ramparts. Other Iron Age finds that may have been either hill-forts or simply fortified homesteads include Castle Ring on Harthill Moor, Ball Cross between Chatsworth and Bakewell, and Burr Tor just north of Great Hucklow.

Romans, Anglo-Saxons and Vikings

By the time the Romans invaded Britain in AD 43, the southern half of Derbyshire was part of the Celtic *Corieltauvi* tribe that stretched from Lincolnshire down to all but the south-western slice of Warwickshire. It thus pretty much covered the complete area of the modern East Midlands region, the exception probably the north-western part of Derbyshire, which may have been aligned to the *Corieltauvi's* northern neighbours, the warlike *Brigantes*. Nevertheless, the Romans had defeated the *Corieltauvi* by AD 45 although they didn't actually settle in the area until after AD 60 – and it was around this time that they built their first fort at Derby. This timber and turf fort was built for 500 legionaries and was located on the west bank of the Derwent

around what is now the Belper Road area of north Derby. However, during the reign of Agricola (78-84), the fort was abandoned in favour of a new one, which became known as *Derventio*. This new fort was situated on the eastern side of the Derwent at the northern tip of modern-day Chester Green – with the name "Chester" deriving from the Old English word *ceaster*, meaning "Roman station or walled town". A civilian settlement, or *vicus*, also emerged to the east of the fort and which in later excavations yielded late first and early second century jars, bowls and dishes made from the local clay, known as Derbyshire Ware, and which had been fired in local Roman pottery kilns; the site of the kilns and a Roman cemetery are at today's north-western end of the Racecourse.

With *Derventio* established, the Romans soon stretched out into Derbyshire, attracted mainly by the prevalence of lead ore in the limestone hills, and this expansion took them towards the southern boundary of *Brigante* territory. Nevertheless, the Romans settled throughout northern Derbyshire with further forts built at Chesterfield, near Glossop in the north-west of the county and near Brough in the Hope Valley. The fort built at Brough was known as *Navio* in Roman times, its name deriving from the Celtic river *Nava* (modern River Noe) on which the fort sat. *Navio* became the second most significant Roman fort in the county due to its strategic importance as lead mining developed in the High Peak; the garrison of a few dozen men would have kept the miners on task and organised the transport of lead along the roads and over this crossing. *Navio's* garrison was moved on to assist with the building of Hadrian's Wall in the 120s, but the *vicus* that grew up around the fort expanded considerably in the 2nd and 3rd centuries. The fort was also reconstructed at various times throughout the Roman occupation, perhaps to quell local uprisings in order to protect the lead trade; it was therefore probably occupied until at least the mid-4th century. Meanwhile, the fort near Glossop was constructed on a spur of land overlooking the confluence of the River Etherow and the Glossop Brook, with the intention of guarding the road from *Navio* to *Mamuciam* (modern-day Manchester and yet another important *ceaster*). The Glossop fort may have been named *Ardotalia* by the Romans, but has been known as Melandra Castle since the 18th century. Its remains are protected under the Ancient Monuments Act 1913-1953, and its foundations form a perfect square when viewed from above. As for the Derbyshire *ceasters* of Little Chester and Chesterfield, it is thought that they were linked by the Roman road, Ryknield Street, which ran from St David's in Pembrokeshire all the way up to York.

Derbyshire's other key Roman site was at Buxton, which was already famed for its warm thermal springs and medicinal properties before they arrived. The Romans named the place as *Aquae Arnemetiae* which means "the spa of the goddess of the grove", named after the Celtic goddess *Arnemetiae*, and the settlement grew into a spa centre that was second in Roman Britain only to Bath (*Aquae Sulis*). Over the years, many coins dating from the 1st to the 4th centuries have been found, plus pottery, bracelets and even a Roman milestone denoting the distance from *Navio*. Conversely, one of the inscribed stones left by soldiers at *Navio* is dedicated to "*Arnementi*" suggesting that the Romans also adopted worship of the goddess, perhaps as a shrewd political move to keep the native Celts happy. Certainly, *Arnementi* would also have been worshipped by the locals at the surrounding *vicus* at *Navio*, as it lay at the confluence of the Bradwell Brook and the River Noe, and confluences were always places of veneration to the Celts. Interestingly, another inscribed stone from *Navio* is dedicated to Mars, the Roman god of war – suggesting that the men were seeking his aid perhaps during the aforementioned uprisings. This perhaps accounts for the archaeological evidence which suggests various re-buildings of the fort. One such re-building is hinted at on an inscription of governor

Initially constructed of wood in the 1st century, Navio was later rebuilt in stone. When viewed from the air, a perfect square is visible formed by Navio's foundations and some remaining stonework such as that shown above on the fort's eastern side.

Julius Verus which was later smashed and buried in debris around AD196. The strong-room in the centre of the fort was also rebuilt during the rule of Severus and by 343 this room was used to store a number of altar stones and 4th century coins – all of which were discovered during 20th century excavations.

As the Romans pushed further north into Scotland, Derbyshire's Roman forts were largely abandoned, with Little Chester the only exception, retaining a token garrison. Here, the fort and its *vicus* were occupied until the mid-4th century, although the site was abandoned long before the final Roman withdrawal from Britain in 410. As for the local Derbyshire population, they continued to be little affected by the Romans, and continued to farm and live in thatched round houses in the manner of their Iron Age ancestors, as is evidenced by excavations from the Trent valley in the south to the fertile soils of north-east Derbyshire. In between, a series of terraces at Chee Tor, Blackwell, provide some of England's most striking physical evidence of farming in Roman times. Meanwhile, along with farming evidence and hoards of Roman coins discovered at Chesterfield, Alfreton, Ripley and Shipley, the prevalence of lead mining in Derbyshire in Roman times has been discovered in the form of cast ingots bearing Roman inscriptions. The earliest stamped ingot dates from Hadrian's time (117-138), with 28 discovered in total and with 20 of them carrying the abbreviated stamp of *Lutudarum*, a place generally believed to be somewhere in the lead-rich Wirksworth region; recent opinion favours Carsington, where traces of a settlement and a modest villa were excavated in the 1980s. Furthermore, two unstamped ingots were found here dating to the late 4th century, suggesting that Briton-controlled lead mining and smelting continued *after* the Romans had departed. However, that said, the Roman departure had a severe effect on both Derbyshire and Britain's economy and it didn't return to similar levels again until the late Anglo-Scandinavian period.

But what of the Derbyshire area after the Romans departed in the early 5th century? This is a difficult question to answer, for once the literate Romans had departed the largely illiterate Britons were unable to record their own progress. What we do know, though, is that the country gradually became settled by the Angles and Saxons of northern Europe. They originally settled in Lincolnshire before pushing their way up the Trent valley into Nottinghamshire and Derbyshire, as evidenced by mid-6th century heathen burial sites found from Newark to Burton-on-Trent. They aren't thought to have settled in the Peak District area, though, until the mid-7th century. Meanwhile, throughout Britain, the Anglo-Saxon ruling class gradually replaced the weak and divided British. Also gradually replaced, were place-names, with only river-names and places deriving from river-names (like Clowne) retaining their Celtic origins, along with topographical features, particularly hills and tors; Derbyshire has 14 of the latter.

By the end of the 6th century, at least half of the Derbyshire area had become part of the Anglo-Saxon Kingdom of Mercia. The Kingdom was centred on the valley of the River Trent and its tributaries, and while it's earliest boundaries will never be known, there is general agreement that its territories covered much of Derbyshire, Leicestershire, Nottinghamshire, Staffordshire and northern Warwickshire. The most authentic source of information at this time was from the Northumbrian monk and scholar who became known as the Venerable Bede, and who describes Mercia as being divided in two by the River Trent. And whereas Tamworth was the acknowledged capital of Mercia for most of its lifetime, and certainly of South Mercia, it is likely that Derby (or Northworthy as it was then known) was the capital of North Mercia, having succeeded the long-abandoned Roman fort at Little Chester.

Over the next three centuries, Mercia fought numerous battles against its Anglo-Saxon neighbours. Its fortunes ebbed and flowed, emerging as a great power in the first half of the 7th century under King Penda, but then losing North Mercia to Northumbria after his death in 655. Mercia then recovered its northern territory again in the second half of the 7th century under Wulfhere before gaining even greater strength under Æthelred. Then for a time throughout the 8th century, Mercia became the dominant power of England south of the Humber, led by Æthelbald (716–757) and Offa (757-796). Alas by 825, Wessex had taken over the dominant mantle, and by the end of the 9th century, Mercia had lost its kingdom status completely with Mercia now ruled by ealdormen serving under the throne of Wessex.

Throughout this period, the Derbyshire town of Repton became the traditional royal burial place of the Mercian kings, including Æthelbald (757), Wiglaf (840) and Wystan (849). It is also likely that Repton was the early capital of South Mercia before it moved to Tamworth in the late 7th century. Repton was certainly the location of the Mercian royal family's conversion to Christianity in 653, when Peada, son of King Penda of Mercia, married the Christian daughter of King Oswy of Northumbria. At this time, the Mercians also invited four priests to join the kingdom as missionaries, with their leader, Diuma, based at Repton. Having converted to Christianity and begun imposing the religion upon their subjects, the Mercians then constructed a double abbey under an abbess. Alas for Derbyshire, the Bishop of Mercia and Lindsey moved his see from Repton to Lichfield in 669.

Today, the centre of Repton is dominated by the church of Saint Wystan, named after the Mercian prince who was murdered by his guardian in 849, but who was later sanctified as the patron saint of the church. Originally built in the 8th century, its even older Saxon crypt served as the aforementioned mausoleum for the Mercian royal family while also housing other notables such as Diuma, Mercia's first bishop. Small surprise,

therefore, that 20th century digs at Repton unearthed rare treasures including what became known as the Repton Stone which dates from around AD 757 and depicts a man riding a horse, carrying a shield and dagger. It is believed to be of King Æthelbald and is therefore the oldest known portrait of any English monarch. As for the 7th century Saxon crypt, it remains intact to this day, as does the later Anglo-Saxon chancel that rises above the crypt with its characteristically tall and narrow design.

Given its importance, it is therefore not surprising that Repton St Wystan became an important Derbyshire minster, or mother church – i.e. one which covered a large area in the days before parishes were introduced. Repton was therefore the minster for southern Derbyshire and its area was adjoined to the north by two minsters in Derby, these being St Alkmund's, and All Saints' church (now Derby Cathedral). The other Derbyshire minsters were St Oswald's at Ashbourne, St Mary's at Wirksworth and St Alkmund's at Duffield, while further north were All Saints' at Bakewell, St Mary and All Saints' at Chesterfield and St Peter's at Hope.

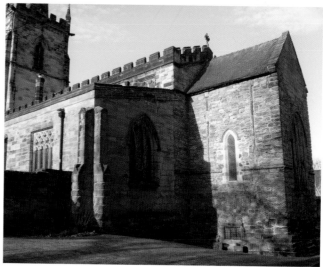

The Anglo-Saxon chancel at Repton St Wystan.

Quirk Alert: A Grave Discovery

Surviving Anglo-Saxon architecture is a rare thing in Britain as most structures built prior to 1066 were wooden. The main exceptions were churches and some elements survive today such as the aforementioned chancel and crypt at Repton. Built as a mausoleum for the Mercian royal family, the 8th century crypt was only discovered 1,000 years later in 1779 when one of the workmen who were digging a grave in the chancel floor, literally dropped in, head first. As for the Saxon crypt itself, it is arguably Britain's most beautiful, but at only 16ft square by 10ft high, many puzzle as to how the bodies could lie in such tiny recesses. The answer, is that the bodies were not placed in the crypt until after the flesh had decayed, after which the skull and long bones were placed into caskets and interred in the crypt recesses.

THE DERBYSHIRE MINSTER SHOW

Here are the successors to four of Derbyshire's nine Anglo-Saxon "minsters" or mother churches. These were all established during the 8th or 9th centuries, but were largely rebuilt in their present styles in the 13th and 14th centuries, at or near to their original sites.

Ashbourne: St Oswald's was named after a Northumbrian king killed in battle in 642.

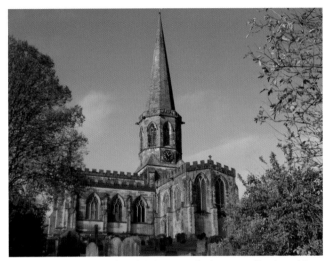

Bakewell: All Saints' church is home to the largest collection of free-standing Anglian and Viking sculpture in Britain.

Chesterfield: The famous crooked spire of St Mary and All Saints' church warped by 32 tons of lead tiling and inefficient 14th century cross-bracing.

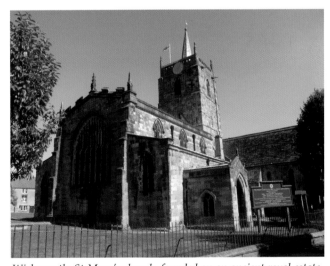

Wirksworth: St Mary's church, founded on an ancient royal estate, and home to a figure sculpture which dates to about AD 800 as well as numerous other Anglo-Saxon carvings.

In terms of Anglo-Saxon remains, the north wall of the nave at Wirksworth St Mary's contains a spectacular figure sculpture that is one of the most important pieces of pre-Norman Conquest sculpture in England, and which interprets a number of scenes from the Bible. It was discovered in 1820 when the pavement was being removed from in front of the altar. The sculpture was found face-down about two feet below the surface and was covering a stone-built vault or grave containing a large, perfect human skeleton. It is thought to date from anywhere between 700 and 900 A.D. However, one explanation for the stone is that it was the lid of the tomb of Betti, one of the four missionary priests who had ventured down from Northumberland in 653, and whose number included Diuma, who was instrumental in converting the heathen Mercian royal family to Christianity at Repton. Meanwhile, Bakewell's All Saints' church contains fragments of sculpted crosses which amount to the largest collection of free-standing Anglian and Viking sculpture in the country. They were discovered in the foundations of the church when part of it was rebuilt in the 1840s, along with medieval grave slabs and decorated tiles. And then St Alkmund's in Derby (whose penultimate 19th century successor was demolished to make way for the ring-road in the late 1960s), contained a richly decorated stone sarcophagus in which the body of St Alkmund himself was believed to have been laid to rest after his murder in around AD 800, and thus making the sarcophagus contemporary with the aforementioned Wirksworth sculpture. Derby's St Alkmund's church was also believed to be the resting place of the Mercian ealdorman Æthelwulf who was killed by the Danes in 871. As for the original

The remarkable sculpture on the north wall of the nave of Wirksworth St Mary's, and which is one of the most important pieces of pre-Norman Conquest sculpture in England.

Part of the unique collection of Anglo-Saxon cross fragments in the south porch at Bakewell All Saints and which comprise the largest and most varied collection of its kind in the country.

church, 20th century excavations have dated it to the 8th and perhaps even late 7th century.

At around this time, a tribe known as the *Pecsætan* populated the Peak District area. They were probably not Anglo-Saxon and are likely to have been Britons descended from the original Neolithic farmers who first settled in the Peak District. Their lands show up in the *Tribal Hidage* of the 7th century, where it is referred to as *Pecsætna lond*. The *Pecsætan* then survive for at least another 300 years, for they appear again in the *Anglo-Saxon Chronicle* of 920 with Bakewell being referred to as being in *Pēak lond*, and a charter of 963 describing Ballidon as being "in the district of the *Pecsætan*." The names all derive from the Old English word, *pēac*, while the ancient name of *Pecsætna lond* means "land of the peak dwellers".

It was also during the Anglo-Saxon period that many of Derbyshire's place-names were established, with many dating from the second half of the 9th century onwards. However, by the end of the 9th century, things had changed and the Vikings were in charge of the area. As a result, a number of Scandinavian place-names appear, not least of which is Derby – a name which probably means "farmstead or village where deer are kept", and would thus derive from the Old Scandinavian words *djúr* and *bý*, meaning "deer" and "farmstead, village or settlement", respectively. That said, some believe that the name is a corruption of *Derventio* – but given that the Anglo-Saxon name for the place was *Northworthy* before the Danes changed it to *Derby*, that seems highly unlikely. The place is then recorded as *Deoraby* in 917, then again as *Deorby* in 959, and then finally as *Derby* in the *Domesday Book* of 1086. As for other Viking place-names in Derbyshire, they are found mainly in the Trent valley – site of their first incursion into the county – and in north-eastern Derbyshire, where a number of places ending in *thorpe* are to be found (derived from the Old Scandinavian word *thorp*, meaning "secondary settlement, or dependent outlying farmstead or hamlet"). What is significant, though, is that the Viking place-name element *by*, only occurs ten times in *Domesday Book* entries for Derbyshire, compared with 22 in Nottinghamshire, 60 in Leicestershire and 225 in Lincolnshire – a trend which emphasises Viking dominance to the east; indeed, there are no names ending in *by* in the district of the *Pecsætan*, indicating that they managed to retain a certain independence from both Anglo-Saxon *and* Viking. Conversely, Derby is the only *city* in England to be named by the Danes and to *retain* that name!

Very little physical evidence of the Anglo-Scandinavian period survives, but one aspect that does is the number of ancient preaching crosses dotted about the county. A number of these, such as those at Bradbourne and Hope, appear in the *Quirky Derbyshire* section, but we can add to those the fine examples shown opposite such as the fragment of the old Anglo-Saxon preaching cross that has been built into the west

ANGLO-SCANDINAVIAN CROSSES

All Saints, Aston-on-Trent.   *All Saints, Brailsford.*   *St Lawrence, Eyam.*

wall of the north aisle at Aston-on-Trent's All Saints church. It was probably used on the site of the current church – which also happens to retain its Anglo-Saxon lower-course stonework on both the tower and the interior pillars. Meanwhile, the shaft of the cross at Brailsford was found buried beneath its base in 1919 outside All Saints' church, after which it was re-mounted in its rightful place. The interlace style of decoration suggests it is Anglo-Scandinavian, as does the figure of the warrior holding his sword. And finally, the 8ft Celtic cross in Eyam St Lawrence's churchyard is a rarity as it still retains its original shape although around 2 feet has been lost from the top of the shaft. Nevertheless, the survival of its cross-head makes it a sculpture of national importance and its vine-scroll carvings are thought to date it to the 8th or 9th century.

Of course, Derbyshire was very much affected by the Vikings for around a century and a half. It all started in the late 860s when after harrying much of England, the Danish army under Halfdan established a base at Nottingham where he was joined by a second army led by Guthrum. This left Mercia appealing to their old enemy, Wessex, but that didn't stop Halfdan and Guthrum, along with Oscytel and Anund invading Derbyshire territory in 873. Under Ivar the Boneless they wintered at Repton in 873-74 where, amongst other things, they sacked and burned the town and severely damaged St Wystan's church – having already done the same to St Alkmund's in Derby. King Burgred of Mercia was unable to dislodge them and was thus expelled by the Vikings who promptly installed Ceolwulf II as the new Mercian king. The Vikings then returned in 877 to partition Mercia and it is at this point in time that the area of Derbyshire began to take shape, along with Nottinghamshire, Lincolnshire and Leicestershire, with each new "shire" named after their respective military stronghold. The west of the Mercian kingdom went to Ceolwulf II, while in the east the area became known as

the Five Boroughs, the name deriving from the Old English word *burh* meaning "fortified place or strong-hold", and the strongholds in question being at Derby, Nottingham, Lincoln, Leicester and Stamford. Then in the following year (878), King Alfred of Wessex and the Danish King Guthrum agreed to carve up England between them following the Treaty of Wedmore and a temporary peace was established. The Five Boroughs became occupied by separate divisions of the Danish army, and the Danes who settled the area introduced their native law and customs known as the Danelaw. Each of the Five Boroughs was ruled as a Danish Jarldom, controlling lands around the fortified *burh*, which served as the centre of political power.

By the end of the 9th century, Mercian links with its old enemy Wessex were cemented by the marriage of Earl Æthelred of Mercia to Æthelflæd, daughter of King Alfred of Wessex. On Æthelred's death in 911, Æthelflæd ruled Mercia as the 'Lady of the Mercians' and set about fortifying Mercia's eastern borders and by 913 she had encroached deep into Danish territory, having established a *burh* at nearby Tamworth. Along with her brother, Edward the Elder of Wessex, Æthelflæd launched her first offensive foray in July 917 and selected the fortress at Derby as her target, expelling the Danes and annexing the whole region back into English Mercia. According to the *Anglo-Saxon Chronicle*, this included Derby "together with the region which it controlled", thus indicating that the county area of Derbyshire had by this stage been established – although we don't actually see the name *Derbyshire* appear until the *Anglo-Saxon Chronicle* of 1048.

Possession of Derbyshire's territory ebbed and flowed over the next century and a half, but it was clearly in the midst of this Anglo-Saxon/Viking struggle that the county was first created, and with very similar borders to those that it has today, plus a number of exclaves in Leicestershire. Internally, the shires of the Danelaw were originally divided up into wapentakes, the equivalent of the Anglo-Saxon hundreds. However, during the 10th century, we see evidence in various charters where distinct areas within Derbyshire are allocated to Mercian thegns and which closely resemble our modern-day parishes. The *Domesday Book* of 1086 then became the first concise recording of towns, villages and estates in Derbyshire, recording most of the county's current settlements, bar those that emerged during the Industrial Revolution. Nevertheless, Derbyshire and its internal areas had clearly taken shape long before the Normans arrived in 1066.

From the Normans to the Elizabethan Era

Following the Norman Conquest of 1066, Derbyshire was soon subjected to the same ruthless overhaul of ruling class that was to be repeated in most other English counties. In other words, out went the previous Anglo-Scandinavian incumbents, to be replaced by Norman gentry. However, there is little evidence of fighting or destruction, and the structure of Derbyshire estates remained largely intact. William the Conqueror himself became the major landowner in Derbyshire as lord of the manor of Ashbourne, Ashford, Bakewell, Chesterfield, Darley, Hope, Matlock Bridge, Melbourne, Parwich and Wirksworth. However, he also bestowed extensive Derbyshire estates upon Henry de Ferrers (150) and William Peveril (23).

The North Midlands also underwent the other standard Norman process, that of fortification – although not so much in Derbyshire, which was not so strategically important to them; the major Norman castles were built just *outside* the county borders, at Nottingham, Tutbury and Tickhill. As for the castles that *were* built in Derbyshire, many of them were hastily erected earthworks surmounted by timber buildings, and were designed to intimidate the locals and act as bases to quell any unrest. Either ring-work or motte-and-bailey in design, the majority were abandoned once the local population were established as benign. Of these early Norman castles, the one at Derby was probably of a motte-and-bailey design, while the earthworks of another near to the shrunken medieval village of

Pilsbury on the west bank of the River Dove are still so defined today that we know that it had *two* baileys.

Pilsbury Castle also stands in a very remote position and is thought to have been one of a trio of defences set up by Henry de Ferrers along with the castles at Tutbury and Duffield – perhaps built to establish control of the area following the harrying of the north during 1069-70. Historians can't be certain of Pilsbury Castle's construction date, though, and other theories suggest that it might have been built by the de Ferrers family around the time of The Anarchy (1135-54), the period of dispute over the English crown between Stephen and Matilda. Pilsbury Castle was possibly destroyed after yet another major English crown dispute, this one due to William de Ferrers' part in the Revolt of 1173-74 against Henry II, but again, historians aren't at all sure. As for Henry de Ferrers' other castle at Duffield, the 11th century timber castle was certainly replaced by a 12th century stone structure which went on to become one of Derbyshire's most important medieval buildings. Indeed, its foundations suggest that its keep was the largest in England after the Tower of London at that time. Alas, like Pilsbury Castle, Duffield Castle was probably one of those destroyed in the 1173-74 rebellion; very little remains today other than one course of foundations, a bit of the motte and part of the ditch.

The other surviving Norman castle in Derbyshire is Peveril Castle which stands majestically over the village of Castleton, and above what is today known as Peak Cavern, but which was recorded in the Domesday Book as Peak's Arse! Like Duffield Castle, Peveril Castle was originally built in the 11th century as a timber fortification before being rebuilt in stone during the 12th century. The original was built by William Peveril who along with his 23 manors was also granted the title of bailiff of the Royal Manors of the Peak. As for Peveril Castle, the replacement stone keep that still dominates above Castleton today was built in 1176 by the first Plantagenet king, Henry II, for alas, the Peveril estate didn't last as long as the de Ferrers estate. This was because it was forfeited to the Crown in 1155 when the third William Peveril retired as a monk (allegedly to avoid the charge of poisoning the Earl of Chester) and therefore he didn't provide an heir.

View at dusk of the earthworks and remains of Pilsbury Castle with its two baileys. The mound to the left is where the motte stood.

Some of the foundations of Duffield Castle. Its destruction in 1173 was a major loss to Derbyshire's heritage.

The keep of Peveril Castle, built by Henry II in 1176.

Quirk Alert: The Devil of Drakelow

In 1085, two of Burton Abbey's Stapenhill villeins did the unthinkable and crossed the Trent to Drakelow, declaring allegiance to Derbyshire's Roger Montgomery. A series of tit-for-tat raids ensued between the two landowners, culminating in a skirmish near a lagoon known as the Blackpool. With neither side proving a tower of strength, the dispute rumbled on until the monks of Burton Abbey sought illumination from their patron, Saint Modwen. Thought to be the only incident of its kind in England, the reliquary containing the saint's remains was taken from her shrine and placed on the floor while the monks implored her to intercede. Geoffrey, Abbot of Burton records in his Life of St Modwen that the next day, the defecting villeins were taken ill, and within hours both men were dead! It then gets seriously bizarre. The bodies were returned to Stapenhill, but were later said to have reappeared in Drakelow carrying their own coffins. They then frequently appeared over subsequent evenings imploring everyone to leave. But they didn't. And lo and behold, other Drakelow folk systematically fell ill and died. Montgomery eventually begged the abbot for help and a surreal ritual followed in order to lay the ghosts to rest. The bodies of the villeins were exhumed and had their heads cut off and placed between their legs, while their hearts were removed and placed on a bonfire. As the flames rose a loud noise was heard and what was taken to be a possessing spirit was seen to fly out of the fire in the shape of a crow. The apparitions then ceased, but Drakelow, with barely anyone left alive, was abandoned, leaving only an unexplained mystery.

Also forfeit by the third William Peveril was Bolsover Castle, although nothing remains of the original Norman castle; the striking structure that you see today when driving up and down the M1 in north-eastern Derbyshire was constructed in the early 17th century on the site of the original Norman castle, by Sir Charles Cavendish and completed by his son, William.

In the years following the Norman Conquest, much of Derbyshire became subject to the forest laws, which applied to areas of the English countryside where Norman kings and barons had exclusive rights to hunt. The term "forest", though, represented more than just dense woodland; it included moor, heath and fen, too. And unfortunately for the resident peasants, a special set of harsh laws were imposed by forest courts, including the prevention of the clearing of new land for farming or from fencing existing crops to keep the game out. As for the "forests" of Derbyshire, they covered more than half of the county. To the north-west of the county was the Forest of High Peak which, unsurprisingly, fell under the custodianship of William Peveril and his descendants. The rest of the county, including the remaining forests of Duffield Frith in central Derbyshire and the Forest of East Derbyshire, was bestowed by King William upon Henry de Ferrers, with Duffield Frith controlled by de Ferrers from his seat at Duffield Castle. The Frith extended from Duffield to Wirksworth on a roughly south-to-north bearing and from Hulland to Heage, west-to-east. However, after Duffield Castle was destroyed in the late 12th century, Belper – or *Beurepeir* as it was then known – took over as the administrative capital of the Frith (the name Belper means "beautiful retreat" and derives from the Old French words *beau* and *repaire*).

As for Henry de Ferrers, he was eventually succeeded by his third son, Robert, who in 1138 became the first Earl of Derby, and the second of seven generations of de Ferrers who remained the major landowners in Derbyshire. However, that all ended in 1266 during the Second Barons War when Robert de Ferrers III supported the barons' cause and subsequently had to relinquish the family estates to Edmund "Crouchback", Earl of Lancaster and son of Henry III. Thereafter, those estates – including Duffield Frith – became part of the Duchy of Lancaster and from 1285 Duffield Frith became a royal forest with its own forest courts. Meanwhile the Forest of East Derbyshire covered the whole county to the east of the River Derwent, but unlike the Forest of High Peak which had been a royal forest since William I's time, the Forest of East Derbyshire didn't become a *royal* forest until the reign of Henry II (1154-1189). Covering the whole length of eastern Derbyshire, it was much larger than the other royal forests; indeed bordering Sherwood Forest as it did, it formed part of an enormous forested area that stretched over 30 miles from the Derwent to the Trent. However, whereas the Forest of High Peak and Duffield Frith both survived until the 17th century, the Forest of East Derbyshire was abolished in 1225, having lasted for only two generations.

We've already mentioned the insignificance of Derby's Norman castle in comparison to Nottingham's and alas, this also reflected the standing of Derbyshire against Nottinghamshire as a county, too. Indeed, a single shire court held at Nottingham served both counties until 1256; meanwhile the sheriff of Nottingham actually had jurisdiction over Derbyshire until the 16th century. Derbyshire's lack of strategic importance to the Normans also meant that abbeys and priories followed a similar pattern to the castles. In fact, no monasteries were established by the Benedictines or Cistercians in the county, and the only Cluniac foundation was a small priory in Derby. The largest and most prosperous of Derbyshire's monasteries was founded by the Augustinians at Darley Abbey around 1146. Very little survives today, bar the pub known as "The Abbey", but which was probably only the guest house of the original abbey. Meanwhile, other Augustinian priories included

NORMAN CHURCHES IN DERBYSHIRE

All Saints' church at Aston-upon-Trent. The lower courses of the tower are actually Saxon, but the rest is largely Norman.

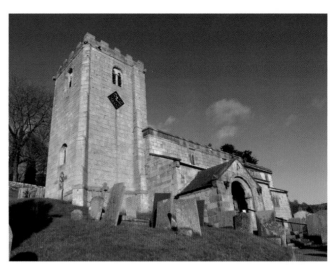

St James's church at Brassington. The tower is Norman except for the parapet and the tops of the buttresses.

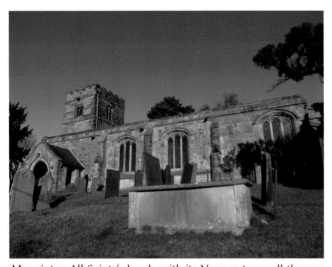

Mugginton All Saints' church, with its Norman tower all the way up to the corbel table.

St Mary's church, Tissington. The tower is largely Norman while the porch shelters a Norman doorway over which is a fine Norman tympanum.

those at Breadsall, Calke Abbey, Church Gresley and Repton – the latter built close to the double monastery that had been destroyed by the Vikings. Finally, the Premonstratensians or White Canons built two medium-sized abbeys in the 12[th]century at Beauchief (now part of south-western Sheffield) and at Dale, several miles east of Derby (see *Quirky Derbyshire [Dale]*). Alas, the income that might have supported impressive abbeys and priories in Derbyshire was diverted instead to monasteries in other counties and to the cathedrals at Lichfield and Lincoln. Meanwhile, estates in the county were granted to religious houses in both neighbouring counties, such as Burton Abbey and Lenton Abbey – but also as far afield as Dunstable Priory in Bedfordshire, with the latter establishment keeping 1,200 sheep at Bradbourne! Of course, all of Derbyshire's monasteries and abbeys perished several centuries later when Henry VIII's Dissolution was implemented between 1537 and 1539. Alas, the subse-

quent efficient plundering of these sites means that little remains today.

As for the process that had begun in the Anglo-Scandinavian period of creating new parishes and chapelries, this was completed under the Normans. Many Norman churches and chapels also survive throughout Derbyshire; in fact 55 of the c.140 founded in the county by 1200 still retain at least a doorway, window, arch or stone font, while Aston-on-Trent, Bradbourne, Brassington, Mugginton, Thorpe, Tissington and Whitwell retain their Norman towers. Add to that list St Michael and St Mary's church at Melbourne which has one of the finest Norman interiors in the country (see *Quirky Derbyshire [Melbourne]*), while All Saints at Dalbury contains a representation of St Michael in a window that is possibly the earliest example of Norman glazing still *in situ* in England. Meanwhile, Steetley Chapel right up in the north-eastern-most corner of Derbyshire is recognised as one

The Abbey pub in Darley Abbey is all that remains of a former Augustinian monastery, originally founded in c.1146.

All Saints' church at Dalbury. The church may date back to the late 11th century which would make its stained glass representation of St Michael the earliest glazing still in situ in England.

of England's finest small Norman churches (see *Quirky Derbyshire [Whitwell]*).

As we have already mentioned, medieval Derby played second fiddle to Nottingham in terms of importance, but the town still flourished as a trading centre in commodities such as wool, lead and wood. In fact, Derby had first been granted a charter in the mid-12th century (1154), and was followed by Hartington (1203) and Chesterfield (1204), although the latter had been a market town since long before then, trading primarily in cloth that was spun, woven, fulled and dyed in the town. Other medieval markets were established at the ancient minster towns of Ashbourne, Wirksworth and Bakewell, while Castleton and Bolsover received market charters in 1223 and 1256, respectively. Early water-powered fulling mills also began to appear in the 13th century such as those at Hartington and Wirksworth, while the latter remained Derbyshire's main lead-mining town. Having said that, lead mining was prevalent elsewhere throughout the county, as was quarrying, too. As for coal mining, that was only mined for local markets, as the 13th century Derbyshire collieries such as those at Denby, Smalley and Swadlincote could not compete with those in Northumberland and Durham. Meanwhile, most Derbyshire families earned their living by the cultivation of small 1-15 acre farms, with rights to cut hay in the meadows and to graze livestock on the common pastures, while adding to their incomes by weaving cloth, mining coal, hewing millstones or smelting lead.

During the two and a half centuries between the Norman Conquest and the early 14th century, the population of England nearly trebled, and Derbyshire prospered, too. In the south of the county, the royal manor of Melbourne was developed into a stronghold, with its castle, bishop's residence, two churches, two parks and a thriving market. Further castles were erected at Codnor (see *Quirky Derbyshire [Codnor]*) and at Horston Castle, a mile south of Horsley – another Norman motte-and-bailey castle built in the first half of the 12th century by Hugh de Buron. However, on the death of Roger de Buron in 1194, the estate passed to the Crown. King John built a stone castle in the early 13th century, adding a keep, chapel, gatehouse and barbican. Only the north wall of the keep and some foundations survive, with much of the castle destroyed by 18th century quarrying. Meanwhile the 13th century saw the foresters of north-western Derbyshire build their own chapel at Chapel-en-le-Frith ("the chapel in the forest"). The place was even granted a royal charter for weekly markets and annual fairs in 1254, joining Melbourne (1230), King's Newton (1231), Higham (1243), Tideswell (1251), Ripley (1251), Ilkeston (1252) and Sandiacre (1252), and followed by Cubley (1255), Aston-upon-Trent (1257), Sawley (1259), Mapperley (1267), Doveridge (1275), Pleasley (1285), Glossop (1290), Overseal (1311), Charlesworth (1328), Repton (1330), Denby (1334) and Monyash (1340). That said, many of these markets either failed to get off the ground, or eventually disappeared due to competition!

Quirk Alert: Splat-Nav!

The Old Glossop Cross is a listed monument which stands in a small square in Old Glossop. It is believed to date from 1290 when the Cistercian monks of Basingwerk Abbey secured the town's market charter which included a weekly market and an annual fair. Unfortunately, the cross fell victim to a dodgy sat-nav in 2012 when a driver – having been misled into thinking he could get to Wesley Street from Old Cross (erm, you can't) – reversed back up the hill and struck the ancient monument, causing damage and movement to the base stones.

The market cross at Bonsall is definitely medieval, but no specific date can be provided – although the ball on top was added in 1671.

This market cross at Repton is thought to date to c.1330 when the town's Wednesday market was first recorded.

Of course, also prospering during this period were the numerous Norman knight and gentry families that were installed after the Conquest, many of whom remained significant Derbyshire landowners through-out the Middle Ages; indeed, some still flourish to this day, such as the Curzons of Kedleston, descended from the Coursons of Notre-Dame-de-Courson and with the current incumbent being the 30th lord. Medieval castles and manors appeared around the county between the 12th and 15th centuries, owned by other families that have stamped their names upon Derbyshire; leading knights of the 14th century came from the families of Bagpuize, Brailsford, Chandos, Chaworth, Curzon, Dethick, Frecheville, Fitzherbert, Foljambe, Gresley, Longford, Mackworth, Meynell, Montgomery, Savage, Shirley, Solney, Tuchet, Twyford and Vernon. However, many of Derbyshire's leading medieval gentry families died out in the male line between the late 15th and 17th centuries. These included the Babingtons of Dethick, the Chaworths of Alfreton, the Foljambes of Walton, the Greys of Codnor, Shirland and Sandiacre, and the Longfords of Longford.

Prominent amongst the surviving Derbyshire gentry families were the Fitzherberts who initially owned the manor house at Norbury, but later owned halls at Padley, Somersal Herbert and Tissington, too. The manor house at Norbury was acquired from the Prior of Tutbury in the early 12th century. Designed in the style that architectural historians call a "first floor hall", it was enlarged in 1305 by Sir Henry Fitzherbert. Meanwhile the early 14th century saw the Fitzherberts putting up considerable sums of money to build the splendid chancel at Norbury St Mary's church. Built in the Decorated Gothic style that was typical of that age, the majority of the chancel windows still contain the original stained glass. This work was followed by the addition of the tower, nave and chapels, built in Perpendicular Gothic style during the 15th and 16th centuries. John Fitzherbert then had Somersal Herbert Hall built in 1564 which was to become Derbyshire's largest and most famous timber-framed house, with the

timbers arranged in a variety of styles including close-studding, herringbone and decorative quatrefoils in the gables. Meanwhile Tissington Hall was built in 1609 by Francis Fitzherbert using limestone with millstone grit dressing, although it has been altered and enlarged since. And just before Somersal Herbert and Tissington Halls were built, the year 1560 also saw the Fitzherbert's acquire Padley Hall – this through the marriage of Sir Thomas Fitzherbert to Anne Eyre, the daughter and heiress of Sir Arthur Eyre of Padley Hall.

Also built during the 13th and 14th century were many of Derbyshire's finest churches including those that were built on or near to the site of their ancient minster predecessors in what were now flourishing market towns. Of course, most of these churches have been subject to later modifications – Derby Cathedral, for example, had its nave and chancel completely rebuilt between 1723 and 1725 and St Alkmund's in Derby was rebuilt completely in the 1840s; however, the majority of those 13th and 14th century minster-successor churches still retain much of their original medieval stone. The same also applies to dozens of town and village churches in Derbyshire which followed throughout the 13th and 14th centuries, some built from scratch and others re-constructed using part of their Norman predecessors, while also built at this time was the magnificent "Cathedral of the Peak", otherwise known as St John the Baptist church at Tideswell.

Alas, the steady growth of the 13th and early 14th centuries came to an abrupt end during the crisis years of 1315-1322 when a number of disasters occurred including cattle plague, sheep murrain and harvest failure. As a result, the national population declined by at least 15 per cent. Furthermore by 1334, Derbyshire was one of the poorest English counties and its taxable wealth ranked 31st out of the 38 counties. Then, as if that wasn't enough, in 1348 the Black Death wreaked devastation throughout Western Europe and the population of England almost returned to its *Domesday Book* level of just over 2 million while Derbyshire's fell to below 40,000. Thus it was that by the 1350s many Derbyshire

MEDIEVAL LEGACY OF THE FITZHERBERT FAMILY

The oldest part of Norbury Manor, which dates from the 13th century.

The charming and asymmetrical Somersal Herbert Hall which was built for John and Ellen Fitzherbert in the mid-16th century.

Tissington Hall, built in 1609 by Francis Fitzherbert.

lead mines lay unworked, fields lay uncultivated and villages began to shrink, sometimes to extinction. This shrinkage explains modern map entries such as "shrunken medieval village", and "deserted medieval village" with the latter designation denoting less than three inhabited houses. Derbyshire has a number of examples of each, with shrunken villages including Rowland (north of Bakewell), Alsop, Cold Eaton and the previously mentioned Pilsbury (all a few miles north of Ashbourne) and deserted medieval villages including Barton Blount and Osleston (both west of Derby).

The process of medieval de-population continued into the 15th century, with the lowlands of south-west Derbyshire particularly hard hit as they lay at the northern edge of the Midland Plain, one of the worst affected districts in the country. Of course, the towns fared even worse, with plague spreading more rapidly, and Derby, in particular, suffered during the 14th and 15th centuries. However, the late medieval period did see a revival in the lead industry in Derbyshire, while the scythe-making and millstone trades grew throughout the county, too. Alongside these industries, pottery production at Derby, Burley Hill, Chesterfield and Ticknall prospered, as did alabaster quarrying at Chellaston with the product used to make some of the finest tombs in both England and France. A number of these alabaster sculptures appear in Derbyshire, including that of Sir Thomas Cockayne (d.1488) at All Saints' church at Youlgreave. Other stunning alabaster wall monuments can be found in Bakewell and Ashbourne churches, while Kedleston All Saints houses fine alabaster figures of Sir John Curzon (d.1456) and his wife Joan, and Wirksworth St Mary's of Sir Anthony Gell (d.1583). Meanwhile, the manufacture of wool spread from the towns into the countryside. Nevertheless, as the Middle Ages drew to a close, the county of Derbyshire ranked a lowly 35th out of the 38 counties of England in terms of wealth.

Quirk Alert: Shrouded in Mystery

Derbyshire is home to many fine alabaster sculptures. However, the most bizarre must be those of Thomas Beresford and his wife at Fenny Bentley's St Edmund's church, as their carved bodies are portrayed in wrapped shrouds, "tied" above their heads and feet – as are their 21 children, too!

Quirk Alert: Building Bridges

Today's picturesque bridge over the River Trent at Swarkestone was built in the 18th century, and adjoins the 13th century causeway to the north. However, regarding the bridge's 13th century predecessor, it is said that two sisters saw their lovers drown trying to cross the Trent on horseback. They thus spent the rest of their lives building the original bridge and died penniless as a result.

MEDIEVAL CHURCHES

Brailsford. All Saints was built in the 11th and 12th centuries on the site of a Saxon predecessor, but the only Norman remains today are an arch and two pillars. The chancel is 14th century and the tower was re-built around 1500.

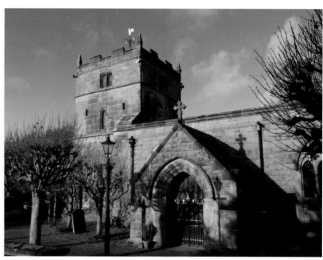

Hognaston. The tower of St Bartholomew's church is 13th century while the belfry is 15th. However, it does still have a Norman doorway sheltered by its porch which includes a fine tympanum.

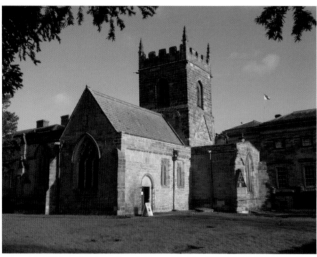

Kedleston. All Saints' church is another 13th century reconstruction of a Norman church, but all that is left of the Norman structure is the south doorway.

Tideswell: The Cathedral of the Peak, or St John the Baptist's church was built in the 14th century.

This medieval five-arched bridge across the River Wye at Bakewell is thought to date from c.1272, and is therefore one of the oldest in the country.

Swarkestone Bridge over the River Trent was built in the 18th century, but succeeded its 13th century predecessor (see Quirk Alert: Building Bridges).

Adjoining Swarkestone Bridge to the south is this 13th century causeway across the Trent marshes. A scheduled ancient monument, it continues to link Swarkestone and Stanton-by-Bridge, while among its 17 arches are many of the 13th century originals.

The gentry, of course, continued to fare much better, although by the end of the 14th century, the Duchy of Lancaster was the largest landowner in the county, having been created in 1351 when Henry, Earl of Lancaster, was made a duke. That said, the county still had relatively few men wealthy enough to become knights – although of those that were knighted, their names live on in many a Derbyshire place name: witness the names of Brailsford, Dethick, Gresley, Longford, Meynell, Montgomery, Shirley, Solney and Twyford, to name but a few. Meanwhile, the Vernons turned their Norman Hall at Nether Haddon (itself, by now, another abandoned medieval village) into the magnificent Haddon Hall, while the other two key 15th century manor houses built in Derbyshire were Padley Hall (built by the Eyres, another successful gentry family who built their fortune from lead mining and sheep grazing) and Wingfield Manor (built by Ralph Lord Cromwell, Lord Treasurer of England, in 1441). The Vernons subsequently became extensive landowners in Derbyshire, profiting from both stock rearing and from the lead industry, the latter of which saw a revival between 1480 and 1540, albeit much of it opencast. The family's increase in wealth was then consolidated further by Henry Vernon who became a prominent member of Henry VII's court. However, when Sir George Vernon died in 1565, he did so without a Vernon heir, and his estate passed to John Manners, the husband of his second daughter, Dorothy, and the hall has been in the hands of the Manners family ever since.

Meanwhile, the family that were to become the greatest Derbyshire landowners that of Cavendish – moved to Chatsworth in 1549 after Sir William Cavendish's marriage to Bess of Hardwick (her second husband). Bess had been born in a small manor house in Hardwick in 1527 on the site of what is now known as Hardwick Old Hall. The family were minor gentry who had taken their name from the manor they had owned for around six generations. However, not only was Bess destined to become the second richest woman in

T'owd Man, now in the west transept of St Mary's church at Wirksworth.

England, she would also play a major role in converting Derbyshire from a county with relatively few grand buildings into one that housed some of the very finest. As was the custom in those days, from an early age Bess worked as a gentlewoman's servant for Lady Zouche at Codnor Castle. She married her first husband aged 16 and, when he died a few months later, inherited a third of his income. It was with her second husband, however, that her most lasting foundations would be built. William Cavendish was already an extremely wealthy man when they wed in 1547, having profited from the Dissolution of the Monasteries and having also landed the wealthy position of Treasurer of the Chamber the previous year. By 1549, Bess had convinced William to sell his lands in Hertfordshire and purchase Chatsworth along with numerous other Derbyshire manors.

Given they had eight children, it is unsurprising that a large number of aristocratic dynasties can trace their ancestry back to William and Bess, including the Dukes of Kingston, the Dukes of Newcastle and the Dukes of Portland, as well as the still resident Dukes of Devonshire at Chatsworth. Before her death in 1607, Bess married four times. Her third husband, Sir William St Loe, was another wealthy man and when he died in 1565, he left much of his property to Bess, much to the chagrin of his blood relatives. Clearly a woman to be reckoned with, Bess married for a final time in 1568, and this time rather sensationally to George Talbot, the sixth Earl of Shrewsbury and who also happened to be the richest and most powerful man in the Midlands and the North of England, having built up his wealth by investing profitably in iron and lead. However, their marriage was somewhat hampered by their responsibility for the custodianship of Mary Queen of Scots, who was moved around between a number of their properties, including Chatsworth, Wingfield Manor and Tutbury Castle – and at great personal cost, too! This was because Mary had a personal retinue of around 50 people, not to mention

---

Quirk Alert: T'owd Man

In the west transept of St Mary's church at Wirksworth, you will find an ancient medieval carving of a lead miner, and which is known locally as T'owd Man – a name from local folklore for a spirit that inhabits mines and caves. The sculpture is believed to be the oldest representation of a lead miner in the world, and depicts a miner complete with his pick and basket, or kibble as it was known then. The sculpture was acquired from Bonsall church in 1863 when the latter was being renovated, but the loss of the sculpture is alleged to have coincided with strange noises emitted from Bonsall's Ball Eye mine, thought to be the muttering spirit of T'owd Man. Determined to reunite T'owd Man with the village, Bonsall Parish Council commissioned a replica of the sculpture to be made in 2001 where it has been set into the wall of the newly restored bandstand overlooking the village's historic market cross.

DERBYSHIRE'S GREAT HOUSES

Haddon Hall, probably the UK's finest example of a fortified English manor house. Dating from Norman times, the hall was progressively improved between the 12th and early 17th centuries. It was then largely abandoned until the 9th Duke and Duchess of Rutland restored it in the 1920s.

Hardwick Hall, built in the 1580s by Bess of Hardwick, arguably Derbyshire's most famous daughter. Ironically, Mary Queen of Scots was never held here despite the Talbots' responsibility to guard her between 1569 and 1584. The building is subject to the saying: "Hardwick Hall, more glass than wall".

Chatsworth House, home to the Cavendish family since 1549. Mary Queen of Scots was a "guest" here on a number of occasions between 1569 and 1571. Both accomplished needle-workers, it was during this time that Mary and Bess worked together on what became known as the Oxburgh Hangings.

the additional security and logistical costs that George had to bear. Ironically, his marriage with Bess broke down in 1584 when George was released from his responsibilities towards Mary.

It was also in the 1580s that Bess finally bought the house and estate where she was born at Hardwick. Following her estrangement from George, she initially built what is now known as the Old Hall on the site of her birthplace. However, when George died in 1590, not only did Bess receive a very large widow's jointure but she also recovered complete control of her pre-final marriage lands. This enabled her to employ Robert Smythson, one of the greatest architects of that era, to build a New Hall alongside the old one. While the Old Hall continued to provide accommodation for guests and servants, the New Hall became Bess's home and very much the jewel in her crown. It was laid out in the grandest of English Renaissance styles as a rectangular block with six square towers arranged symmetrically around it and each topped off by a sculpture that includes Bess's countess coronet above the letters ES (Elizabeth Shrewsbury). Meanwhile, every face of the house is dominated by enormous glass mullioned windows which, given the expense of glass at the time, was an enormous status symbol. Inside, the classical loggia entrance gives onto the two-storey Great Hall, while the Long Gallery that Smythson designed along the entire east front was the finest in the kingdom.

As for the Devonshire title, that was allocated to Bess's second son, William Cavendish in 1618, albeit initially as *Earl* of Devonshire. The title was chosen simply because it was available and because Earl of Derbyshire was out of the question since the Earl of Derby was already in use by the Stanleys of West Derby in Liverpool. By the 1620s, William Cavendish owned nearly 44,000 acres of land in Derbyshire. Meanwhile, Bess's youngest son, Sir Charles Cavendish, was responsible for the transformation of the ruined motte-and-bailey castle at Bolsover between 1612 and 1614, once again engaging the services of Robert Smythson. The structure still dominates the

The Little Castle, Bolsover, with the start of the lengthy Terrace Range shown to the right.

landscape for many miles around, and the façade visible from the M1 comprises the lengthy Terrace Range – which is now largely ruinous – and the Little Castle – which is almost completely intact. The historian Mark Girouard writes: *"by an unlikely miracle the keep at Bolsover has survived into this century as an almost untouched expression in stone of the lost world of Elizabethan chivalry and romances."*

By the time the reign of Elizabeth I came to an end in 1603, Derbyshire had changed considerably since the Norman Conquest. However, it was over the next 200 years that technological improvements would shape not just the country, but the whole world, and Derbyshire was waiting, biding its time, before taking a leading role in making that happen.

The Hunting Stand built in the 1580s and which is located high above Chatsworth House. It is the best surviving structure from Bess of Hardwick's tenure.

From the Stuart's to the Industrial Revolution

By the mid-17th century, Britain's population had begun to recover, rising to around 5 million, but still not quite back to pre-1300, pre-Black Death proportions. In tandem with this Derbyshire's population rose to around 70,000, with the greatest increases experienced in the lead-mining townships of the White Peak. Nevertheless, plague still continued to periodically ravage Derbyshire towns and villages throughout the 16th and 17th centuries, but the number of baptisms still largely exceeded the number of burials. When Elizabeth I's reign commenced in 1558, Derby was a town of around 2,500 residents, and the only other Derbyshire towns with more than 1,000 inhabitants were Chesterfield and Wirksworth, with Ashbourne and Bakewell having around 600 inhabitants each. The borough of Derby, therefore, was the natural centre for the county's administration, and by 1637, borough affairs were run by a mayor and his aldermen and burgesses – a state which lasted until the Municipal Corporations Act of 1835.

The 16th and 17th centuries also saw much of the land enclosed, with upland wastes and open arable fields brought under the private ownership of the nobility and gentry, and regularly at the expense of peasant farmers

and poor cottagers. Alongside this, though, the Derbyshire lead industry had recovered to such an extent that it became the leading supplier of lead in Europe, rising from 3,000 loads of ore a year in the early 1540s, to 120,000 loads by 1640. The population of many White Peak villages therefore rose in tandem with the industrial expansion, as workers flocked into the area. Of course, the smelters and merchants enjoyed huge profits, but the owners also invested in their mines too, particularly in terms of drainage. The most expensive drainage method was to drive a sough into a hillside from a lower point in an adjacent valley; the first in Derbyshire was constructed by the famous Dutchman Cornelius Vermuyden between 1629 and 1636, in order to drain the Dove Gang lead mines between Cromford and Wirksworth. Despite this, Wirksworth lost its status as the commercial centre of the lead trade to Chesterfield, thanks to the latter town's proximity to the smelting mills and being en-route to the inland port of Bawtry on the River Idle.

One fledgling Derbyshire industry of the 16th and 17th centuries was the iron industry, and which was destined to become a major county employer in the following three centuries. The first recorded charcoal blast furnace in Derbyshire opened in 1582 at Loscoe – although it wasn't until the 17th century that Derbyshire's first professional ironmaster, George Sitwell, built furnaces at Plumbley and Foxbrooke, followed by the first Derbyshire slitting mill (1656) and further furnaces, including that at Staveley. Coal production also gradually began to increase with at least 23 pits producing over 10,000 tons a year by the early 17th century. Meanwhile, the timber, limestone and millstone industries complete the industrial picture of the period, with the latter seeing the development of large quarries on the gritstone edges to the east of the Derwent.

As for the poor, Acts of 1597 and 1601 ensured that each parish became responsible for its own paupers. In Derbyshire, public payments of rates became supplemented by private donations, while almshouses for the poor were founded by wealthy individuals such as Sir Roger Manners in Bakewell, Sir John Port in Etwall, Sir

---

Quirk Alert: Sir Samuel Sleigh

Born in 1603 at Ashe Hall, Sir Samuel was a knight, a justice of the peace, a member of parliament, High Sheriff of Derbyshire (twice) and deputy lieutenant of the county. However, despite those achievements, he is most well-known for having first and third wives who died more than 100 years apart. This was because his first wife died young in 1634, while he married his third wife in 1677 when aged 74. She was, of course, very young – 20, in fact – and didn't pass away until 1737, some 103 years after Sleigh's first wife!

Sixteenth century almshouses, Wirksworth.

St Mary's chapel on St Mary's Bridge, Derby, is one of only six surviving medieval bridge chapels in the country. It was also the scene of the gruesome execution of the Padley Martyrs on 24th July, 1588.

Anthony Gell in Wirksworth, Sir Philip Gell in Hopton, Bess of Hardwick in Derby and Jacinth Sacheverell in Morley. The almshouses at Wirksworth were donated in 1584 by Sir Anthony Gell "for six elderly people of Wirksworth", and the houses were constructed by Sir Anthony's brother and heir, Sir Thomas Gell of Hopton. Meanwhile, Philip Gell's Hopton almshouses were built between 1719-1722, "for the life of two poor men and two poor women of Hopton and Carson". Remarkably, many of these Derbyshire almshouses founded in the late 16th and early 17th centuries are still going strong.

In terms of religious matters, the second half of the 16th century saw Protestants dominate Catholics under the reign of Elizabeth I. In 1586, this led Anthony Babington, the young squire of Dethick, to lead a failed plot to assassinate the monarch and to install the Catholic Mary Queen of Scots onto the English throne. Alas, his inner circle of plotters was infiltrated by agents for Francis Walsingham, the Principal Secretary to Elizabeth I and her prime "spymaster". Letters between Babington and Mary were intercepted, decoded and some altered, and were then used as

evidence to try and sentence Babington to death. The poor young squire from Derbyshire was hanged, drawn and quartered for high treason, but the manner of the execution was so brutal that Elizabeth ordered that his co-conspirators be hanged until dead before their disembowelling commenced. Mary Queen of Scots, interned for nineteen years and largely in Derbyshire at the Earl of Shrewsbury's pleasure, was then executed by beheading the following year (1587) for her alleged complicity with the rebellion.

Meanwhile, another year on (1588) and three more Catholic priests were executed in Derby. Two of them – Nicholas Garlick and Robert Ludlam – were arrested on 12th July at Padley Hall, home of the well-known Catholic sympathisers, the Fitzherberts. The raid was conducted by none other than George Talbot who was actually looking for John Fitzherbert; the discovery of the two priests was an unexpected bonus. Thrown into Derby Gaol, Garlick and Ludlam met a third priest, Richard Sympson. All three were tried for "entering the

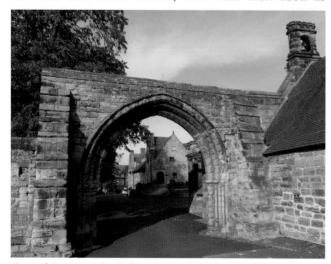

Part of Repton School, founded in 1557 by Sir John Port. This famous arch is reflected in the school's unusual motto, Porta Vacat Culpa ("the gate is free from blame").

Queen Elizabeth Grammar School, Ashbourne, initially founded in 1585 for boys by a group of local gentlemen led by Sir Thomas Cockayne.

kingdom and seducing the Queen's subjects" and were subsequently found guilty of treason. They were hanged, drawn and quartered on the 24th July at St Mary's chapel on St Mary's Bridge.

Despite the unpleasant case of the Padley Martyrs and the Babington Plot, though, Derbyshire supplies little other evidence of religious dissent during these times, despite major countrywide antagonism, elsewhere. A more positive impact of Protestantism was the founding of many grammar schools in Derbyshire, the majority of which survive to this day. The most prominent of those is Repton School, founded in 1557 as a grammar school by Sir John Port, initially on the site of the previously mentioned Augustinian priory. Over the next few centuries it expanded and spread throughout the north-western part of the town, eventually becoming a famous 19th and 20th century school for boys, and particularly excelling in producing top-level sportsmen. These include Bunny Austin, the last British male tennis player before Andy Murray to reach the Wimbledon men's singles final (in 1938), Harold Abrahams, the 1924 Olympic 100 metres gold medallist, and a whole host of professional cricketers. Other alumni include the author Roald Dahl, television personalities such as Graeme Garden and Jeremy Clarkson, and the legendary Sherlock Holmes actor, Basil Rathbone.

Of course, the middle part of 17th century English history is dominated by the English Civil War. However, when the First English Civil War broke out in the summer of 1642, the Derbyshire gentry were largely neutral, and very few rallied to the Crown when Charles I raised his standard in Nottingham. That all changed in December 1642, though, when Sir John Gell of Hopton Hall garrisoned Derby with around 700 Parliamentary troops. Those troops also took part in the defence of nearby Nottingham (which had soon been taken from the Royalists by the Parliamentarians), plus the Siege of Lichfield and the Battle of Hopton Heath. However, all of these incidents took place outside the confines of Derbyshire which didn't see any serious action in the two Civil Wars fought between 1642 and

1651 – although some 1,500 soldiers from Derbyshire were thought to have been killed in action.

In 1662, and two years after the Restoration of the English monarchy, the hearth tax was first levied. This tax charged every household two shillings a year per hearth or stove, and following its first collection, it revealed that Derbyshire was now ranked 30th out of the 38 counties in terms of wealth, while Derby was ranked the 40th largest town in England. Meanwhile, despite the return of the plague in 1665-1666, the year 1700 saw the county's population reach 114,000, nearly half of whom lived in the lead-mining northern Derbyshire wapentakes of High Peak and Scarsdale – a stark contrast to today. As for that Great Plague of 1665, it brings with it one of Derbyshire's most famous tales – and indeed a tale that has undergone a certain amount of scientific revision in the 21st century regarding the cause of, and type of, plague in question. As for the heroism of the inhabitants of Eyam, that is without question.

But we'll start with the traditional tale and which commences in the late summer of 1665, with the arrival in Eyam of a travelling tailor. His name was George Viccars, and he proceeded to sell clothes in the village. Alas, he sold them after having dried some of his wares in front of a fire in the house of Mary Hadfield with whom he was lodging. This was thought to have brought out the rat-based fleas that had been said to have caused the plague in squalor-ridden London, and which had killed many thousands there. Viccars himself was dead within a week, and was followed in September by Mary's two sons and some of her near-neighbours. Another 23 villagers then died in October. Unsurprisingly by this stage, many villagers were keen to flee to Sheffield, but the church leader, William Mompesson, persuaded them not to, fearful of spreading the disease to the north of England which had largely escaped unscathed. In the end, the villagers decided to quarantine themselves, even though it meant death for many of them, and by November 1666, 260 out of the 350 residents had perished. Mompesson himself, survived, but not before he – like so many

---

Quirk Alert: On Me 'Ead, Son

Thanks to a fire at the Royal Shrovetide Committee office in the 1890s, the oldest surviving written reference to Ashbourne's Royal Shrovetide Football match is from 1683, but rumours abound that King Edward III tried to outlaw it in 1349 because it interfered with his archery practice, while it might date back even further to the time of Henry II when such games were known to take place. Regardless of its origin, the match still takes place every year on Shrove Tuesday and Ash Wednesday, and draws spectators from all over the country, as the Up'ards (those born north of the River Henmore) and the Down'ards fight it out to "score" in goals ranged at either end of town, some 3 miles apart. Given the cast of several thousands, the "game" is more akin to a moving brawl – known affectionately as a "hug" – and which passes through the streets of the town, across fields and often through the River Henmore itself where the goals are deliberately placed. The game is played over two eight-hour periods, using a hand-painted leather ball filled with Portuguese cork chippings (to ensure it floats), but ends at 10pm each day. A ball is "goaled" by tapping it three times against a marker board attached to a stone goal plinth. The most popular theory as to the origin of the game is that the "ball" was originally a head tossed into the waiting crowd following an execution!

"Plague Cottage", the home of Alexander and Mary Hadfield, her two children by her first marriage, and – fatefully – the hired hand, George Viccars, who became the first plague victim on 7th September 1665.

St Lawrence's church, Eyam where services were abandoned in 1665 and moved to Cucklet Church, a natural outdoor amphitheatre to the south of the village – and where a plague commemoration service is still held on the last Sunday of August.

others – had buried his entire family in what is clearly one of the most remarkable true stories of personal courage and self-sacrifice ever told.

Today, the splendid little museum at Eyam brings home the extent of the tragedy with many of its exhibits. Statistics are all very well, but the museum offers harrowing individual tales. First and foremost is the tale of Mary Hadfield, who survived, but as well as her two sons, she lost 13 relatives, including her husband, Alexander, who so nearly survived the plague, but died on 3rd Aug 1666, just before it petered out. Then just along from the former Hadfield home is Rose Cottage. Here lived nine members of the Thorpe family. Alas, they *all* died, starting with Thomas Thorpe on 26th September 1665. The plaque outside the cottage lists the date of the deaths of Thomas' wife, parents, sons and daughters. And spare a thought also for the Mortens, for a list at Eyam Museum of all of the dead reveals that the majority of the Mortens perished right at the very end of the plague outbreak. Finally, the museum also offers a graphic that represents all of the houses in the village. Each house on the graphic is marked with stylised figures of the men, women and children that occupied those houses in the summer of 1665. Those who subsequently died of the plague are represented in red and those who survived are represented in green. The graphic appears to be overwhelmingly red.

As for the traditional "Eyam Plague" story, that is now questioned on a number of fronts. It would appear that George Viccars was probably not a travelling tailor after all, but a hired hand of Mary Hadfield's husband, Alexander Hadfield. More significantly, the cause of the plague is now thought to have been down to a lethal virus that was spread directly from person to person via droplet infection and was not related to the bubonic plague that was indeed transmitted by fleas carried on the backs of black rats and which had decimated the country in earlier centuries. It would appear that the

17th century plague lasted for around 38 days between infection and death, but the victim only fell ill towards the end of that period and was usually dead within five days. Alas, they had been infectious for several weeks before, but with no outward signs of the disease…and hence its prevalence. That certainly explains how in March 1666 alone, 56 villagers perished which, in turn, explains why the "passing bell" ceased to toll because deaths were so common, and also why church services were moved out of the potentially infectious St Lawrence's church and into Cucklet Church, an open-air location to the south of the village complete with its natural rock-cum-pulpit. It also explains why food and medicine were deposited at what became known as Mompesson's Well, located high above the village on the northern boundary of the parish, with supplies deposited here in return for payment in coins which were soaked in vinegar to "disinfect" them. And finally, it also explains why the graveyard ceased to take the dead and graves were dug in fields and gardens; dug by the surviving relatives of the loved ones they were forced to bury. Most prominent of these are the Riley Graves of the Hancock family, situated to the east of the village at Riley Side, where a poor woman watched her husband and six children die within eight days of each other before personally burying them all.

Moving forwards another twenty years, and one famous man who settled in Derby in 1684 was George Sorocold, one of England's most talented mechanical engineers. In 1692 he designed a water pumping system in Derby that was so successful, he was invited to install similar water supply systems in other major English towns. He then designed the machinery for the first silk-throwing mill in 1702, built by Thomas Cotchett, followed by John and Thomas Lombe's more famous Derby mill of 1718-1720 – but more on that shortly. In the meantime, the late 17th century also saw the Peak District turned into a tourist attraction for the first time, with public baths improved at Buxton in 1695 and the first public bath opened at Matlock Bath in 1698. Meanwhile, tourist guides began to appear in the form of Thomas Hobbes's *De Mirabilibus Peci* (c.1636) and Charles Cotton's *Wonders of the Peak* (1682).

In terms of religion, an ecclesiastical census of 1676 suggested that 97 per cent of Derbyshire conformed to the Church of England, with 1.8 per cent Protestant and only 1 per cent Catholic. Twelve years later, the Glorious Revolution of 1688 saw Catholic James II displaced by Protestant William of Orange and Mary – an event that was actually plotted in Derbyshire during a meeting on Whittington Moor. That meeting was led by William Cavendish, fourth Earl of Devonshire, MP for Derby and one of the so-called Immortal Seven who signed the invitation to William of Orange. Their plot was that on William and Mary's arrival, Sir Thomas Osborne's men would take York, and Cavendish's

would take Nottingham and Derby – which indeed they did.

It was also during this period that Cavendish developed the south and east wings of Chatsworth, both of which were designed in the newly fashionable English Baroque style. The famous water cascade was then built in 1696 and rebuilt on a grander scale in 1701 with the splendid temple-like Cascade House built at the top of the feature in 1703. Alongside this, the west and north fronts of the house were built – again in the English Baroque style – in 1700-03 and 1705-07, respectively. It was, however, later 18th century *Dukes* of Devonshire who commissioned the overhaul of the grounds, culminating in the stunning efforts of Capability Brown in the 1760s. Also designed and built at this time by James Paine was the stunning Chatsworth Bridge along with Beeley Bridge, which guided the main highway through

CHATSWORTH'S FAMOUS WATER SYSTEM

The upper reaches of Chatsworth's water system, looking down towards the house. The system is fed from a moorland reservoir known as the Swiss Lake.

A little further down, water tumbles off the end of this aqueduct.

At the bottom of the system is the Great Cascade which emerges from the splendid temple-like Cascade House before tumbling 60 feet down 200 yards-worth of steps. In 2004, the Cascade was voted the best water feature in England by a panel of 45 experts organised by Country Life.

The Emperor Fountain was constructed in 1843 by Joseph Paxton, who had been trained at Kew Gardens and was head gardener at Chatsworth. The fountain can reach heights of 290 feet.

The southern and eastern aspects of Haddon Hall.

The bridge over the Wye is known as Dorothy Vernon's Bridge, as legend has it that this is where John Manners waited to elope with Dorothy.

the park. And just for historical completeness, we'll whizz forward to the 1820s when the *sixth* Duke added a new north wing complete with library, theatre and great dining hall, plus a sculpture gallery in which he deposited numerous gifts from Tsar Nicholas whom the Duke had visited in Russia. In anticipation of the Tsar's return visit, he also had the Emperor Fountain constructed and fed by water from a moorland reservoir behind the house, down a channel and tumbling over an aqueduct; alas, the Tsar never saw it with his own eyes for his planned visit never came to fruition. Finally, it was also during the early 19th century that the 6th Duke had the neighbouring village of Edensor re-modelled into probably the finest estate village in the land.

Meanwhile, at nearby Haddon Hall, the early 17th-century saw Derbyshire's finest medieval manor house in its prime. It had initially been constructed as a late 12th century manor house by Richard de Vernon after being granted permission by the future King John. The west wing, including the banqueting hall and kitchens followed in the early 14th century but it wasn't until the late 14th century that the walls were raised and the battlements were added – this by Sir Richard Vernon VI. It was also at around this time that the 12th century parish church of Nether Haddon was assimilated into the building as a private chapel – this after the village had become abandoned, yet another victim of the Black Death. The south and east wings were added between the late 14th and late 16th centuries, while in between, the chapel was extended to include the north aisle. The final elements of the hall, mainly along the north wing, were added in the 1620s. However, by this stage, the hall had passed from the Vernons to the Manners when Sir George Vernon died in 1565 without an heir, and this explains both the Vernon and Manners crests (a peacock and a boar, respectively) that appear throughout the house. Alas, by 1703, the continuous enhancement of Haddon Hall came to an end, when Sir John Manners, 9th Earl of Rutland, was created 1st *Duke* of Rutland and Marquess of Granby by Queen Anne. The

family thus moved to Belvoir Castle in Leicestershire, leaving Haddon Hall suspended in time for over 200 years until the 9th Duke of Rutland instigated a major restoration programme in the 1920s and which is still continuing today.

The first Jacobite rebellion of 1715 received little support in Derbyshire – this being the movement which favoured the son of James II, James Francis Edward Stuart (the Old Pretender) for the British crown following the death of Queen Anne. It wasn't quite the same story in 1745, though, when his son, Bonnie Prince Charlie (the Young Pretender) marched south, arriving in Ashbourne in early December. Here, he was met by cheering crowds to whom he proclaimed his father to be king. On December 3rd, the news reached the Duke of Devonshire's troops, who were billeted in Irongate, Derby, and fearing an alleged "ten thousand-strong army", they retreated to Retford. The following day, Charles Edward Stuart's army entered Derby in a carefully staged and staggered approach, to make his army

Statue of Bonnie Prince Charlie on Cathedral Green, Derby. It was unveiled in December 1995 to commemorate the 250th anniversary of the Young Pretender's march south.

appear more numerous than it actually was (an army of 5,000 is more likely). Charles himself arrived in the evening, on foot, and around 70 highlanders were then sent to secure Swarkestone Bridge, the only crossing point over the River Trent in the Midlands. They reached it four hours ahead of Government troops who had been sent to destroy the historic bridge in order to prevent Charles' advance. With Swarkestone Bridge secured, Charles and his generals held a council of war at Exeter House in Derby, while more troops were sent ahead to Melbourne to prepare billets for their advance. It is at this point, however, that fate took a firm grip on British history. For Charles then received misleading information about an army coming to meet him south of Derby, and although he personally wished to continue with his quest, he was overruled by his fellow officers and they thus retreated back to Scotland. Without doubt, this was a potentially momentous turning point in British history, and there are stories that King George II had packed his belongings and was planning a retreat to Holland; a classic example of the power of misinformation and of history hanging by a thread! Somewhat mindful of this, the Charles Edward Stuart Society of Derby annually commemorates the event in early December, culminating in a parade through the city centre and a battle on Cathedral Green

– which is where you will also find a statue of Bonnie Prince Charlie mounted on his horse, and a plaque underneath with a quote from Samuel Johnson stating: *"It was a noble attempt"*.

The 18th century also saw the wholesale introduction of turnpike trusts throughout Britain – bodies set up by Acts of Parliament with powers to collect tolls in order to maintain principal highways. The first turnpike road in Derbyshire was opened between Buxton and Manchester in 1724, with other Derbyshire sections of this wider important route from London to Manchester also turnpiked over the next 20 years. The route across the moors from Bakewell to Chesterfield followed in 1739 to facilitate the movement of lead to the inland port of Bawtry, while the 1750s saw the turnpiking of most of the other important routes that we recognise today, including the ancient moorland route from Sheffield to Manchester via the infamous Winnats Pass. The turnpiking of roads also supplied a boost to Derbyshire's fledgling tourist industry, particularly at the spa towns of Buxton and Matlock Bath. Indeed, by the end of the 18th century, Matlock Bath provided hotel accommodation for around 500 people, and many of them would have visited the spectacular pleasure grounds at the Heights of Abraham which were opened in around 1800.

Cast-iron mile-marker on what is today known as the A6187 between Sheffield and Manchester but which was turnpiked in the 1750s.

Winnats Pass, the most treacherous stretch of the road.

Quirk Alert: Black Harry

The most notorious highwayman in Derbyshire was Black Harry, who in the early 18th century used to rob pack mule trains between Tideswell and Bakewell as well as travellers on the local turnpike roads. He was eventually arrested by the Castleton Bow Street Runners, and was hung, drawn and quartered on Wardlow Mires gibbet.

In 1759, the Curzons of Kedleston commissioned Matthew Brettingham to design a house in the Palladian style on the Kedleston estate. Robert Adam was then commissioned to design a landscaped park and buildings, but Nathaniel Curzon, the first Baron Scarsdale,

was so impressed with Adam that he was given the house to design, too. Kedleston Hall took 30 years to complete, and although he retained the main features of Brettingham's Palladian design, it soon became recognised as one of Adam's finest works and as one of

The north front of Kedleston Hall with its Palladian design initiated by Matthew Brettingham and built by Robert Adam.

Kedleston Hall from the south, which Adam designed in Classical style complete with the Pantheon dome.

England's grandest buildings. The front is 360 feet long with its central block including six 30 foot high Corinthian columns. As for the rear of the house, Adam went for a completely different, Classical design with the central feature based on the Arch of Constantine and the dome of the Pantheon.

Throughout the 18th century the importance of lead remained paramount in Derbyshire. Many more soughs were constructed to aid drainage, some of them stretching for miles, and requiring extraordinary feats of engineering in their construction. For example, between 1742 and 1764 the two-mile Yatestoop Sough was constructed at Birchover to drain the mines in the Winster area, while the variant branches of the Meersbrook Sough that drained the Wirksworth area has a combined length of 5 miles and today still drains 17 million gallons of water a day. In addition to the soughs, steam or "fire engines" were also employed to pump out water from as early as 1717, especially in the rich mines owned by the London Lead Company around Winster and Elton. Meanwhile coal-fired furnaces known as cupolas were introduced into the smelting process, the first of these being built in Derbyshire in 1735 near Ashover, and once again by the London Lead Company. Alongside these mining developments, the lesser gentry – including farmers, craftsmen and even some free miners – had begun to hold shares in large lead mines and the industry went on to reach its peak in the late 18th century.

As for other Derbyshire industry on the eve of the Industrial Revolution, the charcoal iron industry continued to feed the making of scythes and sickles, the Peak District became the leading producer of millstones and framework knitting became a major growth industry. Meanwhile, coal mining continued to expand, particularly in eastern Derbyshire, and one of its local side-benefits was that towards the end of the 17th century, Derbyshire coal began to provide the fuel for the 17 potteries at Ticknall – and which were flourishing long before neighbouring Staffordshire began to

dominate that particular trade. Finally, dairy farming began to flourish, too, particularly in southern Derbyshire alongside the Trent and the Dove, and this encouraged the London cheesemongers to establish a cheese factory at Uttoxeter. By 1789 nearly 2,000 tons of cheese was exported annually, and by 1841 this figure had risen to 8,000 tons. Meanwhile, livestock dominated elsewhere in the county, particularly in the north-west where sheep farming and the manufacture of woollen cloth thrived.

Of course, this modest amount of industry was about to change with the onset of the Industrial Revolution, as the 18th century saw Derbyshire emerge as a leading industrial light. But the foundations had been laid between the late 16th and early 18th century, with the growth of the lead industry and its ingenious engineering feats, plus the fledgling iron and coal industries and developments in textile production, while the introduction of turnpike roads had greatly improved social and industrial mobility. Nevertheless, that was nothing compared to what came next.

The Industrial Revolution: Derbyshire Leads the Way

The previous chapter briefly mentioned Thomas Cotchett's designs for the first silk-throwing mill in 1702, and John and Thomas Lombe's more famous Derby Silk Mill of 1718-1722, and although these events pre-date the official Industrial Revolution period, this is where the story really begins. For although Cotchett's original timber-framed mill failed to produce thread of a consistent quality, the mill built by George Sorocold for the Lombe brothers on the same site certainly did. More significantly, Lombe's mill became Britain's first ever successfully-water-powered silk mill. There were some rather controversial circumstances, though. This was because John Lombe was reputed to have "stolen" the idea from the Italians who had been using powered spinning since the early 17th century. Lombe had worked between 1716 and 1717 at a northern Italian shop where the secret silk-throwing machinery was used, but he was alleged to have secreted himself into the shop at night and diagrammed it all by candle-light. He is then said to have brought the designs back to England, and begun to put into practise at Derby Silk Mill what he had learned in Italy, courtesy of a patent secured by his half-brother, Thomas, in 1718.

Derby Silk Mill, built by John and Thomas Lombe and the site of Britain's first factory. However, due to serious fires in 1826 and 1910, the tower and the undercroft are the only survivors from the original buildings.

Derby Silk Mill subsequently became home to the first instance anywhere in the world of workers being gathered under one roof to work machinery that was driven by a common power source; without doubt, it was the forerunner to the factories that would soon become commonplace. Unfortunately, though, John Lombe didn't get to enjoy his place in history. He died suddenly in 1722 with his death thought to be down to poisoning, and probably at the hands of a "suspicious" woman who had appeared shortly before his death – and who also happened to be Italian! Certainly, there were rumours that the King of Sardinia, severely miffed by Lombe's alleged treachery, had instructed a female assassin to travel to England and kill both brothers. Whether or not that is true, Thomas Lombe certainly survived – and intriguingly, it had also been Thomas's idea for John to travel out to Italy and "acquire" the plans for the silk-throwing machinery in the first place! Thomas then continued his brother's work and became a very wealthy man as a result of it, while he also received a knighthood in 1727. Nevertheless, when the fourteen-year patent expired in 1732, Thomas's request for an extension was rejected. Yet today, despite Thomas's lengthier stint in the business it is John Lombe who is recognised in Derby, with one statue of him standing at the corner of East Street and St Peter's Street, while there is also a bas relief portrait of him on Exeter Bridge, a few yards down-river from his historic silk mill. What is for sure, though, is that the contribution of the Lombe brothers in terms of a factory system

and silk production in Derby provided the platform for Derbyshire to take on the leading role in transforming the manufacture of cotton into England's leading industry. Throw in the county's long-established framework knitting industry, its fast-flowing rivers, the pioneering genius of Richard Arkwright and the financial acumen of his partner, Jedediah Strutt, and the scene was set; Derbyshire was about to become "the crucible of the Industrial Revolution".

Of those two great names from Derbyshire's history, it was actually Strutt who made the first significant move. For in 1759, he patented a machine for the mechanical manufacture of ribbed stockings, and which became known as the "Derby Rib". The stockings were hugely popular and by the time the patent expired in 1773, Strutt was a wealthy man – and thus ready to take his place in history. In the meantime, Arkwright had developed the water frame or roller-spinning machine by 1769, a device which enabled the continuous spinning of cotton and could be operated by unskilled workers. He then moved to Cromford, which as well as being situated on the River Derwent is also the confluence of a number of other water courses, too. And so it was here at Cromford that he built the first ever water-powered cotton mill in 1771, with the mill largely based on the design of the Lombe brothers' silk mill at Derby. Interestingly, though, the power for his first mill was supplied not by either the River Derwent or the local Bonsall Brook, but by Cromford Sough, one of the aforementioned drainage channels built to drain the lead mines in the Wirksworth area.

Four years later, Arkwright was granted a second patent which mechanised the preparatory spinning process, after which he was able to place the machines into other water-powered mills which were thus copied in many other parts of northern England. But we'll just pop back to his first mill in 1771 again, for in this venture he was crucially partnered financially by Jedediah Strutt. Strutt himself then went onto build the *second*-ever water-powered cotton mill at Belper in 1776 and which would eventually be rebuilt as the South Mill in 1812. This was followed at Belper by further mills in 1786 (this one rebuilt after a fire in 1804 as the North Mill) and 1795 (the West Mill), which along with the mills at Milford (built in 1778), were all Strutt-owned and financed. Further mills on the River Derwent at Darley Abbey were built in 1783 by Thomas Evans whose family of Derby iron founders were linked to the Strutts through marriage.

Meanwhile, Arkwright himself went onto build *his* second mill, the Lower Mill, at Cromford in 1776-77, this time supported financially by Peter Nightingale, a wealthy local lead merchant. This mill was built slightly further down the yard and was thus sourced by a combination of the Cromford Sough *and* the Bonsall Brook, while the wheel which drove the mill was sunk into a deep pit to supply the "head" of water required. With the second mill came a house for Arkwright overlooking the mill entrance, plus cottages for the workers and which were superior to most working-class accommodation at that time. Thus it was that by 1790, Richard Arkwright was employing around 800 workers; men wove his yarn into calico in houses also built by the great man, their wives and children worked in the mills and other men worked in the loom shop or as framework knitters at the mill.

As for Strutt, his Belper and Milford mills included workshops for nail-makers and framework knitters and by 1789 employed 600 workers – a number which had risen to 2,000 by 1833. Like Arkwright, Strutt offered working families superior houses for that day and age, including those built in Belper in the 1790s at Long Row, The Clusters and The Scotches, and in Milford at Hopping Hill. Similarly, the Evans family employed over 500 workers by 1830, with similar property built for workers on Lavender Row, Darley Abbey. Then like Strutt before him, Arkwright's second financier, Peter Nightingale, also got in on the act, building his own mill at Lea in 1784 along with his business partner, John Smedley. Once again, worker accommodation was made available and Lea Mills soon became the basis for John Smedley Ltd, a textile business that is still running

today; in fact, John Smedley Ltd is the oldest manufacturing business in the world while also using the oldest, still-active mill in the world (see *Quirky Derbyshire [Lea]*). And just to complete the late 18th century textile mill picture, Arkwright's other Derbyshire mills were erected at Bakewell (1778), Wirksworth (1780), Cressbrook (1783) and again at Cromford (Masson Mill, 1783). In fact, by 1789, there were 22 cotton-spinning mills in Derbyshire; the Industrial Revolution was very much up and running throughout the county.

Today, the stretch of the River Derwent from Derby to Cromford, upon which these famous pioneers built their historic mills, carries the prestigious World Heritage status. As for the late 18th century product of these mills, this was, of course, mainly cotton which was used to manufacture cheap clothing for the masses, thus improving the general standard of living. Indeed, Sir Robert Peel stated: "*I know of no man who has done more honour to this country than Sir Richard Arkwright, not excluding our military heroes like Nelson and Wellington.*" Similarly, Erasmus Darwin wrote that the Arkwright system of cotton spinning had "*contributed more to the general benefit of mankind, in so short a period of time, than any other single effort of human ingenuity*".

Arkwright's "First Mill", built in 1771 at Cromford. It was initially five storeys high and eleven bays wide, although an extension was built over the Bonsall Brook (shown here) in 1785. The mill was reduced to three storeys following a fire in 1929.

Cressbrook Mill built in 1783 by Richard Arkwright with mill apprentice cottages visible behind it and which typically housed London orphans who worked in the mill. The original mill burned down in 1785 but was re-built by Richard Arkwright Jnr in 1787.

Darley Abbey Mills the first of which was built in 1783 by Thomas Evans, with four other mills added before 1830. Darley Abbey supplies the most intact complex of the original 18th century Derwent Valley mills.

Masson Mill built in 1783 and in continuous use up until 1991. Built on the River Derwent, the original 21-bay, five-storey mill had a power source that was 10 times stronger than Arkwright's first mill.

Quirk Alert: Mashed Up

In 1789, Samuel Slater, one of Strutt's apprentices at Milford, absconded to America carrying Arkwright's system in his head, and therefore somewhat mirroring the escapades of John Lombe, 70 years earlier – although there weren't any English assassins sent after Slater! The former apprentice then settled in Pawtucket, Rhode Island, where he built America's first successful water-powered textile mill and went onto become known as the "Father of the American Industrial Revolution". Anyway, as Slater was born in Belper, the town was thus twinned in the 20th century with Pawtucket – a town which is also the home of toy manufacturer, Hasbro. However, relations between the two towns became "very strained" in 2001, when Belper "rejected" a £6,000 fraternity gift from their twin of a 7ft fibreglass model of Mr Potato Head. Dressed in what the American's deemed to be late 18th century clothing, the garish model was considered "hideous" by Belper residents, and was thus exiled to see out its days at the former American Adventure Theme Park, near Ilkeston. The spurned residents of Pawtucket were reported to be pretty "mashed up" in the American press, while the Sun reported them as being "spuddy furious"!

Despite the late 18th century explosion of cotton mills in Derbyshire, the centre of the industry soon moved to Lancashire thanks to its easier access to supplies of cotton via the Mersey and, when steam-power arrived, to local coal, too. Indeed, by 1901, 85% of the English cotton mill workforce lived in Lancashire, by which stage many of Derbyshire's mills had been long-since converted to other uses or were derelict. The exception to this rule were those Derbyshire mills in the north-west of the county and which were therefore close to the booming industrial Lancashire heartland. These included significant mills to the east of Manchester at places like Glossop, Hayfield and New Mills, and also at Mellor, which was part of Derbyshire until 1936 – for this was where Samuel Oldknow built a six-storey mill between 1790 and 1793, having suitably diverted the course of the River Goyt to meet his needs. At that time, it was the largest cotton mill to be worked on the Arkwright system and by 1804 was employing around 550 people who operated 10,080 spindles. The central building was six storeys high, 210 feet long and 42 feet wide, with three-storeyed extensions at each side, making the total length about 400 feet. Alas, the mill suffered a catastrophic fire in 1892 and the remaining

ruins were largely demolished in the 1930s, after which the site was pretty much reclaimed by nature. However, the site of the wheel pit that housed what was known as the Wellington Wheel in Oldknow's day has recently been restored. As for the boom in the cotton industry in north-west Derbyshire, this brought with it a number of huge population increases with the parish of Glossop, for example, swelling from 8,883 in 1801 to 36,985 by 1901. Partially responsible for these increases was the fact that the parish boundary in those days also included the rapidly expanding settlement of New Mills. Here, the Rivers Goyt and Sett combined to provide a constant fast-flowing water supply and by 1846, the town included eight cotton-spinning mills, four calico printing mills, four candlewick mills and two dyeing mills. The first of these was Torr Mill, built in 1790 by the Schofield family. This five-storey mill harnessed the fast-flowing River Goyt, but it, too, suffered a catastrophic fire and was completely rebuilt in 1838. It was only a stay of execution though, for although cotton production ceased on the site in 1890 and the building was then used by a fustian cloth-cutting firm, a second catastrophic fire completely destroyed it in 1912 and it has remained a ruin ever since.

Torrs Bridge, built in 1884 over the River Goyt to connect the industrial settlements of New Mills and Newtown, which had both expanded rapidly throughout the 19th century. In the foreground are the remains of Torr Mill.

Ruins of Samuel Oldknow's Mill, on the outskirts of the former Derbyshire township of Mellor. Built between 1790 and 1793 it was the largest cotton mill of its time but was destroyed by fire in 1892.

As for those two great Derbyshire cotton mill pioneers and their successive families, Richard Arkwright II sold all but Cromford and Masson Mill in the early 19th century, but the Strutts continued to run their family firm in Belper until 1897, when it was eventually sold to the English Sewing Company. Indeed, Jedediah Strutt's three sons continued to run affairs throughout the majority of the 19th century, with George managing the mills at Belper and William and Joseph managing the business at Derby. They were also social reformers and philanthropists who gave significant donations and founded several important institutions in the Derby area. This included Derby Arboretum, the first publicly owned, landscaped, urban recreational park in England, donated to the town of Derby in 1840 by Joseph Strutt. Other lasting monuments built by the Arkwrights in the late 18th century, include St Mary's church at Cromford, initially built as a private family chapel, and nearby Willersley Castle, intended as a dynastic seat for the family.

Meanwhile, in the decade immediately prior to the birth of Arkwright's mill, another famous Derbyshire son and one of England's most notable engineers, was constructing Britain's first major canal. The waterway in question was the Bridgewater Canal, the years were 1759-61, and its designer was James Brindley who came

SHARDLOW AND THE TRENT & MERSEY CANAL

Shardlow Wharf saw the arrival of several bulk-trading companies following the 1766-77 construction of the Trent & Mersey Canal.

A pub today, the Clock Warehouse at Shardlow was originally built in 1780 to hold stock being shipped along the Trent & Mersey Canal.

from the small Derbyshire village of Tunstead that lies around five miles north-east of Buxton. Brindley followed this major feat by designing the Manchester-Liverpool Canal, but it was 1769 before he designed a waterway in Derbyshire – this being the Chesterfield Canal which ran from Chesterfield to Stockwith, a village which lies on the River Trent just north of Gainsborough. The Chesterfield project was heavily supported by Derbyshire's coal and lead companies who obviously had a vested interest, and the project ran from 1771-77. Alas, Brindley died in 1772, but his legacy for Derbyshire was already in place. The most impressive feature of the Chesterfield Canal was the 2,850-yard long Norwood tunnel in North Derbyshire, while several branches of the canal were added later to link up with Derbyshire's burgeoning coal and iron-works. As a result, the canal noticeably stimulated the growth of these industries, and by 1789, it was aiding the transport per annum of 3,862 tons of lead, 42,379 tons of coal, 7,569 tons of stone, 4,366 tons of corn, 3,955 tons of lime and 1,544 tons of iron.

One of Brindley's most famous projects was the Trent & Mersey Canal, built between 1766 and 1777. It was clearly designed to link the two great rivers, but also brought with it prosperity to southern Derbyshire, particularly to the village of Shardlow. The agents of several bulk-trading companies were based there and as a result, Shardlow's population rose from around 300 in 1789 to 1,306 in 1841. After Brindley's death, further canals appeared in Derbyshire, all of them massively complimenting the burgeoning industry, particularly along Derbyshire's eastern frontier. New canals included the Erewash Canal (1778-1799), the Cromford Canal (1789-1794), and the Nutbrook Canal (1793-1796), while north-western Derbyshire saw the construction of the Peak Forest Canal (1794-1800) and southern Derbyshire, the Derby Canal (1793-1796). By 1830, the Cromford Canal alone was transporting c.290,000 tons a year of which two thirds was coal, while the Erewash Canal was transporting c.170,000 tons of coal per annum.

Clearly then, the late 18th and early 19th centuries saw a proliferation of British mills and canals, with Derbyshire very much at the forefront of the development of both. But on a smaller scale, Derbyshire also saw the pottery industry blossom, partly thanks to local coal mining exposing many new beds of stoneware clays. Leading the way in this industry was Denby Pottery. The business was founded in 1809, although it was known as Joseph Bourne Ltd in those days, named after the owner of the initial business – but it was also a business which soon acquired an international reputation for the quality of its bottles and jars and later for its kitchenware. However, Crown Derby actually preceded Denby Pottery, having been formed in 1750 when Andrew Planché established the first china works in Derby. A London Showroom was opened in 1773 and it was also around this time that Derby porcelain gained its first royal seal of approval from George III, as

he allowed the company to incorporate a crown into its product back-stamp and thus Crown Derby was born. This honour was added to over a hundred years later by Queen Victoria in 1890 when she not only bestowed her own royal seal of approval but also granted the company the title of The Royal Crown Derby Porcelain Company. Meanwhile between 1875 and 1914, the fire-clay deposits in southern Derbyshire also became a major centre for the manufacture of sanitary-ware and salt-glazed drainpipes. The same area along with areas of eastern Derbyshire also supplied clay for brick-making, particularly to the large collieries such as Butterley, Staveley and Stanton.

As for Crown Derby, the business didn't actually move to its current Osmaston Road site until 1878 when it took over the building which had previously been the local Derby workhouse – this thanks to the workhouse relocating to a new building on Uttoxeter Road. And while we're on the topic of workhouses, the Belper Union, which covered 34 parishes from Dethick to Mackworth, opened *its* workhouse in 1840 using the building that is today's Babington Hospital. Of course, as well as the Belper and Derby Unions, there were also seven other Poor Law Unions in Derbyshire, all of which had been created following the passing of the Poor Law Amendment Act 1834. Meanwhile, in Belper itself, the nail-making industry – which had been centred here since the 13th century – peaked around the turn of the 19th century with some 500 workshops in the town supplying nails to the flourishing textile mills. However, the early to mid-19th century saw the industry fall into decline as Belper's workshops were superseded by machinery – although some compensation was that the town continued to prosper in the textile and hosiery industries.

So, we've now talked about cotton mills, canals and pottery as part of the Derbyshire vanguard of the Industrial Revolution in the late 18th century. However, as a brief aside, the same period also saw an increase in Buxton's popularity, triggered by the 5th Duke of Devonshire's desire to see the spa town rival that of Bath. To this end, he commissioned architect John Carr, who amongst other improvements that he introduced in the 1780s, also designed the town's famous Crescent. The centre of this enormous building was intended to become the Duke's "town house", while to the left Carr built St Anne's Hotel and to the right, the Great Hotel with its Assembly Rooms that included card and coffee rooms and a splendid ballroom. However, the Duke's "occasional lodging" was soon turned into the Centre Hotel, with shops, a lending library and other accommodation occupying the ground floor. Further up the hill behind the Crescent, Carr also designed an enormous stable block in 1795, which by 1859 had become the Devonshire Royal Hospital, while later still (in 1881-82) the building was graced with a huge 156 foot dome that at that time was the largest in the world, exceeding the size of both St Paul's Cathedral in

GEORGIAN, VICTORIAN AND EDWARDIAN BUXTON: THE DEVONSHIRE LEGACY

The Crescent designed and built in the 1770s by John Carr for the 5th Duke of Devonshire.

View towards the stable block built by Carr in 1795, and which was converted to the Devonshire Royal Hospital in 1859. Then in 1881-82, it was adorned with this huge 156ft dome that at the time was the largest in the world.

Buxton Pavilion, which along with the Pavilion Gardens was constructed in 1871. Buxton Concert Hall, constructed in 1876, is in the background.

Buxton Opera House, built in 1903.

VICTORIAN MATLOCK: THE SMEDLEY LEGACY

Matlock's former Victorian hydrotherapy spa, built by John Smedley in the mid-19th century, and visited by the rich and famous.

Riber Castle. This famous Derbyshire landmark was built between 1862 and 1868 by John Smedley, following his success with the hydrotherapy business.

London and St Peter's Basilica in Rome. Splendid additions to Buxton's architecture continued throughout the Georgian, Victorian and Edwardian eras such as St John the Baptist's church (1811), the Royal Hotel (1849-52), two new stations (1863), the Palace Hotel (1865), the Pavilion and Pavilion Gardens (1871), the Town Hall (1889) and the Opera House (1903). Of these, the Palace Hotel was designed by Henry Currey in the style of a French chateau and was positioned on the hillside behind the Crescent and adjacent to Carr's stables, while the beautiful iron and glass Pavilion and its Concert Hall (1876) were designed by Edward Milner who had been Joseph Paxton's assistant in the construction of the world-famous Crystal Palace. Unsurprisingly, Buxton's population expanded, growing from 1,569 in 1841 to 6,480 by 1901, while the number of streets in the town doubled. Its role as a tourist centre also blossomed and by 1905, its hotels, hydros, rented apartments and lodging-houses saw more than 4,000 visitors a week in the high season while the town's most prevalent occupation was that of a servant.

During the same period, Matlock Bath also continued to develop as a spa town and holiday resort with many wealthy folk visiting the hydropathic establishment first built at Matlock Bank in 1851. The place was bought two years later by John Smedley, the owner of the nearby Lea Mills spinning works, and by 1867, Smedley's vastly expanded hydropathic establishment was treating 2,000 patients a year, including the likes of Robert Louis Stevenson, Sir Thomas Beecham and Ivor Novello. Out of his profits, Smedley built the rather distinctive Riber Castle which sits at 850 feet above sea-level on the hillside to the south of Matlock overlooking the town. His original intention was to include a 225 foot tower as part of the building but he had to abandon that idea when the telescopes that he planned to place in the tower were too large to fit in! Given its lofty position, the building required locally quarried gritstone to be hauled up the hillside by a series of pulleys. However, despite employing skilled craftsmen, the building ended up looking like a darkly Gothic castle from some 20th century horror movie and was certainly not to everyone's taste. For example, local architectural historian, Sir John Summerson, remarked: *"Had Smedley employed a professional he would have got a house unmistakably, however crudely, shaped with a style – Italian Gothic or baronial. As it was, he produced an object of indecipherable bastardry – a true monster."* None of this fazed Smedley, who had been inspired to construct his castellated mansion by the hilltop fantasies he'd seen while travelling in Europe. The pièce de résistance of the interior was the grand salon, occupying the full length of the building with staircases leading to a gallery and the towers at each end. But Smedley very much cared for the exterior, too, and local folklore claims that he was so taken with his construction that he often took his carriage down into the town at night to admire the sight of his illuminated home on the hillside. As for Smedley's original hydropathic building, this was destined to become the home of Derbyshire

The Old Cheese Shop at Hartington, established by the Duke of Devonshire in the 1870s.

County Council in the mid-20th century while Riber Castle ended up as a zoo!

As the Industrial Revolution passed from the 18th to the 19th century, the countryside landscape was also experiencing major changes, thanks to the enclosure of open fields. These events shaped Derbyshire, and particularly the White Peak, into what we see today, with much of the land divided into square or rectangular fields by dry-stone walls or hawthorn hedges. Alas, much of the 18th and 19th century partitioning was enforced by landowners after securing private acts of parliament with little regard to their impact upon the commoner. Nevertheless, alongside the Industrial Revolution, agriculture still continued to provide plenty of employment in Derbyshire. As the railway network developed, dairy farming prospered and milk began to overtake cheese production in importance. That said, one cheese factory that *did* prosper was the one founded by the Duke of Devonshire at Hartington in the 1870s. It was one of only three sources of Stilton cheese, while it also produced its own unique Dovedale cheese and others such as Buxton Blue. Cattle farming also continued to prosper, and better drainage meant a greater output of crops.

As for the most famous rural incident in Derbyshire during the Industrial Revolution, that occurred in Pentrich during the night of the 9th and 10th of June, 1817. For what became known as the Pentrich Revolution saw an unemployed stockinger called Jeremiah Brandreth lead an "army" of around three hundred local workers in a march on Nottingham. Armed with pikes, scythes and a few guns, their demands included the wiping out of the National Debt, which had spiralled out of control during the Napoleonic Wars. More particularly, increasing industrialisation had combined with mass demobilisation to cause mass unemployment. Locally, the end of the wars also saw a drop in demand for war materials, and thus big combined iron-smelting and coal companies saw the price of iron ore drop and the demand for coal fall – all of which led to the inevitable loss of jobs. The hosiery industry, in particular, had been in decline for a number of years and since 1811, stocking frames had been smashed country-wide in protest at the employment of low-skilled workers to produce low quality stockings. It was thus under this climate, that secret revolutionary committees sprang up around the country, including one at Nottingham to which Brandreth was affiliated. His plan was to march to Nottingham, invading Butterley ironworks on the way, where they intended to kill the three senior managers and then ransack the works for weapons. At Nottingham they planned to take over the barracks and then proceed by boat down the River Trent and attack Newark with Brandreth having informed his fellow revolutionaries that there were sixteen thousand men ready to join them. Of course, it didn't go to plan, with heavy rain causing a number of his "army" to defect during their march on Nottingham. Worse still for Brandreth, one of Lord Sidmouth's informers had long-since infiltrated the group, and at Giltbrook they were met by a small force of the Home Secretary's soldiers. The revolutionaries scattered and, although the leaders managed to escape, they were arrested over the following months, with 85 of the marchers eventually charged with attempting to "subvert and destroy the Government and the Constitution by force of arms." Twenty-three were sentenced, three to transportation for fourteen years and eleven for life. However, Brandreth along with a couple of other ring-leaders was convicted of high treason and sentenced to death by public hanging and beheading, which took place at Nuns Green in front of Friar Gate Gaol in Derby.

UTTERLY BUTTERLEY

The roof of St Pancras Station, London, which was built by The Butterley Company in the 1860s and is still known today as the "cathedral of the railways".

> ## Quirk Alert: Name That Trough
>
> *There are many examples of village water systems around the county, but a series of stone basins at Ible are known as The Twelve Apostles, while the three at Horsley are known as Sophia, Rosamund and Blanche, named after a 19th century vicar's wife and two great nieces.*

The other big Derbyshire industry to flourish during the Industrial Revolution was iron smelting, and this transformed the eastern part of the county with ironworks abounding. Indeed by 1784, Derbyshire and Nottinghamshire were producing 10% of national pig-iron, and by 1806, coke-fired furnaces in Derbyshire alone had an annual output of 10,329 tons making it England's fourth largest county producer. The largest ironworks at this time were the Griffin Works at New Brampton and the Adelphi Works at Duckmanton, both founded by the Smith family, and which between them accounted for a quarter of Derbyshire's annual output. The products of these two Derbyshire ironworks included the cylinders of steam engines, cannons, cannon balls, heating stoves, cooking ranges and grates. Having said that, both sites were closed by 1845, at which point the Smith's turned their attention to one of Derbyshire's other famous ironworks at Stanton-by-Dale, and which eventually became the Stanton Ironworks Co. Ltd in 1878.

Built in the late 18th century, the Stanton site lay on the newly constructed Nutbrook Canal, a waterway originally built to serve the collieries at Shipley and West Hallam. However, it wasn't until 1846 that Benjamin Smith and his son Josiah brought three blast-furnaces into production alongside the Nutbrook Canal, a location that also put the furnaces close to the Erewash Canal, the Midland Railway and numerous collieries, too. Ironically the Nutbrook Canal had been built by William Jessop and Benjamin Outram between 1793 and 1796, both of whom were founders and partners in what would later become Stanton Ironworks' biggest

The twin viaducts over the River Wye at Millers Dale, and both built by The Butterley Company, in 1866 and 1905, respectively.

IRONWORKS AND CANALS: INEXTRICABLY LINKED

Transhipment warehouses at the terminus of the Cromford Canal, Cromford.

Stanton Ironworks dominated the Stanton-by-Dale area from the mid-19th century onwards. However, Stanton's blast furnaces were closed in 1974, and the last pipes cast in 2007. The old steelworks were then dismantled – but relics such as this truck in Ilkeston still serve as a reminder.

Founded in 1849 by Milton Ironworks, Leawood Pumping Station could pump around 28 tons of water per minute up from the River Derwent to the Cromford Canal.

local competitor, the Butterley Company. Nevertheless, by 1848 the Stanton works itself was producing 200 tons of pig-iron a week, just ahead of the output of the nearby Riddings Ironworks and second only to the Butterley Company's Codnor Park ironworks, which produced 210 tons per week. The original three Stanton furnaces were replaced by five more between 1865 and 1867, and just in time for the Franco-Prussian War of 1870-71 which had created a huge demand for iron. As a result, the works expanded rapidly with the construction of new furnaces and foundries alongside the Erewash Canal in the early 1870s.

As a combined iron and coal business, though, it was the Butterley Company which was the largest not only in Derbyshire, but in the East Midlands, too. It was founded by Francis Beresford, a solicitor, and the previously mentioned Benjamin Outram, an assistant surveyor working on the expansion of the Erewash Canal in 1794. Recognising the mineral potential, the two men bought the Butterley Hall estate, and were soon joined in partnership by the canal's chief surveyor, William Jessop and John Wright, a local banker. They initially traded as Benjamin Outram & Co, and they were soon quarrying limestone, mining coal and smelting iron, while using the Cromford and Erewash canals for transportation. In 1807, two years after Outram's death, the company was re-named the Butterley Company and by 1810 the Codnor Park ironworks had been acquired. By 1830, the company employed 1,500 people and accounted for more than a third of Derbyshire's pig-iron output, and by 1848, annual pig-iron exports had risen to nearly 21,000 tons. Their products included cast-iron rails and wagon wheels for tramways and railways, canal lock mechanisms, cast-iron bridges for railways (including Vauxhall Bridge in London), steam engines and locomotives. However, their most famous ironwork was the roof of St Pancras station which covered four acres, weighed 6,894 tons and, at the time, was the largest single-span structure in the world. Meanwhile, their most famous constructions in Derbyshire are the twin viaducts over the River Wye

at Millers Dale. The first of these was the south viaduct, built in 1866, but an increase in traffic saw a second parallel viaduct built to the north in 1905.

Between them, the Butterley Company, Stanton Ironworks and Riddings Ironworks contributed the lion's share of Derbyshire's iron output, which reached 95,000 tons a year by the mid-19th century and rose steadily to a peak of 770,000 tons in 1900. Throughout these times, the production of iron and Derbyshire's canal system became inextricably linked, and nowhere is this more evident than in the construction of Leawood Pumping Station on the Cromford Canal – although it was actually Milton Ironworks in today's county of South Yorkshire that installed a steam engine here in 1849. Its purpose was to pump water up from the River Derwent and into the Cromford Canal, which it did at the rate of four tons of water per stroke at the rate of seven strokes per minute. This was particularly useful in dry summers when it became difficult to maintain water levels – particularly as the Cromford Canal lost huge amounts of water to the Erewash Canal through its adjoining fourteen locks at Langley Mill every time a boat went through.

Also produced by the ironworks was wrought iron, which tended to be preferred by architects and civil engineers for its strength. However, the second half of the 19th century saw ironstone seams become exhausted and the steel industry grow in popularity, all of which led to the Butterley Company eventually closing its blast furnaces in 1902. Meanwhile in Derby, Andrew Handysides had built a brass foundry in 1868 and a malleable cast iron foundry in 1877 and by the turn of the century they had become the second largest employer in the town behind the railway, employing 1,200 workmen. The firm became famous for iron bridges built for railways both at home and abroad, including the Albert Suspension Bridge over the Thames in London, while other products included the Central Station at Manchester along with "smaller" items such as cast iron window frames and Post Office pillar boxes.

It was also during the 19th century that the coalfields along the Derbyshire-Nottinghamshire border became among the most significant in England. These were backed up to a lesser extent by the South Derbyshire coalfields so when the railways opened up the market to London in the mid-19th century, the coal industry exploded and saw Derbyshire competing for the first time on an equal footing with Northumberland and Durham. The railways also brought the famous George Stephenson to Derbyshire, as chief engineer for the construction of the North Midland Railway Company's line from Derby to Leeds. And it was during the blasting of a tunnel at Clay Cross in 1837 that Stephenson saw the exposed coal seams and realised that they could be a rich source of coke fuel for locomotives. He thus bought the estate to mine coal, building coke ovens, blast furnaces and an iron foundry – all three of which by this stage were a typical part of the landscape of eastern Derbyshire, and towns such as Chesterfield, Alfreton, Ripley, Heanor and Ilkeston all grew rapidly as a result.

By 1862, the total coal output from the Butterley Company's 15 collieries had risen to more than 700,000 tons a year and had begun to exceed the output from its iron-works. However, the Clay Cross Company (which had formerly been George Stephenson's company) became by far the largest supplier of coal to London. The company built many houses in Clay Cross, plus a school and a mechanics' institute and the town's population jumped from 564 in 1831 to 6,347 by 1881. Its numerous collieries were mirrored further north with many of them supplying the Staveley ironworks and which ultimately became the Staveley Coal and Iron Co. Ltd. By 1865, the company was producing 743,000 tons of coal a year, which was slightly more than the c.500,000 tons produced by the collieries of the Sheepbridge Coal and Iron Co. Ltd. It is unsurprising, therefore, that by 1870, some 16,405 miners were employed in Derbyshire's coalfields and total annual output reached 5,102,267 tons. That number had risen to 8 million tons of coal per annum by 1880, and peaked in 1913 when 18 million tons were mined by a staggering 48,486 miners; clearly by this stage, coal mining was the county's most prodigious employer. It was, however, also the most dangerous. For although disasters were not experienced on the

Statue of George Stephenson, holding aloft his famous Rocket outside Chesterfield Station. The wheel on which he stands is engraved with the words "LOCOMOTION: THE CONQUEST OVER SPACE AND TIME". The great man spent the autumn of his life in Derbyshire. He died at Tapton House, his home in Chesterfield and is buried at Trinity Church, Chesterfield.

same scale as further north, 23 men were drowned in a Clay Cross pit in 1861, 25 men and two boys died at Renishaw Park Colliery in 1871 and 45 miners were killed in a gas explosion at Parkhouse Colliery in 1882. Understandably, trade unions began to materialise although they were generally opposed by colliery owners. Nevertheless, the Derbyshire Miners Association was created in 1880 to improve their lot. And a difficult lot it was indeed, for as well as the risks of the profession, many pit villages degenerated into slums and by 1901 the infant mortality rate at Shirebrook, for example, had risen to 236 per thousand births. Happily, that trend was bucked at New Bolsover when a model village was built by the Bolsover Colliery between 1891 and 1894. The village included 200 houses, a village green, allotments, schools and an institute, which were supplied alongside a Methodist chapel, an orphanage, co-operative stores and multiple sporting facilities.

Meanwhile, back in Derby in 1839, we finally arrive at the catalyst for the expanding coal, iron and indeed even the tourist industries: the railways. For it was in this year that the North Midland Railway set up its works opposite Derby Station. The North Midland Railway then merged with the Birmingham & Derby Junction and the Midland Counties Railways to become the Midland Railway Company, and Derby became its headquarters in 1840. As a result, the Litchurch Lane area of Derby saw the construction of the largest railway works in Europe. This also encouraged the birth of many new manufacturing companies and thus resulted in an influx to the town of workers from afar, many of whom lived in a new housing community built nearby; indeed, the 1851 census reveals that 43% of Derby's inhabitants were non-Derbyshire born. This new railway-based community resulted in the expansion of Derby's boundaries in 1877 to also include 'Railway Derby' – thus significantly increasing the borough's population. Of course, the railway industry has remained a key industry and employer within the town ever since. Or at least it did until the British government's extraordinary sell-out on a multi-million pound contract to the German company, Siemens, in the summer of 2011 and which has posed the most serious threat to 'Railway Derby' since its rise to significance in the mid-19th century. George Stephenson and all of his brilliant 19th century peers will no doubt be turning in their graves.

We're not quite finished with the great man in Derbyshire, though. For George Stephenson, along with his son, Robert, also engineered the Midland Counties Railway between Derby, Leicester and

Part of the 1,445 foot long viaduct at Dinting Vale that formed part of the railway line built to link Sheffield to Manchester in the 1840s.

Nottingham and which opened in 1839. A year later, and the line from Long Eaton to Rugby connected with the London & Birmingham Railway, thus allowing George Stephenson & Co. to send coal from Clay Cross to London. Also completed in 1840 was the North Midland line which ran through Ambergate, Chesterfield and into what is today known as South Yorkshire. This particular route required a mile-long cutting crossed by ten bridges at Belper, and a tunnel *beneath* the Cromford Canal at Bullbridge. Further railway lines through Derby and into Derbyshire and beyond followed, encouraging the expansion of tourism throughout the county. For example, the first section of the Manchester, Buxton, Matlock & Midland Junction Railway was opened in 1849 between Ambergate and Rowsley, and the extension of that line up to Buxton and then onto Manchester saw the introduction of spectacular features like the five-arched viaduct over Monsal Dale, viaducts over Miller's Dale and the huge tunnels at Cressbrook, Litton and Chee Dale. The line was eventually closed in 1968 and remained unused for 12 years before being taken over by the Peak District National Park. It was then converted into a walking and cycling route known as the Monsal Trail, and which today incorporates all of those impressive 19th century engineering feats as spectacular features. Meanwhile, the 1840s also saw the construction of the railway from Sheffield to Manchester, and which therefore saw most of its track laid in Derbyshire. One of the most spectacular features of this railway was the sixteen-arched viaduct at Dinting Vale over the Dinting Brook, just to the west of Glossop. Completed in 1845, it is 121 feet high and stretches for 1,445 feet – although the elegant 19th century arches are somewhat spoiled today by the interspersing of later brick reinforcements.

Another expanding Derbyshire industry of the Industrial Revolution period was limestone quarrying with major works appearing at Harpur Hill, Dove Holes and Middleton-by-Wirksworth. The limestone would then be processed in limekilns before its distri-

bution by canal and later by railway, mainly to the previously-mentioned ironworks of Derbyshire for use as a flux in the smelting process. Unsurprisingly, the Butterley Company also owned a limestone quarry at Crich and shipped the product to their own ironworks, while George Stephenson built 20 limekilns at Ambergate alongside the Cromford Canal. And sticking with stone, Stancliffe Quarry at Darley Dale produced millstone grit that was used to pave Trafalgar Square while the quarries at Little Eaton provided stone for Derby Cathedral and Birmingham Town Hall.

Unsurprisingly, the Industrial Revolution led to a huge growth in Derbyshire's population throughout the 19th century. The first ever British census of 1801 recorded Derbyshire's population at 161,567 – a *county* total which is actually almost 100,000 fewer inhabitants than today's *city* population of Derby! Having said that, 1801 saw Derby's own population recorded as a mere 10,832, just 4.1% of what it is today. However, these figures at the beginning of the 19th century are also influenced by the fact that Derbyshire's population was largely rural and comprised of folk who rarely moved around, thus giving rise to the local saying: *"He's never once been out of sight of the smoke of his own chimney"*. But as decade followed decade in the 19th century, Derbyshire's population began to rapidly increase across both town and countryside. The county's population reached 272,202 by 1841, and by the turn of the 20th century, it had expanded to 621,636. During the same period, Derby's population trebled between 1801 (10,832) and 1841 (32,741), and more than doubled again to 69,266 by 1901. Meanwhile, Chesterfield's population didn't quite keep in step, moving from 4,267 in 1801 to 14,688 in 1901, while Wirksworth's went from 2,978 in 1801 to 4,122 in 1841 before falling as a result of the decrease in the popularity of lead mining in the 19th century. Without any heavy industry, Bakewell's population rose only gently whereas the similarly non-industrial Ashbourne saw its population drop from 2,246 in 1831 to 1,795 in 1901.

Intriguingly, though, all of the county's secondary towns were briefly overtaken by Belper at the beginning of the 19th century, with the early Industrial Revolution boom years seeing its population rise to 4,500 by 1801 and to 10,082 by 1851. However, the adverse fortunes of the cotton industry thanks mainly to the American Civil War saw Belper's population drop to 8,527 by 1871 although it did rise back to 10,934 by 1901. Of course, Belper was soon overtaken in the Derbyshire population league table by those towns surrounded by the coal, iron and steel industries in the east of the county. In this region, Heanor's population rose from 3,058 in 1841 to 12,418 in 1901, Ripley's from 2,515 to 9,239 and Ilkeston's from 5,326 to 25,384. In addition to the towns, other east Derbyshire *parishes* also mirrored those population growth figures between 1841 and 1901, with Alfreton growing from 7,577 to 17,505, Staveley from 2,688 to 11,420, Eckington's from 4,401 to 12,895 and Killamarsh from 906 to 3,644. The only other area of Derbyshire to keep population pace with the towns in the east of the county was in the far north-west where the cotton mills continued to prosper thanks to their proximity to the booming cotton heartland of Lancashire. Glossop, in particular, benefited during this period with the Duke of Norfolk's agent developing what became known as New Glossop, and which we know today simply as Glossop; the original settlement less than a mile to the east eventually became known as Old Glossop. The development

Victoria Mill at New Mills was built in 1860 alongside the Peak Forest Canal.

Also known as Victoria Mills, these mills at Draycott were built in 1888 to commemorate Queen Victoria's Golden Jubilee the previous year. The mills became one of the most important lace factories in the world.

Lace was also the main product of Springfield Mills at Sandiacre and which were also built in 1888.

included the building of the Town Hall in 1837, the Market Hall in 1844 and the railway station in 1847 each of which contributed towards the town's designation as a municipal borough in 1866. Meanwhile, in tandem with the population growth in the north-west and the east of the county, the decline in the lead and agriculture industries saw many other areas of *rural* Derbyshire's population peak in 1841 before steadily falling. And while the north-west continued to prosper, fortunes at Shardlow were as diametrically opposed as its county location, for this area of south-east Derbyshire, which had boomed at the end of the 18th century, saw its population fall as its canal port felt the impact of the railways.

Back to the north-west, though, and we've already covered Samuel Oldknow's six-storey mill built at Mellor (1790-91), but many others had followed at Glossop, Hayfield and New Mills in the early 19th century. By 1851, the parish of Glossop contained 60 mills while nearby New Mills was home to another 18. Of these, Wren's Nest Mills at Glossop employed 1,400 workers operating 123,000 spindles and 2,541 looms, while Victoria Mill at New Mills flourished courtesy of its construction in 1860 alongside the Peak Forest Canal. Towards the end of the 19th century, though, the rest of the county had seen the textile industry decline dramatically and between 1860 and 1890, the number of silk mills in Derbyshire dropped from 42 to 14. However, the trend was bucked in Long Eaton where the lace industry flourished in the late 19th century, assisted by the town's proximity to Nottingham, the lace capital of England. The Harrington Mills were built between 1885 and 1887 and by the early 20th century, the lace industry employed 4,000 people in Long Eaton, a quarter of its population. Lace mills were also built nearby. For example, Victoria Mills at Draycott were built in 1888 to commemorate Queen Victoria's Golden Jubilee the previous year. However, a devastating fire delayed construction and it wasn't completed until 1907 after which it became one of the most important lace factories in the world and the largest manufacturing mill in Europe. Similarly, Springfield Mills at Sandiacre were built alongside the Erewash Canal as lace mills in the same year (1888), this time by Terah Hooley, a local entrepreneur and former owner of nearby Risley Hall. Meanwhile, today, many of these featured mills are long-since closed to industry but still very-much in use. For example, Wren's Nest Mills at Glossop ceased trading in 1955 but is now home to apartments and a number of major retailers, while Victoria Mills at Draycott ceased lace manufacture in 1970 but along with Springfield Mills has now been converted into luxury apartments.

Quirk Alert: Deal or No Deal?

In 1848, a man allegedly sold his wife at Repton market cross for a shilling!

The Magpie Mine near Sheldon was worked from 1740 and closed for the last time in 1954. Its remains are probably the best example in the UK of a 19ᵗʰ century lead mine.

One final industrial facet of the 19ᵗʰ century was that it saw the decline of the lead industry which, for so many centuries before, had been one of Derbyshire's main employers. The industry was still largely thriving in the first half of the century, with the Magpie Mine at Sheldon mining a record for a Derbyshire mine of 800 tons of lead in 1827. It was also located at the junction of three veins and was one of several mines exploiting them and which thus led to a number of disputes. The worst came in 1833 between the Magpie Mine and the Maypitt Mine. It had become common practise to light fires underground to smoke out opponents, but the action on this occasion resulted in death by suffocation of three miners from the Maypitt Mine. Twenty four Magpie miners were put on trial for their murder, but all were acquitted because of the difficulty in identifying the individual culprits. Nevertheless, it is said that the wives of the "murdered" men put a curse on the mine, and it never really prospered thereafter! Water, in particular, was a problem in the Magpie Mine and so when the price of lead fell, the cost of pumping made the mine unprofitable and it closed in 1883. It was worked again at intervals until 1923 and reopened in a limited way in the 1950s but only ever employed a few men and rarely made money. A similar story of decline occurred elsewhere, with the final blow for many lead mines delivered in 1885 following the breakthrough in mining cheap lead-zinc ores in Australia. Inevitably, lead mining villages began to see a drop in their population and the majority of those who remained became poor. Demographically, Derbyshire had 2,333 lead miners in 1861. That number had dropped to only 285 by the end of the century, although many of those worked for the still-flourishing Mill Close Mine in Darley Dale, which by 1887 accounted for 85% of the county's iron ore, and actually remained productive until its closure in 1940. As for the Magpie Mine at Sheldon, it is the only Derbyshire lead mine with a significant part of its buildings still standing today, including the Cornish Engine House (built 1869) and adjacent tower (built 1840); indeed, its surface remains are probably the best example in the UK of a 19ᵗʰ century lead mine

And that's about it for the Derbyshire Industrial Revolution. During this period, great names associated with the county undoubtedly shaped the future of the world, from John and Thomas Lombe in the 1720s to Richard Arkwright, Jedediah Strutt and Thomas Brindley in the late 18ᵗʰ century. Other great innovators continued their work in the 19ᵗʰ century, with local families such as the Smedleys and the Nightingales complementing the Outrams and the Jessops, and they were joined in the mid-19ᵗʰ century by the great George Stephenson who was destined to work his later years and then be laid to rest in Derbyshire. Little wonder, therefore, that many of these great names are perpetuated today by the World Heritage Site that is Derwent Valley Mills.

From the Late Victorians to Present Day

It was during the 19ᵗʰ century that Derbyshire's towns began to take on the social identity that they have today. This included the first appearance of police stations, hospitals, banks and railway stations, accompanied by a boom in shops and which ranged from small family businesses to large department stores. Leisure facilities also began to appear, such as public parks, swimming baths, libraries, museums and art galleries. Examples of new parks in Derby include the 11-acre arboretum which was funded by the Strutt family, and Sir Michael Bass's recreation ground that still bears his name today, while Queen's Park was opened in Chesterfield in 1887 to commemorate Queen Victoria's Golden Jubilee.

By the end of the 19ᵗʰ century, the Derby Grand Theatre had also opened (1886) and Thomas Barton had started his public bus service in the Derby area, commencing in 1898. Unfortunately, as town populations increased, this brought with it sanitation problems. These had initially been tackled following the Municipal Corporations Act of 1835 with the Act introducing a corporation headed by an annually elected mayor, 12 aldermen and 36 councillors. Then local boards of health were set up to deal with sewerage and sanitation matters following the Public Health Act of 1848, which then became urban sanitary authorities in 1872 and ultimately urban and rural district councils after 1894.

Sticking with the social scene, a number of present-day customs and recreations came to the fore in the 19ᵗʰ century. Well dressings, which had been suppressed during the Reformation, were initially revived at Tissington during the 17ᵗʰ or 18ᵗʰ century by the Fitzherbert family. The ancient origins of well dressings are not fully known, but are suspected to have developed from the pagan custom of offering a sacrifice to the gods of wells and springs to ensure a continued

DERBYSHIRE'S EARLY PUBLIC PARKS

The Arboretum, Derby, was a gift from Joseph Strutt to the town in 1840. It was also the first public park in the country and was thought to have been one of the inspirations for Central Park in New York.

Queen's Park, Chesterfield, opened in 1887 to commemorate Queen Victoria's Golden Jubilee. As well as its boating lake and botanical gardens, it is also home to one of English First Class cricket's most picturesque grounds.

The Pavilion Gardens in Buxton were opened in 1871, thanks to donations from the seventh Duke of Devonshire, and have gradually expanded to 23 acres thanks to later ducal gifts.

Manor Park in Glossop was not converted into a public park until 1927, when it was acquired by the Borough Council of Glossop. The park was formed from the ornamental grounds of the manor house owned by the Dukes of Norfolk.

supply of fresh water. By the time the tradition was revived at Tissington, the meaning had changed to giving thanks to God for the gift of water and, at Tissington, for their deliverance from the plague. In the 19th century, the custom began to spread, firstly to nearby Wirksworth (1827), and then Youlgreave and Tideswell (1829), and then throughout Derbyshire, with each town and village generally adopting the same process of creating scenes from the Bible from petals and other soft vegetation pressed into soft clay which, in turn, was pressed onto boards. At Tissington, the boards are still soaked in the famous village pond and the clay is actually trodden upon to develop the correct consistency. The clay is then pressed onto the boards and the picture is traced onto the clay

One of the six wells that are dressed annually at Tissington.

and in-filled with alder tree cones, coffee beans and flower petals. Unsurprisingly, well dressing is a fairly laborious process and takes around three days to complete. Each of the wells is then blessed by the clergy on Ascension Day following the morning service at St Mary's church, and the well dressings remain in place for one week until the following Wednesday evening. Today, the website www.welldressing.com lists c.100 locations of Derbyshire well-dressings and which are spread across the majority of the county.

As for the county's most famous song, *The Derby Ram*, that was committed to print in 1867 by Llewellyn Jewitt, although it had been previously performed since the 18th century by farm-workers in pubs as an annual plough-play between

Christmas and Plough Monday. The song was then adopted by the 95th Derbyshire Regiment who also took a ram as their mascot. Of course, the most famous Rams of all were formed in 1884 in Derby. Originally based at the Racecourse as an offshoot of Derbyshire County Cricket Club (founded 1870), Derby County FC adopted its nickname of The Rams thanks to their links to the local regiment, although they didn't move to their famous Baseball Ground until 1895. And no turn of the century Derbyshire football reference is complete without mentioning the legendary Steve Bloomer. Having joined Derby in 1892, he went onto score 293 goals for the club in 473 games spanning two periods, and an astonishing 28 goals in 23 games for England – a ratio that has never been surpassed. Also, his 317 first division goals position him second only to the similarly legendary Jimmy Greaves – which goes some way to explaining Derby County's anthem: *Steve Bloomer's Watching*. Alas, Steve Bloomer isn't a son of Derbyshire, though; he was born in Cradley Heath, then part of Worcestershire…although there are a number of Bloomers in Derbyshire including the famous bakers in Bakewell and, as it happens, my own cousins who are also Derbyshire Bloomers, and probably share some of Steve Bloomer's sporting genes, given the amount of impressive county and national success they and their children have achieved in a number of different sports. Back to Derbyshire football, though, and for completeness, Derbyshire's other current football league club, Chesterfield FC, were formed in 1919. They have enjoyed a somewhat less illustrious past than their more southerly county neighbours, but they were certainly robbed of an FA Cup Final appearance in 1997, thanks to bungling officials and lack of goal-line technology! Then located half-way between Derby and Chesterfield is Alfreton, where Alfreton Town are currently riding high in English football's fifth tier and potentially knocking on the door of becoming only Derbyshire's third ever professional football team – although Glossop North End did grace the First Division in season 1899/1900 – the smallest town ever to reach English football's top league. They changed their name to Glossop at this point to avoid confusion with Preston North End, but alas, they finished bottom that season. Their last complete season in the football league was 1913/14 when they finished 17th in Division II; they were not re-elected after the war.

Back to the 19th century again, though, for it also saw slight changes made to Derbyshire's county boundaries. For starters, in 1844, a number of Derbyshire-related exclaves were tidied up – exclaves being areas of land belonging to one county but which were completely surrounded by another county. Many of England and Wales's exclaves were absorbed by their surrounding county thanks to the Counties (Detached Parts) Act 1844, although this didn't included Derbyshire's exclaves in Leicestershire at this time. However, part of the township of Foston and Scropton (in the parish of Scropton) was transferred to Staffordshire at this time, while the part of the parish of Glossop on the Cheshire side of the River Etherow was declared to be in Derbyshire, as its previous status had been uncertain. Then in 1884, the three separate detached parts of the parish of Packington, including the chapelry of Snibston were transferred to Leicestershire, where they formed part of the new parish of Ravenstone with Snibston. Finally, the last Derbyshire exclave, known as the Donisthorpe-Measham exclave, was transferred to Leicestershire in 1897, including the parishes of Appleby Magna North, Chilcote, Measham, Oakthorpe and Donisthorpe (partly in Leicestershire), Stretton en le Field and Willesley. At the same time the parishes of Netherseal and Overseal were transferred from Leicestershire to Derbyshire. Before that, Derbyshire's south-eastern boundary with Leicestershire would have been interesting and confusing in equal measures. Indeed, in the early 18th century, William Woolley wrote of Appleby Magna: "*The two counties are so mingled here that the houses, to an ordinary passenger, cannot be distinguished asunder, which be of either shire, there being no direct meer between them.*"

Quirk Alert: Bottoms Up

In 1877 the five Longdendale Valley Reservoirs, built in what is now the far north-west of Derbyshire, made up the largest expanse of inland man-made water in the world at that time. From top-down, they are Woodhead, Torside, Rhodeswood, Valehouse and Bottoms.

The end of the 19th century also saw Derbyshire follow suit with most other English counties, as the Local Government Act 1888 heralded the modern era of local government. Thus it was that in 1889, Derbyshire was formalised as an *administrative* county, which was based very closely on its *historic* county boundaries. Derbyshire County Council controlled almost the entirety of the administrative county area with the exception of Derby, which was declared a county borough in 1889. And that is how things remained right up to 1st April 1974 when the Local Government Act 1972 was implemented – but more on that a little later.

The start of the 20th century saw the quarrying and stone industries continue to thrive. The most significant development using Derbyshire stone came when Bole Hill Quarry near Upper Padley supplied 1.2 million tons of stone to the early 20th century dams that were being built in the Derwent valley, by the Derwent Valley Water Board, a company formed in 1899 and which employed 2,753 workers by 1908. Even more remarkable was the temporary settlement built between Howden and Derwent Reservoirs at Birchinlee to house the navvies and their families. By 1909, it housed 967 people and included schools, hospitals, pubs and shops, but which were largely made up of corrugated iron huts and hence the place became known as Tin Town. The place even had its own post office, plus a recreation hall which was the venue for cinema, concerts, dances and whist drives. However, all of Tin Town's buildings were demolished once the reservoir building was complete and nothing remains of the place today.

As for Howden and Derwent Reservoirs, they were built in the narrow Upper Derwent and Ashop valleys, their build having been commissioned by the authorities of Sheffield, Derby, Nottingham and Leicester. In order to facilitate their construction, though, a number of villages, hamlets and farmsteads had to be submerged. It was a similar story when the third of these prominent reservoirs was built at Ladybower between 1935 and 1943, with the villages of Ashopton and Derwent also submerged. The buildings in Ashopton were demolished before the reservoir was filled, but parts of Derwent village such as Derwent Woodlands Church and Derwent Hall remained intact, and still became visible during dry summers; indeed the clock tower of the church had been left standing and the upper part of it was permanently visible above the water level until 1947, when it was seen as a hazard and was demolished.

Quirk Alert: An Echo from the Past?

This is a personal "close but no cigar" tale and which relates to the three photographs above. The "incident" took place one afternoon in late October 2011 when I happened to be in the Upper Derwent Valley. I'd already driven alongside the northern finger of Ladybower Reservoir (shown left, taken from Win Hill). I was then making my way towards the dam at the end of Derwent Reservoir when I heard these deep, throbbing engines approaching. I had no idea what the occasion was or why it was happening on that particular day, but the hairs on my arms went straight up! Unfortunately, I only had about three seconds to get my camera out and to try and focus on the approaching aircraft (centre). If I'd had time to prepare, I'd have got the whole dam into the photograph or, better still, a view of it flying between the dam's towers from the side (right). Poised by the west tower, I awaited a re-run for another hour, but it didn't come back – prompting a workmate to later question whether or not I'd been subject to a temporary Time Slip! What made me briefly consider the phenomenon was the fact that I do recall a vague sense of detached reality, plus the area was completely deserted at the time, too. So if this was a planned flight, wouldn't there have been crowds about? I then found references online to the Legend of the Ghost Flier which is apparently famous in these parts! This certainly sent a few tingles down my spine – but "my plane" wasn't silent, wasn't anywhere near to crashing, and didn't then suddenly disappear like the Ghost Flier is said to do. Of course, when I got home and looked at my photograph, I soon realised that I'd not snapped an ethereal Lancaster Bomber, but probably a Hercules, and presumably a Hercules on exercises.

For the benefit of those who don't understand the significance of this ramble, the three Upper Derwent reservoirs, Howden, Derwent and Ladybower, played a major part in one of wartime aviation's most famous stories. For it was here that 617 Squadron tested the viability of the famous bouncing bomb, invented by Ripley-born Sir Barnes Neville Wallis – albeit tested using bags of flour, I hasten to add! But the squadron's subsequent assault on the dams of the Ruhr Valley in Germany's industrial heartland was one of the most significant factors in the eventual defeat of the Germans in World War II. And hence the rare anniversary fly-throughs by surviving Lancaster Bombers – to hundreds of onlookers, of course, and not one belatedly spooked Derby lad!

As for the dam itself, it is a stunning sight and an impressive feat of human engineering in its own right, constructed in the early 20th century by hundreds of workers from nearby Tin Town.

The start of the 20th century also saw a number of key businesses start up in the Derby area. This included the Trent Motor Traction Company which from 1913 ran several services from Derby to Ashbourne, Chesterfield, Burton-upon-Trent, Melbourne and Ilkeston. However, the biggest name of all was Rolls-Royce, which was formed in 1906 by Charles Stewart Rolls and Henry Royce. Fortunately, it was an offer of cheap electricity from Derby's borough council that resulted in their decision to base their car production in Nightingale Road to the south of Derby. The new factory opened in 1908 building just the one model and which was later to be named as the Silver Ghost. However, faced with falling Silver Ghost sales in the depressed 1920s, the company introduced the smaller, cheaper Twenty in 1922. Then in 1931, the company acquired rival car maker Bentley. Both Rolls-Royce and Bentley car production moved from Derby to Crewe in 1946.

The loss of car manufacturing left just the aero-engine division in Derby, which had initially been set up during the First World War. The company's first aero-engine was the twelve-cylinder Eagle, first produced in 1915 and quickly followed by the smaller six-cylinder Hawk, the 190hp Falcon and, just before the end of the war, the larger 675hp Condor. In fact, around half the aircraft engines used by the Allies in World War I were made by Rolls-Royce and production began to accelerate after the war to such an extent that by the late 1920s, aero engines made up most of Rolls-Royce's business. As for Henry Royce, his last design was the Merlin aero-engine, which came out in 1935, albeit two years after his death. A powerful supercharged V12 engine, the Merlin was fitted into many World War II aircraft such as the Hurricane, Spitfire, Mosquito, and the Lancaster, plus the American P-51 Mustang. Over 160,000 Merlin engines were eventually produced.

After the Second World War, Rolls-Royce also made significant advances in gas turbine engine design and manufacture, while in the late 1950s they also moved into the manufacture of nuclear reactors for Britain's submarine fleet. The aero-engine division continued to grow, though, and by 1966 the company had acquired Bristol Siddeley with its principal factory at Filton, near Bristol. A strong manufacturer of military engines, Bristol Siddeley also manufactured the Olympus 593 Mk610 which went on to be used in Concorde. Rolls-Royce also used Leavesden Aerodrome in Watford for the manufacture of helicopter engines until the site closed in June 1993. But the company had dark moments, too – like in 1971 when financial problems

The original façade of Rolls-Royce Main Works on Nightingale Road, Derby. The factory opened in 1908 initially manufacturing cars, but as more sites sprang up around the city, the Nightingale Road works diminished in importance. The site was finally vacated in 2008 and was largely demolished in 2010 with the above exception due to its listed building status courtesy of its historical importance.

caused largely by set-backs in the development of the RB211 aero-engine led to the company being nationalised by the government and many workers were made redundant. The main business then remained in public ownership until 1987, when it was privatised as Rolls-Royce plc. Two years later, the company merged with Northern Engineering Industries since when it has thrived as a world-class aero-engine and turbine manufacturer, commanding 25 per cent of the world market for civil aviation engines. The company remains Derby's largest single employer.

Back to the first half of the 20th century, though – a time which was of course dominated by war. The First World War saw the death of 11,409 members of the county regiment, The Sherwood Foresters, and their deaths are commemorated by the war memorial at Crich Stand. Meanwhile, the Second World War didn't see so many Derbyshire servicemen and women killed, but it did see more civilian deaths. For example, 74 people were killed and 350 wounded from the bombing of Derby, with the city a German target due to its strategic railway industry and more particularly Rolls-Royce's manufacture of the Merlin aero-engines that were to play such a vital role in the Battle of Britain. Interestingly, though, despite its strategic industries, Derby suffered relatively little damage in both world wars, possibly due to the effective deployment of decoy towns built mainly to the south.

Quirk Alert: Tibshelf Crude

Britain's first inland oil well was sunk at Hardstoft, Tibshelf in 1919. It was a 3,070ft well that for eight years produced high quality lubrication oil.

In between the world wars, the 1920s marked the beginning of a lengthy depression for the entire country, and by 1932, 23 per cent of Britain's labour force were out of work, with that figure being even higher in the industrial hotbed of eastern Derbyshire. In fact, the core industries in this region never really recovered to their pre-war peaks thanks to foreign competition. The coal mine owners' response was to lower wages, thus provoking a number of strikes throughout the 1920s. That said, coal-mining still employed 50,000 Derbyshire workers in 1924, and the Staveley Coal & Iron Co. was still expanding, still taking on extra workers, and still building homes for its workers, as was the Butterley Company. Meanwhile, The Stanton Ironworks Company Ltd supplied a large number of artillery shells during the First World War while the Second World War saw them mass produce shell and bomb casings, gun barrels, concrete air-raid shelter components and experimental concrete torpedo casings.

The Derbyshire coalfield also played an important role in the Second World War and remained the main source of work for many years after that. However, the opening of deeper pits in Nottinghamshire began to tempt workers over the border and the Erewash Valley was no longer one of Britain's most prosperous mining areas. After the war, the coal industry was nationalised with the National Coal Board taking over in 1947 and inheriting a workforce of 704,000 men working in 959 pits in British coalfields. By 1955, over 30 of those pits were located in north-east Derbyshire with another five located in the south of the county; indeed Markham Colliery at Staveley became the largest in Britain at that time. Alas, the coal industry still harboured its fair share of disasters. In 1938, 79 men were killed and 58 injured by an explosion at Markham Colliery, while 80 men were killed as a result of an underground fire at Creswell in 1950. The industry also continued to suffer from foreign competition, particularly when in 1956-57 cheap imported crude oil began to arrive, and some mines were closed while in others, machines replaced men. But when in the 1970s cheap oil came to an end, the National Union of Miners began to exert their influence via a number of strikes, not to mention electing parliamentary Labour candidates such as Dennis Skinner, who has been MP for Bolsover since 1970. The coal-mining renaissance was relatively short-lived of course, as anyone who watched the scenes unfold on their TVs in 1984 will confirm. The north-east Derbyshire miners largely supported the national strike of that year, but picket lines were crossed daily in neighbouring Nottinghamshire leading to ugly scenes. It was all in vain, too, as the near year-long strike ended in defeat for the miners. Then during the late 1980s and early 1990s, Derbyshire's pits were systematically closed, culminating in the last at Markham Main in 1994. Though they were prevalent, and still evident today, Derbyshire's pit villages actually lasted for only 100-150 years; a mere blip on the scale of time. Some purists might also see the remnants of their industry as a blot on the landscape – particularly where open-cast

mining was practised during the second half of the 20th century. But the coal miners left their Derbyshire legacy, having triggered a major shift of the population over to the east of the county.

Quirk Alert: The Bombed Boar

In 1806, Joseph Strutt commissioned a copy of the Renaissance Boar from Marketo Nuovo, Florence, and which became known as the Florentine Boar. It was moved from Strutt's home in St Peter's Street, Derby, to the Arboretum when it was unveiled in 1840 but was beheaded by flying masonry during a German bombing raid 101 years later in 1941.

Meanwhile, the 20th century iron industry fared even worse, with steel now favoured over wrought iron. Small ironworks went out of business and by 1930, 17 out of Derbyshire's 35 blast furnaces had been closed. The Clay Cross Company hung on for longer but closed down its furnaces in 1958 and the Butterley Company closed its last furnaces at Codnor Park in 1965 – which also happened to be the year that the Stanton and Staveley works merged having been taken over by Stewarts and Lloyds Ltd. This also meant that when in 1967 Stewarts and Lloyds became part of the nationalised British Steel Corporation, Stanton and Staveley was also incorporated. Alas, both the Stanton and Staveley blast furnaces only lasted another seven years, for they were both closed down in 1974. And just to complete the sorry industrial tale, the Derbyshire lead and millstone industries also breathed their last before the Second World War, while the cotton industry thrived only in the far north-west of the county.

The only traditional Derbyshire industry to continue to flourish was the quarrying of quality millstone grit at Stancliffe, Stanton and Birchover. Alongside the grit-

IN MEMORIAM

Built in 1923, this is The Sherwood Foresters War Memorial, known locally as Crich Stand, and which is dedicated to the memory of the regiment's soldiers.

These pit wheels are all that remain of the former colliery at Clay Cross, along with a pair of pit wagons, flowerbeds and a stone sculpture commemorating all NE Derbyshire miners who "lost their lives working to keep the home fires burning and the wheels of industry turning". Similar wheels can be found at Alfreton, Codnor, Denby and Loscoe.

BEAUTY AND THE BEAST

View from Black Rocks towards Dene Quarry which lies just off Cromford Hill, and produces crushed limestone aggregates for road-stone and concrete. To the right is Ball Eye Quarry at Bonsall.

Bradwell Cement Works, founded in 1929, some 22 years before the Peak District was founded.

stone quarries, limestone quarrying actually expanded after the Second World War and is still much in demand today. Interestingly, Derbyshire's limestone quarries are also responsible for the strange shape of the Peak District National Park, formed in 1951 – for it has a large slice missing on its western flank around the Buxton quarries, plus it doesn't include the largely stunning countryside around Wirksworth and Matlock to the south-east, too. The main exception to that rule is the Cement Works at Bradwell, whose chimney can be seen from most points in the Hope valley but which continues to be a major employer in that area.

The limestone quarries of Derbyshire are, of course, controversial as even the most industrially-minded person would have to concede that they despoil the landscape. However, the Council for the Protection of Rural England (CPRE) and the Peak District National Park organisations find themselves battling against limestone and gritstone quarrying companies who use mineral permissions granted before the creation of the national park in order to expand their sites. They are also battling against pragmatism, too, for the limestone and lime produced is of the top-most quality and Derbyshire's limestone quarries now produce around 20 million tons of output a year which represents about 15 per cent of national production. They also supply a major source of employment in the White Peak. For example, the Tunstead Quarry just east of Buxton, and which was opened in 1929, produces 5.5 million tons of limestone a year and employs around 400 people. It is also the largest producer of high-purity limestone in Europe, as well as the largest producer of lime in the

REDEVELOPMENT: TWO AWARD-WINNING ROUNDHOUSES

Derby Roundhouse. This Grade II listed building is the world's first and oldest surviving railway roundhouse. Initially built in 1839 by Robert Stephenson (son of George) for £62,000, it was renovated in the 21st century and opened in late 2009 as an exhibition and conference centre.

Michael Hopkins' award-winning Round House at Hathersage, now a cutlery works and visitor centre, but converted from an abandoned old gas cylinder. In 1990, the conversion saw Hopkins win a BBC design award, plus awards from the Civic Trust and the CPRE.

UK. So, therein is the dilemma, for since the beginning of the 20th century, quarrying has replaced lead as the major employer in the Peak District and its adjoining areas. Add to that the fact that Derbyshire is also the major producer of fluorspar and gypsum in the country, and that the south of the county supplies gravel and sand on a large scale, and the debate of countryside despoiling vs. county employment will surely rage on for some time to come.

The CPRE and the Peak District National Park also fight against uncontrolled building in the countryside, and where building does go ahead, the Peak Park Planning Board strive to ensure that new buildings conform to Peak District style and materials. As for conversion of old buildings, the Civic Trust and the CPRE bestow awards upon the designers of the best of these, with a fine example being Michael Hopkins' conversion of an abandoned gas cylinder at Hathersage. The building, which is now known locally as the Round House, is the site of David Mellor Cutlery which contains a cutlery works and visitor centre.

Back to industry, though, and it is true that most traditional industries in the county declined in the first half of the 20th century, and the rural population suffered as a result. However, the County Borough of Derby largely prospered, and certainly did better than most places in the depressed 1920s and 1930s. Led by Rolls-Royce, engineering became the borough's leading industry during the inter-war years, followed closely by railway rolling stock and British Celanese's synthetic fibres and chemical products which by this stage were being produced at their site in Spondon. Formed in 1912, the latter company initially produced fireproof celluloid out of cellulose acetate for the film industry. However, the company soon diversified into paints, synthetic fibres and chemical products, and became known as British Celanese Ltd in 1918 – a name that stuck until the latter part of the 20th century when it became first Courtaulds, then Acordis until returning full circle back to just "Celanese". In its heyday, the company employed around 20,000 people at its 360-acre site in Spondon. Alas, it became yet another Great British employer to fall foul of new American owners when they closed the site in November 2012 with the loss of hundreds of jobs, citing high energy costs and a shift in demand to the Far East. That said, while there are thousands who have benefitted from the company's employment over the best part of a century, there are also plenty of Spondon residents who won't mourn its passing, thanks to the infamous aromas that have been produced over the years!

Throughout the 20th century, Derby continued to expand, absorbing rural parishes and creating new suburbs and it was to here that people gravitated. Many moved from the centre of a town that was being cleared of its Victorian slums, to the town outskirts and into 6,852 council houses that were built between the wars. The borough council also assumed responsibility for hospitals, schools, colleges, libraries, museums, art galleries and swimming baths, while Markeaton Park and Darley Park were also acquired and developed. The site of the former had been owned by the Mundy family since 1516, but in 1929, Derby Borough Council acquired 20 acres of land including Markeaton Hall (later demolished in 1964). A further 180 acres followed, as did boating lakes, golf courses, paddling pools, tennis courts, numerous gardens, woodlands, a steam railway and children's recreation areas.

One of the boating lakes at Markeaton Park. The land was acquired by Derby Borough Council from the Mundy family in 1929.

It was also at this time that Derby built one of the most advanced bus stations in the country – although that has now been demolished and replaced by a 21st century state-of-the-art bus station instead! One negative side to the slum clearance, though, was the demolition of a lot of important architecture along with the poor-quality housing. Much of fine Georgian Derby has now gone, replaced by modern, unattractive architecture. Since the Second World War, the town has also continued to expand, initially with the Chaddesden and Mackworth estates. An inner ring-road was added in 1967 to complement the pre-war outer ring-road, and the A52 between Derby and Nottingham was made into a dual carriageway in the 1970s. Meanwhile, service industries were starting to rival engineering, a number of which would eventually be based at Pride Park following its development to the east of the city in the 1990s. What is for sure, though, is that since its replacement by Matlock in the 1950s as the administrative centre for the *county*, Derby has had a diminishing influence on the northern half of Derbyshire which looks more towards Sheffield and Manchester and doesn't even consider itself part of the East Midlands. In the meantime, Derby and Nottingham continue to converge, with large parts of the Nottingham Urban Area already extending well into south-eastern Derbyshire, covering the towns of Heanor, Ilkeston, Long Eaton and Sandiacre.

Many of the other towns in the county followed suit in terms of the clearance of slums, the appearance of ring-roads and new housing estates. Meanwhile, the former coal-mining towns and villages have undergone considerable redevelopment. Pit-head buildings and winding engines have been demolished to be replaced by industrial estates such as those built on former colliery sites at Alfreton, Clay Cross, Codnor, Dronfield, Ilkeston, Pinxton and Tibshelf, while the "greening" of former colliery tips and open-cast sites further pushes this former great industry out of sight and out of mind. Meanwhile, many of the huge textile mills in the north-west and south-east of the county, along with those in the Derwent valley have been converted into apartments, shopping malls or sites for small businesses.

> ## Quirk Alert: The Muggle and the Full-Blood Princes
>
> *Over the years, many famous dignitaries have "turned up the ball" at the annual Royal Shrovetide Football match at Ashbourne, including two Princes of Wales: the future Edward VIII in 1928, and Prince Charles in 2003. However, the first woman to "goal" a ball was Doris Mugglestone in 1943 – suggesting that there wasn't anything particularly "muggle" about this woman!*

RAILS AND TRAILS

The Ecclesbourne Valley Railway, looking north from Lower Hazelwood.

The Engine House at Middleton Top on today's High Peak Trail. A monument of national importance, this stationary engine raised and lowered wagons containing goods, between High Peak Junction and Middleton Top. Today, cycles are hired here, thus avoiding that murderous climb from High Peak Junction!

Hartington Station on the Tissington Trail, where this signal box has been beautifully restored.

One of the engines on the Peak Railway at Rowsley Station.

As for former railway tracks that were closed in the 1960s, many have been reinvented as walking, cycling and horse-riding trails, while other sections have been re-opened by railway enthusiasts. For walking and cycling we've already mentioned the Monsal Trail, the former Matlock to Buxton stretch of railway with its spectacular viaducts and tunnels, and similarly the High Peak Trail which follows the course of the 19th century High Peak Railway that linked Cromford to the canals at Whaley Bridge, but another stunning alternative is the Tissington Trail which follows the former railway line between Ashbourne and Buxton and actually meets the High Peak Trail just south of Parsley Hay. As for restored railway lines, Peak Railway runs from

Rowsley to Matlock but, like today's Monsal Trail, back in the 19th century it was yet another part of the Derby to Manchester line. Closed in 1967, the short section from Matlock to Rowsley was re-opened as a steam railway in the 1990s. Then there is the Ecclesbourne Valley Railway. Initially opened in 1867 as a branch line to Wirksworth on the Midland Railway, the line was closed to passengers in 1947 and to freight carrying Wirksworth's quarry product in 1989. However, the Ecclesbourne Valley Railway Association along with WyvernRail plc, have recently restored the 8.5 miles of track that runs through the Ecclesbourne Valley from Duffield to Wirksworth, and the line opened again in April 2011.

> ## Quirk Alert: The Beast of Lumsdale
>
> *From the 1960s to September 2000, Riber Castle became a tourist attraction that was home to a wildlife park known locally as Riber Zoo. However, on its closure, animal activists are thought to have released several Lynx into the wild with later local sightings earning the moniker of The Beast of Lumsdale.*

Ecclesiastically, the diocese of Derby was created in 1927 to cover the whole county, having previously been affiliated to the diocese of Southwell. To authenticate the diocese, the previous parish church of All Saints became Derby Cathedral. Meanwhile agriculturally, farming continued to suffer in the face of foreign competition and, for the first time, the gentry began to suffer, too, as death duties and inheritance tax began to bite, forcing many families to give up their manors and halls. In fact, only 13 Derbyshire landowning families still occupy one of their original seats, amongst them the Devonshires of Chatsworth, the Rutlands at Haddon Hall, the Fitzherberts at Tissington and the Scarsdales at Kedleston Hall. The latter, however, is now mostly owned by the National Trust, while a number of grants and investments have enabled the Curzons – who have held their seat since Norman times – to continue to live in one of the pavilions. Also typical of this 20th century pattern is Calke Abbey, which came into the possession of the National Trust after Charles Harpur-Crewe's death in 1981, and which left his brother to face death duties of £8 million. Meanwhile, it

was the death of the 10th Duke of Devonshire in 1950 which forced the Cavendish family at Chatsworth to sell eight of Chatsworth's most valuable works of art; indeed the Devonshires didn't pay off the duty and its interest until 1974. Thankfully, the family survived, and turned the house and estate into arguably the finest tourist attraction in the land.

> ## Quirk Alert: Get Me Out of Here!
>
> *In 2001, Ken Edwards of Glossop broke the world record for the number of cockroaches eaten in one minute. Ken has also had 47 rats down his trousers, simultaneously. Incidentally, these two feats weren't achieved at the same time. That would have been really stupid!*

As we come towards the end of Derbyshire's history, it is worth clarifying the local government changes and county border changes implemented towards the end of the 20th century, and which still remain in place today (2014). The first and third of the maps below show the vague change in county shape following the Local Government Act 1972, and which came into force on the 1st April 1974. In summary, there were some small gains and losses incurred, all of which were confined to the north-west of the county. Here, Cheshire had ceded the majority of its north-eastern territory to the new metropolitan county of Greater Manchester. However, Cheshire's most north-easterly strip of land around Tintwistle and Longdendale valley went to the new non-metropolitan *district* of High Peak, which became part of the new non-metropolitan *county* of Derbyshire. Conversely, the western-most hump of pre-1974 Derbyshire around Marple Bridge went to Greater Manchester, and thus the current north-western Derbyshire border now heads straight upwards in a northerly direction, and a little further than it did before. The only other shape difference between historic and contemporary Derbyshire is the stretch along the county's northern boundary with South Yorkshire. Here, the city of Sheffield had already acquired historic areas of Derbyshire earlier in the 20th century, such as Mosborough, Totley and Dore.

Moving onto the middle of the three maps, this demonstrates the potential impact of the Redcliffe-

Historic Counties

Redcliffe-Maud Proposals, 1969

Ceremonial Counties, 1974-1996

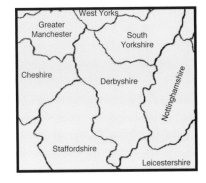

Maud Report, should it have come into play. This report marked the culmination of the Royal Commission on Local Government in England, which had run from 1966 to 1969 under the chairmanship of Lord Redcliffe-Maud, and had been looking at restructuring local government in England. The report's proposals were generally much more radical than what eventually transpired in 1974 – and that certainly proved to be the case where Derbyshire was concerned, although gains and losses would have largely offset each other. On the loss front, Derbyshire would have ceded much of that north-western bulge to what the Redcliffe-Maud Report had christened as SELNEC (South East Lancashire/North East Cheshire). This would have included the towns of Glossop, Whaley Bridge, New Mills and Chapel-en-le-Frith, while some sacrilegious minority report even had the gall to suggest that Buxton should be included, too! On the gain front, though, Derbyshire would have inherited Burton-upon-Trent and its surrounding areas from Staffordshire. However, in 1970, the incoming Conservatives rejected the Redcliffe-Maud Report and created their own White Paper instead. The subsequent Local Government Act 1972 thus introduced the new non-metropolitan county of Derbyshire, which was comprised of nine districts, eight of which have since remained as non-metropolitan districts, while Derby became a unitary authority in 1997. The latter is thus no longer administered by Derbyshire County Council, and has its own City Council which runs its own affairs, while the other eight districts of the county are administrated via the standard two-tier system; an upper tier (education, main roads, public transport, policing, fire services, etc.) is controlled by Derbyshire County Council from its head offices at Matlock, while the eight District Councils are responsible for local planning, local roads, council housing, refuse collection and so on. Of course, the eight districts *plus* the City of Derby still collectively form the *ceremonial* county of Derbyshire and all answer to the same Lord Lieutenant. The ceremonial county therefore contains 30 towns with between 10,000 and 100,000 inhabitants, plus Derby itself (c.258,000), and thus with so many sparsely populated upland areas in the county, 75% of the population lives in 25% of the area.

Statue of the legendary Brian Clough and Peter Taylor outside Derby County's Pride Park Stadium (now the iPro Stadium). Here they are holding the Football League Championship trophy that they won with Derby County in 1972.

> ## Quirk Alert: Bath Time
>
> *In 2005, Wirksworth's Tim Fitzhigham became the first (and currently the only) person to cross the English Channel in a bath! The journey took two months, while his tin bath was complete with Victorian shower heads and taps, and a compass in the plug hole!*

One final boundary change is worth noting, for in 1968, the county borough of Derby was expanded into large parts of the rural districts of Belper, Repton and South East Derbyshire. This resulted in a dramatic reported population increase for Derby between the 1961 and 1971 censuses, increasing from 132,408 inhabitants to 219,578. Shortly after that, it may seem difficult to believe now, but Derby County FC were crowned English League Champions not once, but *twice* in the 1970s. The first occasion was 1972 under the stewardship of the legendary Brian Clough and Peter Taylor – the former quite simply "the best manager England never had", and the subject of numerous biographies, books and even a highly acclaimed film, *The Damned United*, which was released in 2009. Starring Michael Sheen as Brian Clough and Timothy Spall as Peter Taylor, the film follows the progress of Derby County from Clough and Taylor's arrival in 1967, to their acrimonious departure in 1973 and Clough's subsequent turbulent 44 days in 1974 at Derby's hated rivals, Leeds United. The film therefore covers the majority of Derby County's glory years, also highlighting the sinister goings-on during the European Cup semi-final of 1973 when later proven corruption robbed the Rams of a place in the final and a very real chance of being European Champions. Despite Clough's departure, though, Derby went on to be crowned English League Champions again in 1975, this time under the similarly legendary Dave Mackay, who had previously been instrumental in guiding Derby to promotion from Division Two in 1969 as a player. But that was pretty much it for long-suffering Rams fans. A "watershed" defeat to Manchester United in the semi-finals of the FA

Cup in 1976 was followed by a slide from top to fourth in Division One. This triggered a spectacular decline from League Champions in 1975 to Division Three in 1984 – and the opportunity for Chesterfield to put one over on their southern county rivals in the mid-1980s – although that pitch was never playable! Brief flickers followed under Arthur Cox in the late 1980s and Jim Smith in the 1990s, while the previously-mentioned 1997 FA Cup semi-final was Chesterfield's recent main highlight. 1997 was also the year that Derby County moved from the Baseball Ground – their home for over one hundred years – to a new 33,000 all-seater stadium at Pride Park, an impressive stadium that has since hosted international football. Finally, as a footnote to this section, Derby, Chesterfield and Alfreton are all currently in very strong positions half-way through the 2013-14 season! We all live in hope!

Throughout all of Derbyshire's history, Derby remains the main settlement of the county and its only city – and even that status is relatively recent, having been bestowed in 1977 as part of the Queen's Silver Jubilee celebrations. Since then, the city has continued to modernise at pace, commencing with the Eagle Centre Market in 1975 and the New Assembly Rooms built in the market square in 1977, and culminating in the massive development to the east of the city at Pride Park in the late 1990s, and the huge Westfield Shopping Centre built at the southern end of the city centre in the mid-2000s. Meanwhile, the mid-1990s also saw Toyota open a huge car manufacturing plant to the south-west of the city near Burnaston, where its two assembly plants employ over 3,000 employees making around 220,000 vehicles a year. Then in 2004, JCB Power Systems opened a manufacturing plant and assembly line for diesel engines at Dove Valley Park on the A50 near Foston.

As we finish our chronological Derbyshire journey in the early part of the 21st century, the county still remains a tourist hot-spot, with the Peak District National Park pulling in around 10 million visitors a year, making it one of the most visited national parks in the world. The walking, cycling and horse-riding trails also continue to pull in the visitors, as do the county's historic towns and villages. And tourism in the area was given a further boost in 2001, when the Derwent valley from Cromford down to Derby was added to the list of UNESCO World Heritage Sites.

Quirk Alert: Busted by a Phantom!

When Derbyshire County Cricket Club's one-day side were named the Derbyshire Phantoms, following a competition run by Ram FM in 2005, I rang in and proposed the Derbyshire Dambusters (see page 48 for historical justification). I was most disappointed when they went for the Phantoms (which is a nod to Derby being the Ghost Capital of the UK), as the Dambusters is alliterative, uplifting and represents the whole county and not just the city! It is a *county* cricket club, after all! And think of that rousing music they could have played every time the team took to the field, or took a one-day wicket! Seems as if the alliterative/county-wide lesson wasn't taken on board in 2010, either, when they re-named the team the Derbyshire Falcons – this time named after the famous peregrine falcon which perennially nests on Derby Cathedral.

Finally, here are a number of geographical "honours" that Derbyshire holds. Its University of Derby campus at Buxton is the highest in England, while Titan Cave at Castleton is the largest in Britain, and Peak Cavern (also at Castleton) is the deepest cave and has the largest natural cave entrance in the British Isles. Meanwhile, Bleaklow has been classed as England's only true desert, Haddon Hall has the country's oldest rose gardens, Chatsworth is home to the highest gravity-fed fountain and Ashbourne the largest Highland Games gathering outside of Scotland. Add to that Derby which is officially the most haunted city in Britain, Buxton which is home to England's oldest hotel, Hathersage the highest open-air lido and Five Wells the highest and oldest megalithic tomb. Then we have Ripley and Heanor which have been designated the most English towns in the UK, based on surnames with an English origin, Ault Hucknall which is England's smallest village with four dwellings and a church, and Brackenfield which claims to have the largest village green in the country.

As for Derbyshire itself, the county contains both the central point of England plus the furthest point in England from the sea – the latter having been officially named as a farm near Coton in the Elms in the south of the county. Conversely, it is also something of an island in terms of its location. That may seem a strange thing to say, but much of Derbyshire contains relatively wild and unpopulated land, and yet the county is hemmed in on all sides by a sea of conurbations totalling around 7 million people!

Quirk Alert: Chocolate Baa!

In 2008, the Thornton's factory at Somercotes produced the world's first edible billboard which, at 15ft high, announced a Happy Easter from Thornton's. In the same year, they produced a white chocolate Lenny Lamb – but seem to have missed the obvious subtitle!

Quirky Derbyshire

Introducing the Shire-Ode

So, a Shire-Ode tells the story – in rhyming verse – of fictitious, eccentric inhabitants of the county in question. However, in so doing, it also incorporates into the flow of the verse, many place-names that can be found within that county – places which then go on to form a county almanac, of sorts. Each place in the almanac appears in roughly alphabetical order, although some of the smaller places are batched up into trios on a single page known as a "Threes Up" page. The location of all of the places is also pinpointed in the maps that follow the Shire-Ode.

As for the *Derbyshire* Shire-Ode, this tells the tale of Brad and Mel, the former a recluse who is devoted to his trees, but who is also afflicted by the need to incorporate Derbyshire place-names into his every-day speech, and the latter a lady who becomes a cook of national repute, but who fails to find love...until a chance meeting with Brad...by a Ford...on the Dove...

Derbyshire Shire-Ode: Brad and Mel

They were born in **The Forties** – in fact, '43
Melbourne in **Cromford** and **Bradbourne** in **Lea**
Though Brad was the **Kinder** there was great **Hope** for Mel
Who excelled in the kitchen and sure could **Bakewell**.

But in youth, our **Bradley** was a bit of a **Clowne**
Liked to pepper his speech with **Derby** village, **Dale** and town
But his jokes didn't **Wash**; folks'd **Flagg** him as odd
Thus the **Bradway** meant spending more time on his tod.

Then a job with **Peak Forest** Commission bore fruit
And by thirty he'd become a tree surgeon of repute
In his job he had faves; preferred **Ashover** oak
And **Oakover** birch, but still **Birchover** folk.

By forty, a recluse, he'd speak only to tree
In his **Oakwood**, **Birchwood** or **Hazelwood** at Lea
See, **The Brushes** with past loves sent him **Halfway** to hell
So for him, only trees would now treat **Bradwell**.

Meanwhile, Mel's cooking led to the expected role
Though she'd never cook fish: neither trout, **Codnor** sole
But she made marvellous soups which with **Crewton** were blessed
Was inspired with a **Bramley** – her pies were the best.

So she opened a diner on apt-named **Glutton Bridge**
Where folk flocked to her **Dore** for delights from her fridge
And though **The Gutter Press** critics tried to so **Knockerdown**
Her business did **Flourish** and soon spread to town.

Determined to thrive, and **Calver** career
She opened a new shop on **Pye Bridge**, that year
You just couldn't **Curbar** fervour for food
And **The Banks** were impressed with the profits accrued.

By fifty she became a name **Biggin** food
Though she **Sawley** missed love, but couldn't find the right dude
Her parents despaired they did truly believe:
"If you don't settle down, love, we fear that **Youlgreave**."

Now a **Littleover** fifty, himself, Brad was low
And **Wye**: alone **Woodside**, he missed ladies so
He'd not took a **Birdholme** since brash **Fernilee**
Who with large **Wigley** rear was too **Common Side** for he.

So he marked out his **Boundary**; put a **Boulton** that door
Thus **Fallinge** in love was unlikely any more
Then his daily neat **Scotches** hit the three, then **Foremark**
Yes, he'd **Hopton** the wagon, as life lost its spark.

Plus he'd not use his **Whitwell** – he'd go **Backmoor** and more
To the bar; he'd eat less, then he'd drink a **Littlemoor**
So with so **Little Eaton**, his belts they got **Slack**
His skin became **Callow** – his moods they got black.

As his diet got worse, alas **Breadsall** he'd eat
But salvation was nigh, for Mel he'd soon meet
Though neither **Heanor** her were looking for love
It came at first sight, by a **Ford** on the **Dove**.

With Brad being so **Birley**, Mel's knees became weak
When she smiled he just fell for that **Dimple** on each cheek
They were wed in six months at the foot of **Crich Stand**
Said their vows at the altar with a **Cross o' th' Hands**.

Mel's parents were there: that's **Shirley** and **Cliff**
She had her best **Hatton**; he coiffed his best quiff
The bridesmaids wore **Oker** with bows of **Oaks Green**
Whilst the Best Man, that's **Stanley**, wore a **Woolley** suit of cream.

At reception, Brad swore it was: "No more the clown,
"No **Woodville**, drink excess, or speech full of town,"
Then with scotch raised in toast, he winked at his wife
Said: "**Whatstandwell** today, love, will last us for life!"

To hear the Shire-Ode in musical format, go to www.andybeardmore.com

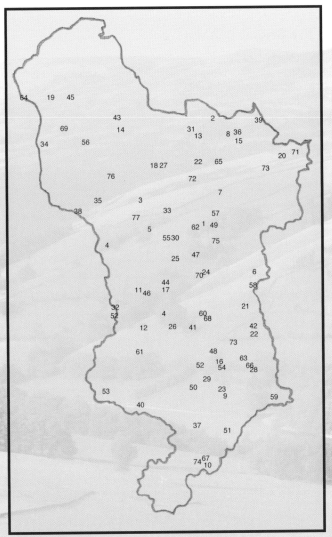

LOCATION MAP FOR BRAD AND MEL
Historic Derbyshire

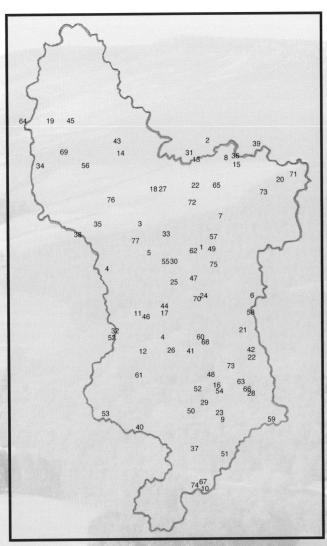

LOCATION MAP FOR BRAD AND MEL
Modern Derbyshire

PLACE-NAME TABLE FOR BRAD AND MEL

1 Ashover	17 Callow	33 Fallinge	49 Littlemoor	65 The Brushes
2 Backmoor[2]	18 Calver	34 Fernilee	50 Littleover	66 The Flourish
3 Bakewell	19 Cliff	35 Flagg	51 Melbourne	67 The Forties
4 Biggin[1]	20 Clowne	36 Ford	52 Oakover/Okeover[1]	68 The Gutter
5 Birchover	21 Codnor	37 Foremark	53 Oaks Green	69 Wash
6 Birchwood	22 Common Side[1]	38 Glutton Bridge	54 Oakwood	70 Whatstandwell
7 Birdholme	23 Crewton	39 Halfway[2]	55 Oker	71 Whitwell
8 Birley	24 Crich Stand	40 Hatton	56 Peak Forest	72 Wigley
9 Boulton	25 Cromford	41 Hazelwood	57 Press	73 Woodside[1]
10 Boundary	26 Cross o' th' Hands	42 Heanor	58 Pye Bridge	74 Woodville
11 Bradbourne	27 Curbar	43 Hope	59 Sawley	75 Woolley
12 Bradley	28 Dale	44 Hopton	60 Scotches	76 Wye
13 Bradway[2]	29 Derby	45 Kinder	61 Shirley	77 Youlgreave
14 Bradwell	30 Dimple	46 Knockerdown	62 Slack	
15 Bramley	31 Dore[2]	47 Lea	63 Stanley	
16 Breadsall	32 Dove	48 Little Eaton	64 The Banks[2]	

[1] Appears twice in Derbyshire

[2] Place is situated just outside the Derbyshire county boundary today, but was historically part of Derbyshire until the 20th century.

Brad and Mel –
A Derbyshire Shire-Ode Almanac

NAME (STATUS):	**ASHOVER** (Village)
POPULATION:	1,796
DISTRICT:	North East Derbyshire
EARLIEST RECORD:	*Essovre*, 1086 (*Domesday Book*); *Esshovere*, 1252
MEANING:	Ridge where ash-trees grow
DERIVATION:	From the Old English words *æsc* (ash-tree) and *ofer* (flat-topped ridge, hill or promontory)
FAMOUS RESIDENTS:	**Sir Joseph Banks** (1743-1821), botanist on *The Endeavour* after whom Banks Island is named. **The Bassett Sisters**, descendants of the Liquorice Allsorts confectioners. Some of **Harry Potter's owls** from Honeybank Animal Actors.

Ashover Pub: Old Poets Corner

Adorning one of the walls at the Old Poets Corner are the words: *We quaff thy balmy juice with glee, and water leave for France*. And indeed, this Ashover pub is the venue for monthly poetry nights hosted by a Derby-based man known only as "The Pub Poet", while even the resident chef is a poet, too. Formerly known as the "Old Red", the current pub name comes courtesy of the latest owners who also ran a similar establishment in Holbrook called "Dead Poets".

Ashover Church: All Saints

Little remains of the Norman church other than a tiny piscina in the chancel and a fine mid-12th century font, with the tower and spire dating from the 15th century. Meanwhile, between 1621 and 1942, All Saints' church had only *eight* rectors, thanks to lengthy lifespans. In fact, Joseph Nodder and his son, John, saw *six* monarchs during their tenure, from William IV to George VI. Something in the Ashover water, perhaps?

As for that 12th century font, it is a rare example of a stone basin encased entirely in lead and is the only one in Derbyshire. Perhaps this is why 17th century rector Immanuel Bourne buried it in his garden at Eastwood Hall during the English Civil War, as Parliamentarian soldiers had already demonstrated their intentions by demolishing the windows of the church and using the lead to make bullets. Alas, Bourne's reward for his industry was the burning down of his hall, followed by further vandalism of the church and the destruction of the parish registers...

Ashover Historic Trivia:
The English Civil War

Ashover's experience of the Royalists was little better than of the Parliamentarians, for in 1646, they slaugh-

The Crispin Inn, scene of an infamous English Civil War altercation in 1646, when landlord, Job Wall, was thrown out of his own pub by drunken Royalists.

Meanwhile, a bunch of Parliamentarians ransacked All Saints' church and when failing to find the hidden font, promptly burned down the rector's hall!

tered livestock and drank all the wine and ale in the cellars of Eddlestow Hall while the owner, Sir John Pershall, was away. They then moved onto the Crispin Inn. However, the landlord, Job Wall, refused the Royalists entry claiming they were too drunk – at which point they threw him out, drank most of his ale and then poured what was left down the street. Meanwhile, the commander of those scurrilous Roundheads who had vandalised the church, allegedly followed this up with a sermon, to which rector Immanuel Bourne registered a marvellous response: "*Lord what stuff and nonsense he did talk, and if he could have murdered the King as easily as he did the King's English, the war long since would have been over.*" As for the destruction of Eastwood Hall, Bourne's clerk records the incident in verse, as follows:

The Crispin Inn was founded in 1416 when Thomas Babington of Dethick and his men returned from the Battle of Agincourt, which was famously fought on St Crispin's Day.

> *The Roundheads came down to Eastwood Hall,*
> *And they tried it with mattocks and they tried it with ball,*
> *And they tore up the leadwork and splintered the wood,*
> *But as firmly as ever the battlements stood,*
> *Till a barrel of gunpowder at last did the thing,*
> *And then they sang psalms for the fall of the King.*

Ashover Quirk Alert: The Fabrick

High above Ashover is the gritstone boulder known as "The Fabrick" or Ashover Rock. It sits on an area of heathland at 982ft (300m) above sea level and from here you can see *eight* different counties. Of these eight, three are subdivisions of Yorkshire, including – aston-

ishingly – *North* Yorkshire! Now, geographers may be sceptical of this claim, given the main bulk of North Yorkshire lies many miles to the north of Ashover; in fact, the county town of Northallerton is located some 82 miles distant! But the claim is true thanks to a quirk of North Yorkshire's shape, which has a protruding foot that stretches down further south than the River Humber and which borders the South Yorkshire metropolitan district of Doncaster. And in that "foot" is Drax Power Station, the cooling towers and chimneys of which are visible from The Fabrick with binoculars. However, you cannot see the *buildings* of the power station due to the curvature of the earth! Meanwhile, closer to home are the key landmarks of Chesterfield's crooked spire, Bolsover Castle, Hardwick Hall and Ogston Reservoir, but also visible with binoculars some 40 miles to the east is Lincoln Cathedral, too.

The Fabrick is also home to a topograph, erected in 1990 by the Rotary Club of Clay Cross, and which announces the places that you can see and their distance from this spot; this including Clay Cross itself which lies around three miles due east of The Fabrick. The topograph also states that it stands here: "By the kind permission of the Misses Bassett", this courtesy of the fact that these descendants of the family made famous for creating Liquorice Allsorts actually own the land around The Fabrick. They also allow the land to be graced by Morris dancers on certain dates of the year, too!

The Fabrick, also known as "Ashover Rock" is a gritstone boulder that sits on high ground above the village of Ashover.

Looking east towards first Hardwick Hall, then Nottinghamshire and then Lincolnshire – two of eight counties that can be seen from The Fabrick!

NAME (STATUS):	**BAKEWELL** (Town)
POPULATION:	3,979
DISTRICT:	Derbyshire Dales
EARLIEST RECORD:	*Badecan wiellon*, 924; *Badecanwelle*, 949; *Badequella*, 1086; *Bauquell*, mid-13th century
MEANING:	Spring or stream of a man called Badeca
DERIVATION:	From the Old English name, Badeca, plus the Old English word *wella* (spring or stream)
FAMOUS RESIDENTS:	**Stephen Downing**, victim of the longest-serving "unsafe conviction" following his conviction for murdering Wendy Sewell in 1973; the conviction was quashed in 2001.

Bakewell Pub: The Rutland Arms

Not only is the Rutland Arms the birthplace of the famous Bakewell Pudding in c.1860, but Jane Austen also penned part of *Pride and Prejudice* during her stay there in 1813 – and indeed, Bakewell actually features in the novel as Lambton, while the hotel has named one of its suites after her. However, the inn was known as the White Horse Hotel in those days, having been a very popular 18th century tavern and coaching inn. It was then rebuilt in 1804 into its current incarnation by John Manners, the 7th Duke of Rutland.

Bakewell Church: All Saints

Built on the site of a former 9th century Anglo-Saxon minster church, the various facets of today's All Saints' church date from a Norman west doorway, pillars and arcades, to a 13th century chancel, all the way up to the rebuilt 19th century tower and spire. The churchyard is also home to two Anglo-Scandinavian crosses, one of which is 8ft high and contains pagan, Anglo-Saxon and Scandinavian carvings while *inside* the church you will find the oldest alabaster statue in Derbyshire (dated 1385), this being of Sir Godfrey Foljambe and his wife, Avina. Meanwhile, in the south porch of All Saints, you will find the largest and most varied collection of ancient stonework in the country, largely discovered in

the foundations of the church when parts of it were rebuilt in the 1840s. The collection includes a number of pre-Conquest crosses, an array of stone gargoyle heads, 12th century carved grave slabs, and 13th century decorated tiles.

Bakewell Historic Trivia:
Some Jolly Good Manners

Bakewell was granted Derbyshire's first chartered annual fair in 1254 and it still takes place every year, although since 1819 it has run under the banner of the Bakewell Show. It attracts around 65,000 visitors a year at the beginning of August, making it the county's largest agricultural and horticultural show. Back to c.1300, though, and this was when the famous five-arched bridge over the River Wye was built, although some experts date it as far back as c.1272, which would probably make it the oldest road bridge in the county. Much later in the 18th century, the bridge became part of the turnpike road to Chesterfield while nearby Holme Bridge (built 1664) on the packhorse route, offered a toll-free alternative over the Wye. This latter bridge also sat just in front of Lumford Mill, built by the great Sir Richard Arkwright in 1778, along with his usual high-standard mill-worker cottages. As for the main bridge, this was widened on its upstream side in the 19th century

The Rutland Arms, host to Jane Austen in 1813 and birthplace of the famous Bakewell Pudding in 1860.

Bakewell All Saints, viewed from the south-west.

and still carries modern traffic on the A619 between Bakewell and Chesterfield.

Bakewell has also profited from the generosity of the Manners family of nearby Haddon Hall over the centuries. Roger Manners founded some almshouses in 1593 for four poor men who had to be "sole, unmarried and uncontracted", Sir John Manners founded St John's Hospital in 1602 while a later Sir John Manners founded the larger almshouses on South Church Street in 1709. However, the most lasting legacy is Lady Manners School, a grammar school founded in 1636 by Lady Grace Manners and still going strong today.

Bakewell Quirk Alert:
The Secret of the Pudding

Bakewell is undoubtedly most famous for its puddings, selling over 12,000 a week during the summer. The popular belief is that the Bakewell Pudding was first created in around 1860 at Bakewell's coaching inn, the White Horse (now The Rutland Arms). Allegedly, the landlady, Mrs Ann Greaves, usually did the cooking when entertaining important guests, including the making of a legendary strawberry tart. However, on the monumental day, the cooking was left to an inexperienced assistant, who subsequently omitted the egg and sugar mixture when making the pastry. The strawberry jam was then spread over what was now the wrong pastry base, with the egg and sugar mixture then added on top of the strawberry jam, complete with an extra – but secret – ingredient. Thus the tart became a pudding, the customers loved it, and the rest is history.

Today, a number of shops in Bakewell claim to own the original recipe. One story goes that Mrs Greaves left the recipe in her will, to a Mr Radford, who in turn passed it on to Mr Bloomer – whose descendants still make and sell the pudding today at "Bloomers – The First And Only Original Bakewell Pudding Shop" on Water Street. The latter shop proudly announces: "Recipe Dated 1889" and "Handed Down Over Four Generations". However, the "Old Original Bakewell Pudding Shop" in Rutland Square, claim that Mrs Annie Wilson, the 19th century owner of the cottage/shop, acquired the recipe from the blundering assistant cook at the White Horse, and *this* was the true recipe passed down through the ages. It is even said that, as a guest at the hotel on the momentous day, Mrs Wilson wrote down the recipe in pencil in a small notebook which is still kept today in a fire-proof safe.

Finally, for culinary completeness, there is also "The Bakewell Pudding Factory – Pudding Parlour and Shop", which sells a "Bakewell Pudding" and an icing coated "Bakewell Tart", the latter being baked in a short-crust pastry base. Meanwhile, "The Bakewell Tart & Coffee Shop" on Matlock Street also sells Traditional Bakewell Tart, Iced Bakewell Tart, Moist Bakewell Tart and Traditional Bakewell Pudding – with the Bakewell Tarts again completely different from the puddings, both in flavour and appearance! Of course, *supermarket* Bakewell Tarts are a different confection yet again, made with short-crust pastry, an almond topping and a sponge and jam filling – and which are different again from Mr Kipling's *Cherry* Bakewells, but which are also regularly misnamed as Bakewell Tarts, too! Anyway, that's enough Tart Talk for now…

Long view towards the five-arched medieval bridge over the River Wye, thought to date from c.1272 and probably the oldest road bridge in the county.

The Old Original Bakewell Pudding Shop in Rutland Square and which has the words "The Original Shop With The Original Pudding" above its door.

NAME (STATUS):	**BIGGIN** (1 Village; 1 Hamlet)
POPULATION:	Biggin-by-Hartington (c.400); Biggin-by-Hulland (107)
DISTRICT:	Both Derbyshire Dales
EARLIEST RECORD:	*Newbiggin*, 1233
MEANING:	A new building
DERIVATION:	From the Old English words *nīwe* (new) and *bigging* (building)

Biggin Geographic Trivia: Depressive Saucers

The two Derbyshire Biggin's are situated about ten miles apart with the larger of the two – also known as Biggin-by-Hartington – lying about 5 miles *inside* the Peak District National Park and the smaller – also known as Biggin-by-Hulland – located around 5 miles *outside* the National Park. Biggin-by-Hartington is located just to the west of the A515 roughly half way between Ashbourne and Buxton. Situated at over 1,000 feet above sea level, the village still manages to find itself in a saucer-like depression and thus the village is entered by a gentle descent from all sides. Meanwhile, Biggin-by-Hulland is situated between Hulland Ward and Kirk Ireton.

The eastern approach to Biggin-by-Hartington.

Biggin Pub: The Waterloo Inn

The Waterloo Inn is located at the western end of Biggin-by-Hartington, and is actually the only pub in both Derbyshire Biggin's. It is a haven for walkers, particularly in the summer, and is also the location of a popular camping site…while it manages to be the subject of some rather unwitting trivia, too (see *Quirk Alert* for more).

Biggin Church: St Thomas

The church of St Thomas at Biggin-by-Hartington was built to a design by E. H. Shellard between 1844 and 1848 and is comprised mainly of local limestone. As for Biggin-by-Hulland, the place is so tiny that it doesn't have a church, so the locals would have to travel to nearby Christ Church at Hulland, St Philip and St James at Atlow, or Holy Trinity at Kirk Ireton.

Biggin Historic Trivia: Old and New Buildings … and 14,000 Sheep!

The name Biggin probably derives from the Middle English word *bigging* meaning "a building" – although which buildings this may relate to in the case of the two Derbyshire villages is not clear. The larger Biggin also used to be known as Newbiggin, a common place-name in the north of England and which usually means "new building". The place was certainly recorded as *Newbiggin* in 1233 when it was home to a monastic settlement of the Cistercian order, established by the monks of Garendon Abbey, near Loughborough in Leicestershire. The monks also established a sheep ranch at Biggin Grange, which still has one ancient outbuilding standing today. However, nothing else remains from this period with the 16th century Grade II-listed Biggin Hall perhaps the oldest building in the

The Waterloo Inn, Biggin-by-Hartington.

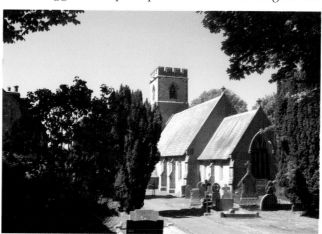

St Thomas' church, Biggin-by-Hartington.

The Grade II-listed Biggin Hall, built in the 16ᵗʰ century … and sporting one spooky-looking tree shadow!

village – unless you count Liffs Low, a Stone Age barrow which still lies to one side of nearby Liffs Road! Moving forward to the 18ᵗʰ century, and as was the case with so many of the villages in the White Peak, Biggin had become a lead-mining village but saw its population fall in the second half of the 19ᵗʰ century as the lead mining industry declined. Sheep farming was also important throughout these years and Biggin was particularly noted for its sheep and cattle markets, of which there were several throughout the year with up to 14,000 sheep sold there a day, on occasion. Sheep farming continues to this day, but its importance has diminished following the consolidation of all animal sales to nearby centres such as Bakewell and Derby.

Biggin Quirk Alert: 1815 and Polly's Kettle

Just to the east of Biggin-by-Hartington a bridge carries the Tissington Trail over the main approach road. This walking and cycling trail is part of the former railway line from Ashbourne to Buxton and stretches for 13 miles from Ashbourne to Parsley Hay. Anyway, when I recently cycled the Tissington Trail, I bumped into a couple walking their two Labradors on this very bridge, and who were called Wellington and Napoleon (the dogs, not the couple). And by extraordinary chance the one-and-only pub in both Biggin's is called the Waterloo Inn! Tenuous, admittedly, but it's all I've got!

Hoonwell Lane, Biggin-by Hulland.

In terms of less anecdotal quirky trivia, though, Biggin-by-Hartington was recently home to the National Dry Stone Walling Champion two years on the bounce while it was also home for most of the last century to Polly Webster who ran the village's Café and General Store. Polly was renowned far and wide with cyclists and walkers visiting her for meals and tea and she would happily accept business late at night, even serving meals after midnight. The shop and café remained open until Polly was well into her eighties.

NAME (STATUS):	**BIRCHOVER** (Village)
POPULATION:	362
DISTRICT:	Derbyshire Dales
EARLIEST RECORD:	*Barcovere*, 1086 *(Domesday Book)*; *Birchoure*, 1226
MEANING:	Ridge where birch-trees grow
DERIVATION:	From the Old English words *birce* (birch-tree) & *ofer* (flat-topped ridge, hill or promontory)
FAMOUS RESIDENTS:	**Eddie Shimwell**, first full-back to score in a Wembley FA Cup Final. He scored for Blackpool in their defeat to Manchester United in the 1948 final, and went on to appear in two more FA Cup Finals for Blackpool, including the famous 'Matthews Final' of 1953.

The Red Lion Inn, Birchover

Birchover Pub: The Red Lion Inn

One of over 900 Red Lion pubs in Britain, Birchover's version was recently voted in the top four! It was built in 1680, originally as a farm and alehouse and was granted its first license in 1722 – when licensing became law. Some of its original 300 year-old oak beams are still in place as well as its 30ft well that is situated just inside the main entrance to the pub and which sports a thick glass cover. Despite all of that, though, the more famous of the two pubs in Birchover is probably The Druid Inn – see *Quirk Alert* for more!

Birchover Church: St Michael and All Angels

St Michael and All Angels' church was actually a chapel originally built by Rev. Thomas Eyre in the 18th century, but which eventually became a Church of England parish church in 1870. Lying in the shelter of Rowtor Rocks, it is a highly unusual building in that there are only windows on the east and south sides. Thomas Eyre also carved three seat-like carvings at Rowtor Rocks, thought to have been created to commemorate the ascension to the English throne of William of Orange and Mary in 1689.

Birchover Historic Trivia: Ancient and Modern Stones

The area around Birchover is very atmospheric as it is home to numerous prehistoric monuments and stone circles and it has formed the backdrop to a number of horror and thriller novels over the years. The most well-known stone circle is The Nine Ladies on Stanton Moor (*see page 9 for more*), which is said to represent nine ladies turned to stone for dancing on a Sunday. Also nearby, and in the Birchover parish, is Nine Stone Close on Harthill Moor. This stone circle is known as the Grey Ladies, so-called because they are said to represent ladies who dance at midnight. Once a 45ft circle of stones, only four standing stones remain today but they do have the distinction of being the tallest in Derbyshire, ranging from 4ft to 7ft in height. Then just north-east of Birchover, there is Doll Tor, another stone circle of around 20 feet in diameter and consisting of just six stones each of no more than a metre in height. The stones were set at the edge of a platform which probably staged seasonal and family ceremonies. Cremations, urns and other funerary goods were discovered when the site was excavated in the 1930s.

Stone and minerals have also dominated Birchover's history since those ancient stone circles were built, firstly with Rowtor Rocks and its druidic worship (see *Quirk Alert*), and then by lead mining, with the 2.25 mile-long Yatestoop Sough constructed between 1742 and 1764 to drain the lead mines in the Winster area. However, Birchover is also famed for its quality of

One of Rev. Thomas Eyre's three seat-like carvings at Rowtor Rocks.

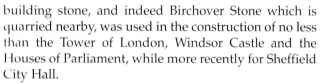

Nine Stone Close on Harthill Moor. Behind the stone circle is Robin Hood's Stride and which is also known locally as 'Mock Beggars Hall'.

Doll Tor, a small Bronze Age stone circle built around 2000-1500 BC.

building stone, and indeed Birchover Stone which is quarried nearby, was used in the construction of no less than the Tower of London, Windsor Castle and the Houses of Parliament, while more recently for Sheffield City Hall.

Finally, The Millennium Stone was constructed at the turn of the 21st century and is said to exemplify the former industry of millstone production in the village. The carved motif on the base is a copy of a Romanesque carving discovered in a stone wall at Uppertown, a deserted medieval village that lies just south of Birchover. It is thought that the carved stone was used in a church at Uppertown that no longer exists, but which was built in the 11th or 12th century.

Birchover Quirk Alert: Druids, Prizes and Broad Horizons

Given the Birchover backdrop, it is unsurprising that the area is reputed to have been used by ancient Celtic Druids as a ceremonial worship site, and that Rowtor Rocks, situated at the western edge of the village, was the site of their temple. Certainly with its hewn stones, tunnel, chimney, steps, caves, man-made chambers and Bronze Age stone carvings, it isn't hard to imagine. Meanwhile, sitting at the foot of Rowtor Rocks is The Druid Inn and which was actually named in reference to the Ancient Order of Druids, a friendly society founded in 1781 who held their meetings there. As for today, no doubt the druids would enjoy the "gastro pub", with its classy restaurant built onto the side of the inn, and which offers the lure of

"Derbyshire Tradition: Contemporary Style". Such offerings were certainly enough for *The Sunday Times* to award the restaurant a score of ten out of ten back in 2002!

Next up is a familiar type of story, but still worth an airing. Apparently, just before the war, the local Birchover Brass Band won third prize in a brass band competition in Ormskirk, Lancashire. For many years after that, they proudly announced themselves as the Birchover Prize Band…right up until someone eventually leaked the information that there had only been three bands in the Ormskirk competition!

Finally, the Village Hall was built in 1907 and was initially made available for the local menfolk only, where they were provided with newspapers in order to help them "broaden their horizons". Presumably, their tea would have been ready and waiting for them on their return home!

The Druid Inn, named in the late 18th century by the Ancient Order of Druids who held their meetings there. Behind the inn is Rowtor Rocks, thought to be an ancient Druidic temple.

Threes-Up!

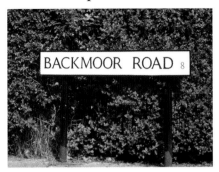

	BACKMOOR	BIRCHWOOD	BIRDHOLME
STATUS:	Suburb	Hamlet(s)	Suburb
POPULATION:	c.4,000	c.30	c.2,000
DISTRICT:	Sheffield	Amber Valley	Chesterfield
MEANING:	Place at the ridge on the moor	Wood where birch-trees grow	River-meadow where young birds are found
DERIVATION:	From the Old English words *bæc* (back or ridge) and *mōr* (moor, marshy ground or barren upland)	From the Old English words *birce* (birch-tree) and *wudu* (wood or forest)	From the Old English word *bridd* (young bird) and the Old Scandinavian *holmr* (island, promontory, raised ground in marsh or river meadow)

Threes Up Trivia!

Today's Sheffield housing estate of **Backmoor** lay within the boundaries of the historic county of Derbyshire for nearly 1,000 years until it was eventually annexed by the expanding Sheffield in the 1930s, along with other former Derbyshire villages like Dore, Totley and Bradway. Today, it is just a suburb of south-western Sheffield, including the eponymous Backmoor Road and Backmoor Crescent. Prior to being absorbed into the Sheffield metropolis, it is likely to have been an isolated settlement on a ridge on the moor.

As for **Birchwood**, a certain poetic license was invoked in the Shire-Ode, as its usage is in reference to the twin settlements of Upper Birchwood and Lower Birchwood, which are located in east Derbyshire in between a quadrangle of Alfreton, South Normanton, Pinxton and Somercotes. Linking the two hamlets of Upper and Lower Birchwood is Birchwood Lane which, in turn, links Somercotes with South Normanton. Lower Birchwood even has its own hamlet announcement, albeit half-obscured by foliage, but Upper Birchwood – which only appears to consist of Birchwood House – does not. There is also a private road called Birchwood a few miles away in Loscoe.

Moving onto **Birdholme** and today, it is a relatively deprived suburb of southern Chesterfield with the large St Augustine's council estate making up much of its area – although there are a few wealthier enclaves such as the beautifully tree-lined Langer Lane (*shown top right*). In years gone by, the Bryan Donkin valve factory used to dominate the landscape of the area. The company was founded in 1803 by inventor and engineer Bryan Donkin, who went onto assist Charles Babbage in the development of his ground-breaking Difference Engine – widely acknowledged as the world's first computer. Alas, the factory in Birdholme closed in 2004 and the area has since been redeveloped into the Alma Leisure Park.

NAME (STATUS):	**BIRLEYHAY** (Hamlet); **BURLEY HILL** (Hamlet)
POPULATION:	Birleyhay: c.20; Burley Hill: c.75
DISTRICT:	Birleyhay: North East Derbyshire; Burley Hill: Amber Valley
EARLIEST RECORD:	Birleyhay: *Unknown*; Burley Hill: *Burleye*, 1251
MEANING:	Woodland clearing by or belonging to a fortified place
DERIVATION:	Birleyhay: from either the Old English word *byr-lēah* (woodland clearing near a byre or cow-shed) or the Old English *byrh-lēah* (woodland clearing near a fortified place or stronghold). Burley Hill: from the Old English words *burh* (fortified place or stronghold) and *lēah* (wood, woodland clearing or glade).

Birley/Burley Trivia

The place called **Birley** that is pinpointed on the Shire-Ode map is actually called Birleyhay. However, there are still a number of other Birley's in Derbyshire: Birley Wood lies a mile or so north of Birleyhay, right on the Derbyshire border with South Yorkshire. It also lends its name to Birley Wood Golf Course, which lies sandwiched between Birley Wood and Birley Lane. All of these places lie alongside the Birley ward of Sheffield, part of which used to be in Derbyshire in the early 20th century, including the Birley housing estate which, in turn, was built on what was formerly Birley Moor – an area that must be an absolute nightmare for a postman, as there are five different roads starting with "Birley Moor" within a half-mile radius, but each suffixed differently with Avenue, Crescent, Drive, Road and Way. Add in Birley Wood Drive, Birley Community College, Birley Spa, Birley Spa Lane and Birley Spa Wood, and there surely can't be anyone living in this area that is anything less than well-built! As for Birley Spa, this is a Grade II-listed building that was constructed in 1842 around a spring of mineral water.

Meanwhile, **Burley Hill** is a tiny settlement just north of Allestree and comprises a couple of farms on the right-hand side of the road going up the hill and 25 attractive homes, all on the left-hand side and numbered from 1 to 25. Recorded as *Burleye* in 1251, it was home to a medieval pottery site in the 13th and 14th centuries where four coal-fired pottery kilns produced glazed and unglazed jugs and pitchers, cooking pots and dishes. In fact, amongst the finds at Roystone Grange, near Ballidon, one of the three granges that the Cistercian Abbey of Garendon possessed in the Peak District, there were a number of fine glazed jugs crafted from the potteries at Burley Hill. Around the area today, you will also find Burley Brook, Burley Grange, Burley Wood and Burley Meadows while right in the middle of all of these places, is Bunkers Hill, with its strange mounds and hollows. Since 2000, Bunkers Hill has also been home to a topograph to celebrate the Millennium along with the hill's spectacular 270 degree panorama.

Burley Hill, located just north of Allestree.

View to the north-east from Bunkers Hill.

Burley Wood from the topograph on Bunkers Hill.

NAME (STATUS):	**BRADBOURNE** (Village)
POPULATION:	116
DISTRICT:	Derbyshire Dales
EARLIEST RECORD:	*Bradeburne*, 1086 (*Domesday Book*)
MEANING:	Broad stream
DERIVATION:	From the Old English words *brād* (broad or spacious) and burna (stream)

Bradbourne All Saints' church.

More of Bradbourne All Saints' ancient stonework.

Bradbourne Church: All Saints

The ancient church of All Saints still possesses its Norman tower all the way up to the Norman corbel table, while the parapets are 15th century. It also still retains fine Norman doorways to the tower, porch and church. The finest of these is the south doorway to the tower which is carved with three orders of moulding, one of beak-heads, the other two of birds and animals. However, the doors and the tower aren't the oldest

Close-up of some of the Norman mouldings over the south tower doorway of All Saints' church.

elements of the church, as the Norman part of the tower is built on the lower courses of its Anglo-Saxon predecessor, while evidence of typical Anglo-Saxon long-and-short work is visible on the north side of the nave.

Bradbourne Historic Trivia: The Cross and the Lamp

The churchyard of Bradbourne All Saints is also home to an ancient Anglo-Saxon preaching cross. The shaft is carved with scenes of the crucifixion, an archer and typical Anglo-Saxon-style vine-scrolls, and since the shaft contains no evidence of Scandinavian influence, it almost certainly dates to the late 8th or early 9th century. The cross was broken into three pieces at the Reformation and two of the pieces were re-fashioned

into a churchyard stile while the other was partially buried under the west wall of the porch. The shaft was then re-erected in its current form in 1886.

Dipping back even further in time, a late Neolithic and early Bronze Age burial site called Wigber Low can be found just south of Bradbourne. It is the site of Derbyshire's only so-far discovered exposure platform which were used by Neolithic people to accelerate the decomposition process by exposing dead bodies to the open-air on top of such platforms. When excavated, Wigber Low turned up the remains of cremated human bones that had been scattered over a flat-topped, oblong cairn, encircled by blocks of limestone.

In the 13th century, Bradbourne, like many other Derbyshire estates, was owned by a religious house. But whereas many estates were understandably owned by institutions closer to home – like the cathedrals at Lichfield and Lincoln and the abbeys at Burton and Lenton – Bradbourne belonged to Dunstable Priory in Bedfordshire, which in 1284 owned 1,200 sheep on the estate! However, in 1552, the estate was bought from the priory by Sir William Cavendish.

Moving forward to the 19th century, and a lamp was erected in front of the entrance to All Saints' church and

This Anglo-Saxon cross in Bradbourne's churchyard dates to c.800.

The Old Parsonage to commemorate Queen Victoria's Diamond Jubilee. The lamp's stone pillar is carved with the words: "To commemorate the sixty years reign of Queen Victoria 1837 – 1897. Erected by the inhabitants of Bradbourne and Ballidon." Above that is a much later plaque which declares that: "This lamp was renovated by the parish council and switched on by Mrs M. Trafford on 15th August 1981."

Bradbourne Quirk Alert: Unimaginable Conflicts…and Inflation!

Inside Bradbourne All Saints' church is a memorial to Thomas Buckston of Bradbourne Hall. He died in 1811 at the age of 87 and was one of the British army's oldest officers. That also means that he was one of very few soldiers who served during both Culloden (1746) and Trafalgar (1805). Perhaps the only one! That's today's equivalent of a soldier having served in both World War II and Afghanistan in the 21st century, which is pretty much unimaginable. And talking of war, Bradbourne is also one of the 51 Thankful Villages of England, having suffered no losses during World War I. In fact, it is the only village in Derbyshire to bear this title, thanks to the fact that 18 men left to fight and 18 came back home again.

Finally, here's a silly fact for you. The *Domesday Book* of 1086 lists Bradbourne as belonging to Henry de Ferrers. But as all *Domesday Book* entries do, it also names the Lord of the Manor in 1066, which is invariably an Anglo-Saxon nobleman who was deposed by William I after the Norman Conquest – poor Aelfric of Bradbourne in this particular case. However, the *Domesday Book* entry also lists the value of the estate in both 1066 and 1086 and intriguingly, those values are 80 shillings (£4.50) and 30 shillings (£1.50), respectively. But we're not going to theorise on the twenty-year depreciation. Instead, be enlightened by the fact that those values of £1.50 and £4.00 are what it now costs to park your car at nearby Carsington Water's main carpark for two hours and the whole day, respectively. So in summary, what you park your car for in 2014 for two hours, would have bought you the entire manor of Bradbourne in 1086!

The shadow of Bradbourne's "Magic Lamp", rather handily tells the time for you. The above photograph was taken at 15:02 (14:02 GMT) on 22 April!

NAME (STATUS):	**BRADLEY** (Village)
POPULATION:	260
DISTRICT:	Derbyshire Dales
EARLIEST RECORD:	*Braidelei*, 1086 (*Domesday Book*)
MEANING:	Place at the broad wood or clearing
DERIVATION:	From the Old English words *brād* (broad/spacious) and *lēah* (wood/woodland clearing)
FAMOUS RESIDENTS:	**Hugo Meynell** (1735-1808), father of fox-hunting, MP for three constituencies between 1762 and 1780, and High Sheriff of Derbyshire, 1758-1759. **Thomas Bancroft** (1596-1658), poet.

Bradley Pub:
The Fox and Hounds/The Jinglers

The Fox and Hounds – which was presumably named after local 18th century landowner Hugo Meynell's favourite pastime – used to be the only pub in the Bradley parish, but alas, it was closed in 2000. The building is still there, though, and is located on the eastern edge of the Bradley parish on the A517 by the turn for Mercaston. This former public house had the unusual distinction of having two names: The Fox and Hounds if approaching from Ashbourne, and The Jinglers if approaching from Belper.

Bradley Church: All Saints

The 14th century All Saints' church at Bradley is described in numerous books as an odd, squat-like structure on account of the fact that it doesn't possess a tower; however, others feel it has great charm. The shape of the building certainly wasn't helped, though, when its wooden tower was struck by lightning in the 18th century and had to be demolished. The single bell is now hung from a structure on the west wall of the church while also present in the churchyard is the three-foot shaft of yet another ancient Derbyshire cross. As for the interior of the church, this has an aisle-less nave and chancel all under one roof and a 13th century font with

an octagonal bowl, while there are numerous memorials to the Meynell family who lived in Bradley Hall, directly opposite the church. The present hall was built in the late 18th century by Hugo Meynell whose family had acquired the old hall (now demolished) from Andrew Kniveton after the English Civil War – the latter being a rare Derbyshire Royalist who thus found his estate sequestered by Parliament.

Bradley Historic Trivia:
Fox Hunting, Dictionaries and Epigrams

Sticking with Bradley Hall, we've already mentioned that the present hall was built in the late 18th century by Hugo Meynell (1735-1808). Hugo went on to be known as the father of fox-hunting, particularly after he became Master of Fox Hounds for the Quorn Hunt in Leicestershire in 1753, a post that he held for 47 years. In this role, he pioneered the extended chase at high speeds through the countryside and also bred a new form of hound with greater pace and stamina and a better sense of scent. But apart from his vulpine-related activities, he also represented three constituencies as Member of Parliament in the House of Commons between 1762 and 1780, and served as High Sheriff of Derbyshire in 1758-1759.

It was also to Bradley Hall that Dr Samuel Johnson

The former Fox and Hounds – but only if approaching on the A517 from Ashbourne! If approaching from Belper, the pub was known as The Jinglers!

Bradley All Saints' church dates from the 14th century, but lost its tower to a lightning strike in the 18th century.

(1709-1784) used to visit Hugo's mother and her daughters when staying at Ashbourne with his friend Dr Taylor. He first visited the Meynells in 1739 when Hugo Meynell was only four years old and it is thought that Johnson was a great admirer of Hugo's sister, Mary, but who later married William Fitzherbert of Tissington. Dr Johnson also began his friendship with Miss Hill Boothby at Bradley Hall, and she went on to provide much encouragement to him as he prepared his great *Dictionary*.

Meanwhile, Bradley was also home to 17th century poet, Thomas Bancroft, who lived in the village up until his death in 1658. He was also famed for addressing poems and epigrams to famous people in which he embedded clever puns with his targets including William Shakespeare and Ben Jonson.

Bradley's famous Hole in the Wall seen from the south.

Bradley Quirk Alert: The Hole in the Wall

The building known as the Hole in the Wall is located in the Moorend area of the Bradley parish. This archway spans the road between two cottages that date from 1750-51 and it has therefore been suggested that it was a toll house. This theory is backed up by the fact that Bradley is mentioned as being on the route of the 18th century turnpike road from London to Manchester, plus the facing walls beneath the arch contain a blocked-up doorway and a small window apiece.

Perhaps these were used to check passage through the arch, although the fact that there are no windows *facing* approaching traffic would make this a pretty unconventional toll house! Then again, there was clearly once a gate here, too, as the hinges remain – so perhaps the traveller had to approach the "toll house" window to ask for the gate to be opened while also paying their toll. Alternatively, the structure could have been a gatehouse to Bradley Hall.

Bradley Hall, home to the Meynells in the 18th and 19th centuries.

NAME (STATUS):	**BRADWELL** (Village)
POPULATION:	1,423
DISTRICT:	High Peak
EARLIEST RECORD:	*Bradewelle*, 1086 *(Domesday Book)*; *Bradewell*, 1230
MEANING:	Place at the broad spring or stream
DERIVATION:	From the Old English words *brād* (broad or spacious) and *wella* (spring or stream)
FAMOUS RESIDENTS:	**Samuel Fox** (1815-1887), inventor. **Evans Bros**, 19th century producers of telescopes, opera glasses and spectacles. **Hannah Bradwell**, founder of Bradwell's Ice Cream in 1899. **Denis Avey** (b.1919), WWII veteran and British Hero of the Holocaust.

Bradwell Geographic Trivia: The Hotchpotch

Located in the Peak District's Hope valley, Bradwell marks the spot where the Dark Peak meets the White Peak. Other early settlements on Bradwell Hills and Smalldale have now merged with the original Bradwell resulting in a hotchpotch of charming and individual buildings accessed by a maze of narrow lanes, ginnels and alleyways. Indeed, 19th century Bradwell chronicler Seth Evans, wrote: *"Its steep winding streets – if streets they can be called – and all sorts of queer little out of the way places running in and out in all directions, break neck, oblique, skew-tilted, beginning everywhere, leading nowhere, make the stranger feel that he is living in mediaeval times."* He then goes on to state that: *"This romantic spot was never troubled with a surveyor"*, and *"Every man was his own architect"*. It was the boom of the lead industry in the late 18th century that led to this haphazard growth. There were several large mines on Bradwell Moor and numerous small mines in the hills around the village; in fact, the road back to the village from the south-west is still known as Hungry Lane, so-named as this was the return route used by the tired and hungry miners at the end of each day!

Bradwell Pub: Ye Old Bowling Green Inn

Bradwell actually has five pubs, including The New Bath Inn, which marks the site of a medicinal Roman spring that was revived in Georgian times. As for Ye Old Bowling Green Inn, the pub is actually situated in the hamlet of Smalldale, up the hillside to the west of Bradwell and with fine views overlooking Bradwell Edge. The inn dates back to 1577 and is known to locals simply as "The Green".

Bradwell Church: St Barnabus

Bradwell's church is called St Barnabus, but was built relatively recently in 1868, thanks to the donations of Bradderite Samuel Fox who donated land for the site of the churchyard and vicarage along with £100 to go towards the building of the church. He also provided for the poor of the parish by leaving a trust fund of £1,000, with the interest allocated annually to those in need. Fox's own house is marked with a plaque and lies just off the main road, while a pub in his name – The Samuel Fox Inn – lies *on* the main road.

Bradwell Historic Trivia: Bloody Battle and a Famous Fox

A mile north of Bradwell is the village of Brough where the remains of the Roman fort of Navio can be found, although Roman remains have been found at Bradwell, too. These include a Roman bath, coin hoards and a cast lead ingot – presumably because Bradwell was the first stop on the Roman road from Brough to Buxton. It is

Bradwell, taken from Bradwell Edge and exposing its sprawled hotchpotch of houses.

St Barnabus' church built in 1868 following a donation from Samuel Fox.

A stretch of the c.7ᵗʰ century Grey Ditch, to the east of Bradwell.

The Samuel Fox Inn, named after Bradwell's most famous son.

also reputed that the Romans often imported French or Italian convicts to do "hard labour" in the lead mines of Bradwell – a fate which became known as *damnati in metalia*.

Bradwell is also thought to be one of three possible locations of the Battle of Heathfield in 633, a critical moment in early Anglo-Saxon history when King Penda of Mercia defeated King Edwin of Northumbria. The other two locations – Hatfield in Yorkshire and Edwinstowe in Nottinghamshire lay claim through their names; Bradwell's claim is Grey Ditch, an impressive linear earthwork running from Mam Tor to Shatton Edge that dates from the correct period and may have been constructed as a battle defence. The earthwork is still visible in four distinct sections that bisect Bradwell between Mich Low to the north-west and Bradwell Edge to the south-east. The aptly-named Gore Lane also passes nearby where archaeological finds include many bones and old weapons. Then there is also an ancient tree known as the "Eden Tree" or "Edwin's Tree"; local folklore suggests this is the tree from which King Edwin's body was hung as proof of his death in order to end the battle and prevent further slaughter. Today, the tree lends its name to Bradwell's Eden Tree House and Eden Tree Caravan Park.

Many centuries later, the year 1815 saw the birth of Bradwell's most famous son, Samuel Fox, who invented the folding umbrella mechanism, complete with U-shaped ribs known as the paragon umbrella frame. In 1842, he set up Fox Umbrella Frames Ltd in Stocksbridge and his company became the largest umbrella frame manufacturer in the world around the turn of the 20ᵗʰ century, plus it also went on to become one of the largest steel makers in the UK, too. Alas, what had become Hoyland Fox Ltd in 1988 was acquired by The Activa Group in 2008, and they promptly transferred the brand name, patents, technology, tools and machinery to its China factory ending 166 years of British tradition.

Bradwell Quirk Alert: Falcons, Ghosts and Gliders

The oldest building in the Bradwell parish is Hazlebadge Hall, built in 1549. The Strelleys lived in its predecessor from 1154, and also held a mill at nearby Brough, given by Edward III – but only on the condition that when visiting Derbyshire, a member of the family would attend him on horseback carrying a Heron Falcon! The Vernons then took over in 1421 until Margaret Vernon, last of the line, was said to have gone insane after witnessing her lover's marriage to a rival at Hope church. Her ghost is said to haunt the hall and also the valley where she is sometimes alleged to gallop on a white horse at midnight between Hope and Hazlebadge!

Meanwhile, the hill overlooking Bradwell was the starting point for the UK's longest ever paraglider flight on August 9ᵗʰ, 2011, and which completed around 160 miles away in Suffolk!

The surviving wing of Hazlebadge Hall, home of the Peverils, Strelleys and Vernons from the 11ᵗʰ to the 18ᵗʰ century. The Vernon family crest still survives above the upper window.

Threes-Up!

	BOULTON	BOUNDARY	BRADWAY
STATUS:	Suburb	Hamlet	Suburb
POPULATION:	13,876	c.100	c.5,000
DISTRICT:	Derby	South Derbyshire	Sheffield
EARLIEST RECORD:	*Boletune*, 1086; *Boletun*, 1176	*Bondary*, 1870	*Bradweye*, 1300
MEANING:	Bola's farmstead	Place at the boundary	Place at the broad road
DERIVATION:	From the Old English personal name, *Bola*, plus the Old English word *tūn* (enclosure or farmstead)	From its position as a village on the boundary between Derbyshire and Leicestershire	From the Old English words *brād* (broad or spacious) and *weg* (way, track or road)

Threes Up Trivia!

Although **Boulton** is first recorded in the *Domesday Book*, it was inhabited by Stone Age people as evidenced by the oldest flint tools discovered in Derbyshire on adjoining Boulton Moor. Meanwhile, Boulton's St Mary's church (*shown top left*) dates from early Norman times, having been built in around 1090 by the de Sacheverell family who were Lords of the Manor of *Boletune* at that time. Almost 200 years later in 1271, the church became the subject of a protracted dispute when the post of chaplain became vacant. Sir Robert de Sacheverell claimed the right to nominate the new chaplain, believing Boulton Church to be independent, but the abbot of Darley Abbey believed it was *his* right as owner of St Peter's church in Derby to which Boulton was deemed to be a chapelry. However, although it was true that the first Norman overlord of Boulton, Ralph fitzHubert, owned both churches, this was at a date *prior* to the building of Darley Abbey to which St Peter's was later gifted. The dispute went on for ten years, before the abbot finally got his way – although control came to an abrupt end during the Dissolution of the Monasteries in the late 1530s. Nevertheless, it wasn't until 1730 that Boulton St Mary's status as a chapelry of

The Toll House at Boundary lies on the A511, a former toll road between Ashby-de-la-Zouch and Burton-upon-Trent.

St Peter's came to an end and it finally became the parish church of Boulton.

As for **Boundary**, this tiny place is located about a mile south-east of Woodville and dates from the 19th century when the place grew up alongside the former toll road between Ashby-de-la-Zouch and Burton-upon-Trent. The 1857 *Trade Directory* lists the Greyhound Inn on today's A511 as belonging to Elizabeth Cooper of Boundary, while John Marius Wilson's *Imperial Gazetteer of England and Wales* of 1870-72 describes the place as: *"BONDARY, or Barton-Road, an extra-parochial tract in the district of Ashby-de-la-Zouch and county of Derby; 2 miles N of Ashby-de-la-Zouch. Pop., 52. Houses, 9."* Sometime after this, the village was

formally recognised as a parish and by 1881 its population recorded as 102.

Finally, **Bradway** is a Sheffield suburb comprising the three former Derbyshire villages of Upper Bradway, Bradway, and Lower Bradway, each of which was annexed by Sheffield in the 1930s, thus making each now part of the ceremonial county of South Yorkshire. Bradway is also the site of the 2,027 yard-long (1,853m) Bradway Tunnel, which was opened in 1870 when the village was still part of Derbyshire. During its excavation, the natural water table became an issue and a number of small heading tunnels had to be constructed. Remarkably, these drained around 16,000 gallons of water an hour.

The Greyhound Inn at Boundary, and also on the A511.

NAME (STATUS):	**BREADSALL** (Village)
POPULATION:	750
DISTRICT:	Erewash
EARLIEST RECORD:	*Brægdeshale*, 1002; *Brægdesheale*, 1004; *Braideshale*, 1086
MEANING:	Nook of land of a man called *Brægd*
DERIVATION:	From the Old English personal name, *Brægd,* plus the Old English word *halh*, (nook or corner of land). Mr Brægd himself may have been named after the Old English words *brægd* (trick or deceit) or *brægden* (crafty)
FAMOUS RESIDENTS:	**Erasmus Darwin** (1731-1802), physician, botanist, philosopher, inventor, author, poet. **Sir Francis Sacheverel Darwin** (1786-1859), physician, traveller. **Joseph Whittaker** (1813-1894), naturalist, botanist. **Edward Darwin** (1821-1901), author. **Henry Harpur-Crewe** (1828-1883), naturalist, botanist.

Breadsall Pub: The Windmill Inn

Breadsall village doesn't actually have a pub, but The Windmill Inn at Breadsall Hilltop just about qualifies – although plenty of folk may argue that it is located in the expanding Oakwood, these days. Either way, the pub offers stunning views to the north across the Derwent valley.

Breadsall Church: All Saints

All Saints' church at Breadsall has a very distinctive 14th century recessed spire which rises from its 13th century tower. Alas, all that remains of the Norman church is its fine south doorway with its carvings of the necks and heads of birds. The chancel and north arcade were built in the 13th century while the nave arcade, the south walls of the nave and chancel, and the porch date from the 14th. Meanwhile towards the end of the 19th century, an alabaster carving of Our Lady of Pity was found under the floor and is thought to be nearly 600 years old.

Breadsall Historic Trivia:
Erasmus Darwin & Co

Opposite the church is Breadsall Old Hall, a medieval gentry or manor house that combines stone-work with timber framing. Meanwhile, a mile up the road is Breadsall Priory, a splendid Elizabethan house built in the late 16th century, and where the Darwin family lived from 1799 to 1858. The site's predecessor dates back to around the mid-13th century when the original Breadsall Priory was founded for a prior and two canons. The priory remained small and poor up until its dissolution in 1536 after which the site was granted by the Crown to the Duke of Suffolk. However, it was Sir John Bentley who built the Elizabethan house that still stands today, with subsequent extensions and alterations carried out by architect Robert Scrivener in about 1861, and a new wing added in 1906. Today, the house is a hotel and country club with two 18-hole golf courses, while it also hosted a G8 summit meeting in 2005.

Of course, the most famous resident of Breadsall Priory was Sir Erasmus Darwin (1731-1802) who lived there for the last three years of his life and was buried at All Saints' church, Breadsall. Darwin was first and foremost a physician, who had practiced for over fifty years and who had actually turned down an invitation to be physician to King George III during his career. However, he was also a famous botanist, natural philosopher, slave-trade abolitionist, inventor and poet,

![Breadsall All Saints' church.]

Breadsall All Saints' church.

Breadsall Old Hall.

Breadsall Priory which dates from the 17th century.

facets which surely laid the foundations for his more famous grandson, Charles. Indeed, Erasmus's most important scientific work, *Zoonomia*, talks about evolution from an associationism perspective and also tips its hat towards natural selection, while his final long poem, *Temple of Nature* (and originally entitled *The Origin of Society*), was packed with references to natural history and evolution. Then in *The Botanic Garden*, not only does he speculate on cosmological theories such as the Big Bang Theory, but he also appears to be somewhat blessed with technological foresight particularly with respect to these famous lines:

Soon shall thy arm, unconquered steam ! afar
Drag the slow barge, or drive the rapid car ;
Or on wide waving wings expanded bear
The flying chariot through the field of air.

Erasmus Darwin was also a founder member of the Lunar Society in 1765. This brought together many of Britain's leading scientists, industrialists and inventors of the age, including James Watt, Josiah Wedgwood and Joseph Priestley, plus leading writers such as Anna

Rectory Lane, Breadsall.

Seward and Thomas Day. The society's purpose was to share ideas and knowledge and was so-named because they used to meet in Birmingham at full moon. Darwin was also a friend of Dr Samuel Johnson who has already cropped up in Bradley's *Historic Trivia*, while coincidentally Samuel Fox (see Bradwell's *Historic Trivia*) was also Erasmus Darwin's brother-in-law. Meanwhile, Erasmus's own inventions included a horizontal windmill which he designed for Josiah Wedgwood, a carriage that didn't tip over, a steering mechanism for his carriage that would be adopted by cars 130 years later, a speaking machine, a canal lift for barges, a copying machine, a variety of weather monitoring devices and an artesian well.

Breadsall Quirk Alert:
Famous Botanists and Kevin the Peacock

Remarkably, as well as Erasmus Darwin, Breadsall was home to two more celebrated 19th century botanists. Breadsall-born Joseph Whittaker was school-master at Breadsall Boys School while Henry Harpur-Crewe became rector of All Saints in 1857. The pair produced many papers and twice collaborated, once in 1846 when they jointly reported on the extinction from Derbyshire of the Lady's Slipper Orchid, and again in 1864 when they produced a list of the principal flowering plants and ferns of Derbyshire. Today, Henry Harpur-Crewe's plant collections can be found in the Natural History Museum and his letters can be found at Kew Gardens. Meanwhile 300 of Joseph Whittaker's plants acquired during his South Australia trip can be found in Kew Gardens and 2,200 pressed British plants, mostly from Derbyshire, are held in the herbarium at Derby Museum and Art Gallery. Furthermore, the species of sundew *Drosera whittakeri* is named after him.

Throughout 2013, Breadsall became home to a mystery peacock called Kevin. Whether he was wild or had escaped from a stately home, no one knew. What they did come to know, though, is how loud a 115 decibel mating call is – and usually at around five o'clock every morning! And that was just for starters. Several months later, Kevin had clearly taken up permanent residency in Breadsall. As well as causing mass sleep deprivation, he also proceeded to endear himself to the locals by eating garden vegetables and foliage, recycling his meals on pristine patios, bringing traffic to a halt, and terrifying the local cleaning lady who promptly locked herself into the village hall lavatory while he stalked about outside; in short, the locals had ceased thinking how beautiful he was and had started to wonder what he tasted like! Alas, attempts to either capture him or trace his owners have failed and so Kevin's stranglehold on the village continues to tighten, whilst residents are forced to align their sleep patterns to his, and plan their car journey's around Kevin's meanderings!

NAME (STATUS):	**CALLOW** (Hamlet)
POPULATION:	30
DISTRICT:	Derbyshire Dales
EARLIEST RECORD:	Not known; however, the place was recorded as one of the chapelries affiliated to Wirksworth in the early 12th century
MEANING:	Place at the cold or bare hill
DERIVATION:	From the Old English word *calu* (bald, bare, lacking vegetation or bare hill) in a dative form

Callow Hall, Callow.

Callow Park with the hill behind it rising up to the village of Callow.

Callow Church: Callow Hall!

Callow is so small that it doesn't have a church, although it must have once had a chapel, since the place was recorded as one of the chapelries affiliated to the medieval parish of Wirksworth during the reign of Henry I (1100-1135). The hamlet does, however, still have an old manor house, a private residence located down the hill to the south of the village. Callow Hall is also unusual in that it still has its ancient moat and retains the medieval stone undercroft that originally belonged to the de la Laund family many centuries ago.

Callow Historic Trivia: Callow Park

This relatively recent history revolves around what is now called Callow Park College and which nestles in the valley underneath the village of Callow and alongside the B5023 from Duffield to Wirksworth. Originally known as just Callow Park in the second half of the 20th century, it was a country club complete with squash courts, a small swimming pool, two outdoor tennis courts and rooms for visitors to stay the night. It was also used for functions, and one of my wife's most vivid memories is of being a teenage bridesmaid at a reception there, having arrived in a horse-drawn carriage on a beautiful summer's day. The wedding had taken place at Belper, and the carriage arrived having travelled down the steep road from Ashleyhay just over the road from Callow Park. For anyone who knows that area, you'll appreciate just how special that would have been.

However, the country club closed in 1993, and the site was taken over by Alderwasley Hall School. Today, it is a private sixth form college targeted at individuals with learning difficulties, plus it caters for younger students specialising in Art and PE.

Callow Quirk Alert: The Callow Connection

Although the village of Callow only amounts to a cluster of remote houses, it lends its name to two establishments that are situated 5 or 6 miles to the south-west of the village. Callow Country House Hotel is located on Mappleton Road half way between Ashbourne and Mappleton and it was built between 1849 and 1852 in two parallel ranges, with two storeys and a four bay front. That said, it was originally *designed* as a much more ambitious Jacobean-style three storey house by H.I. Stevens in 1848 for John Goodwin Johnson, but was later reduced in scale. The house passed through a number of families until purchased by the Spencer family who began renovating the building into a country house hotel which opened in 1982. Today, it describes itself as *"a unique country house hotel with an unrivalled setting and renowned restaurant, situated in the heart of the Derbyshire Dales and Peak District, close to the lively market town of Ashbourne. Surrounded by 35 acres of private garden, fields and woodland overlooking the Bentley Brook and vale of the River Dove, this ivy-clad luxury Victorian hotel really is a haven of peace and tranquillity."* Are you hooked yet?

As for the other establishment, this one is also related to leisure and is known as Callow Top Holiday Park. It is located a mile to the north of Callow Country House Hotel on the A515 as it heads out of Ashbourne, bound for Buxton. It has won numerous top awards and, as well as the ample facilities that they have, they quite rightly dangle the main carrot, as…*"Situated in a delightful, elevated setting in the Derbyshire countryside, Callow Top is perhaps the most picturesque of all caravan parks and campsites in Derbyshire. Just north of the famous market town of Ashbourne, Callow Top is perfectly located for exploring the most attractive areas of the Derbyshire Peak District National Park. Alton Towers, Dovedale, Tissington & the Tissington Trail, the High Peak Trail and the Manifold valley are all within easy reach, making the park an ideal base for your family break or weekend away."*

Anyway, leaving the Callow Tourist Board behind, the odd thing about these two places is that neither appears to have a connection with Callow village. What's more, neither of them appears to be related to the most likely etymological derivation, as neither of them resides on a "bare hill" and neither is lacking in any vegetation!

Callow Country House Hotel is actually located around six miles to the south-west of the village of Callow.

Part of Callow village which is little more than a cluster of stone houses on top of a hill.

NAME (STATUS):	**CALVER** (Village)
POPULATION:	1,800
DISTRICT:	Derbyshire Dales
EARLIEST RECORD:	*Calvoure*, 1086 *(Domesday Book)*; *Caluore*, 1199; *Calfover*, in 1239
MEANING:	Slope or ridge where calves graze
DERIVATION:	From the Old English words *calf* (calf) and *ofer* (flat-topped ridge, hill or promontory)

Calver Pub: The Eyre Arms

The Eyre Arms is named after a local medieval gentry family who made their fortune from lead. The first lead mine was opened in the Calver area in the 1420s following a new vein that was discovered north of the River Wye. The Eyres soon cashed in and by the late Elizabethan period, the main beneficiary was Rowland Eyre, whose manors of Rowland, Hassop and Calver were not subject to the royalties of lot and cope. Not known for his compassion, he built nearby Hassop Hall out of his profits, enclosing the land and converting farms to pasture in the process. You will also find an Eyre Arms in nearby Hassop and Bakewell – again, named after the same family.

The Eyre Arms, Calver.

All Saints' church, Curbar/Calver.

Calver Church: All Saints

The 19th century parish church of Calver is dedicated to All Saints, although it is located a few paces over the Calver border in the neighbouring village of Curbar where it serves both villages as well as the nearby village of Froggatt. It is located alongside the local school – with the latter also serving the three villages.

Calver Historic Trivia:
Lead, Cotton and Corn

The earliest settlement at Calver probably began near the old bridge across the Derwent where several ancient east-to-west trading routes forded the river while evidence of an early Anglo-Saxon settlement was revealed when skeletons were found in 1860. From the Middle Ages up to the end of the 19th century the ford and later bridges were used by jaggers leading pack-horse teams across the river, before climbing the steep eastern bank up through Curbar Gap and on across Big Moor to Sheffield and Chesterfield. The settlement grew in importance when the ancient ford was superseded by the first bridge at Calver, and then later in the 1420s when the first lead mine was opened there. Known as the Cheprake, this lead vein also saw mining commence at nearby Great and Little Longstone, Rowland and Hassop – to the benefit of the local Eyre family who owned them all. However, the terminal decline of the lead industry in the 19th century saw the population of Calver drop significantly between the censuses of 1841 and 1901 (from 621 to 379).

Calver was also one of the first places in the country to benefit from the Industrial Revolution, as it became home to one of the early cotton-spinning mills following Richard Arkwright's first at Cromford in 1771. Calver's first mill was opened in 1778 by John Gardom of Bubnell and John Pares of Risley and in 1785 Gardom built another, much larger mill close by. Alas, disaster struck twice at the turn of the 19th century when first the 300 year-old bridge was swept away during the catastrophic floods of 1799, taking part of the smaller mill with it, and then the larger of Gardom's two cotton mills burned down completely in 1802. However, both bridge and mill were rapidly rebuilt with the latter recommencing production in 1804, and by 1830 it employed 200 workers. The mill finally ceased producing cotton in 1923.

All of the aforementioned 19th century industry had its effect on Calver, of course, and it certainly wasn't the pretty village that it is today. In fact, in 1870, James Croston comments in his book *On Foot Through The Peak* that the air at Calver was *"full of pale blue smoke that wreathed itself into a variety of fantastic looking clouds"*, while sixty years later, travel writer Thomas Tudor remarked, *"Calver is not pretty for it has mills and lime works and ugly houses, and gives little suggestion of the rural charm which agriculture and its attendant interests can throw over these Derbyshire dales."*

Calver Quirk Alert:
Colditz, Cricket and Fishy Bill!

Calver Mill went on to be used as a storage depot during WWII and as a plant for crushing and washing fluorspar used in steelmaking. However, Calver Mill's connection with WWII was to re-surface around thirty years later when it was used in the role of the infamous Colditz Castle during production of the television series *Colditz*. Ironically during the *actual* war, lights were lit on the moors nearby, fooling the German bombers into harmlessly releasing their payloads onto the empty moors rather than their intended target of Sheffield. Then in 1947, Calver Mill was bought by W. & G. Sissons to produce stainless steel hollow-ware. Today it has been converted into private apartments.

Meanwhile, it is possible that Calver is the home of the oldest cricket club in Derbyshire. Princess Victoria is certainly recorded as having attended a cricket match here in 1832, and Ilkeston Rutland Cricket Club's

records certainly refer to a Calver Cricket Club in their 1829 records. This means that Calver Cricket Club precedes Derbyshire CCC by at least thirty years.

Finally, "The Little Shop" on Hassop Road dates back to 1919. Today it sells sweets and ice creams, but it was formerly the domain of Fishy Bill, the local fishmonger. Alas, he acquired his nickname thanks to his reputation of offering the previous week's unsold fish during his weekly fish rounds. Local folklore also has it that his sales of ice creams hit the skids, too...after he was caught washing his feet in the ice cream bucket!

View towards the pavilion of Calver Cricket Club.

View of Calver Mill from the rear. It isn't too hard to imagine it adorned with swastikas!

NAME (STATUS):	**CLOWNE** (Village)
POPULATION:	7,447
DISTRICT:	Bolsover
EARLIEST RECORD:	*Clune*, c.1002; *Clune*, 1086 (*Domesday Book*)
MEANING:	Named after the ancient river *clun* which rises nearby
DERIVATION:	*Clun* is an ancient Celtic river-name of uncertain origin

Clowne Pub: The Anchor Inn

There are a number of pubs in the village of Clowne, including The Angel Inn, The Nags Head Hotel, The White Hart Inn and The Travellers Rest. However, the pub chosen here is The Anchor Inn, which is situated in the centre of the village on the B6417 where High Street merges into Mill Street and also at the point where both are joined by Church Street. Originally built in the 17th century, the pub faces the village's market cross, which sits in the centre of all three roads. The market cross is Grade II listed with the base dating from probably as long ago as the 14th century and the cross shaft probably the 17th century.

The old market cross in Clowne with The Anchor Inn behind.

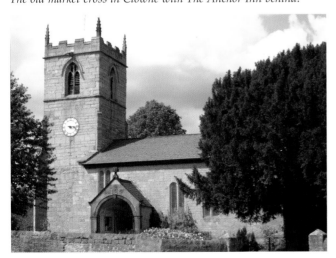

St John the Baptist church, Clowne.

Clowne Church: St John the Baptist

The church at Clowne is dedicated to St John the Baptist. It is also one of a number of Derbyshire churches that are intriguingly sited apart from the village centre, alongside what is now a minor road, suggesting that the settlement has moved since the 12th century when the church was built – perhaps due to the plague which badly struck Clowne in both 1586 and 1606 with the victims buried away from the village at Monument Field or Plague Field. As for the church, it has a 15th century Perpendicular Gothic tower, but the interior of the building reveals much earlier work going back to Norman times, including the south door, the chancel arch, the priest's doorway and the font. Fast-forwarding to the 20th century, and the Norman chancel was actually rebuilt and enlarged in 1955 when two chapels were added, one of which was dedicated to those who lost their lives in local coal mines.

Clowne Historic Trivia: Markland Grips

Markland Grips is a Site of Special Scientific Interest that lies just to the south-east of Clowne, and which is managed by the Derbyshire Wildlife Trust. It is an area where Neolithic discoveries have been made, including flint arrowheads and scrapers, polished stone axes and pottery. The term "grip" is a geological one describing a vertical cliff-like side formed by the melt-water left behind by the receding glaciers at the end of the last Ice Age. In the cliff sides at Markland Grips are several small caves, rock shelters and fissures where human bones have been discovered and which have been carbon dated also to the early Neolithic period. Markland Grips is also the site of the only Derbyshire Iron Age hillfort found outside of the Peak District. This was an impressive ten and a half acre promontory fort located on the magnesium limestone here. Set between two wide ravines or "grips" that converge to the east, it was defended at the western end by three lines of ramparts. Fragments of both Iron Age and Roman pottery have been found here.

Much later, the c.1002 dating of *Clune* is courtesy of a rare piece of pre-*Domesday Book* documentary evidence thanks to the Mercian thegn, Wulfric Spot. The founder of Burton Abbey, his will dates from c.1002 and it is in this document that he bequeaths a number of estates in north-eastern Derbyshire, including Clowne, to a certain Morcar.

By the beginning of the 19th century the inhabitants of Clowne worked in agriculture, or mined the shallow coal seams there, while others were employed at the mill, which made candlewick, sacking and sail-cloth. However, during the Industrial Revolution, the population of Clowne exploded, increasing from 484 in 1801 to 3,896 in 1901 – although it actually peaked due to the coal mining industry in 1911 (6,037). As the village grew, it swallowed up the tiny neighbouring villages of Hickinwood and Markland, eventually becoming a typical North East Derbyshire colliery village. The sinking of the 1,000 foot Southgate Colliery actually took place in 1877, and at its peak, the mine employed 400 men and produced 600 tons of coal per day. At the end of the 19th century, rows of Victorian terraced houses were built to house the mining families, while a school was also built in 1895. As for the colliery, although it survived a fire in 1920, it was only a short stay of execution as it closed in 1929 after the pit flooded.

Clowne Quirk Alert:
Two Stations, Two Spellings

It was also coal that brought the railways to Clowne in the 19th century – double-fold, as it happens. This is because the Lancashire, Derbyshire and East Coast Railway (ultimately the Great Central), and the Midland Railway lines both ran through the village in order to provide easy export of the coal. This also meant that the village had not one, but *two* stations, with one station on each line – and somewhat quirkily, both were spelt differently, one as Clown and the other as Clowne. Of the two, Clowne South railway station was opened by the LD&ECR in March 1897 and eventually closed in 1964. It was actually built side by side with the Midland Railway's station, with the latter's line running between Staveley and Elmton, while to the south there was a connection between the two lines.

Part of Markland Grips, an area of steep-sided ravines located just south-east of Clowne and home to both Neolithic people and an Iron Age hill-fort.

The LD&ECR line then continued north, crossing the Midland line near the branch to Barlborough Colliery, then dropped steeply to the Rother valley through Spinkhill Tunnel. The station was actually re-named to Clown and Barlborough (note spelling) in 1939 before being named as Clowne South again in 1951.

The former Clowne South railway station, closed in 1964 and since put to other uses!

NAME (STATUS):	**CODNOR** (Village)
POPULATION:	4,966
DISTRICT:	Amber Valley
EARLIEST RECORD:	*Cotenoure*, 1086 (Domesday Book); *Codenoura*, c.1200
MEANING:	Ridge of a man called Cod(d)a
DERIVATION:	From the Old English personal name, *Cod(d)a*, plus the Old English word *ofer* (flat-topped ridge, hill or promontory)
FAMOUS RESIDENTS:	**Chanel Cresswell** (b.1990). actress. **Eric Grainger** (1906-1987), boxer. **James Hunt** (b.1975), footballer. **Joseph Millett Severn** (1860-1942), writer, historian, phrenologist. **Arnold Warren** (1875-1951), cricketer. **Nick Wright** (b.1975), footballer.

The Poet and Castle, Codnor.

Codnor Pub: The Poet and Castle

The Poet and Castle is located in the centre of Codnor at the top of Alfreton Road that heads northwards towards Riddings, Somercotes and ultimately Alfreton. It is one of several pubs owned by the Ashover Brewery, including Ashover's own pub, The Old Poets Corner.

Codnor Church: St James

St James' church was built at Cross Hill to the south of Codnor in 1844 when Codnor and Loscoe were made into one ecclesiastical parish. The church was built from public subscriptions and grants of around £2000, and was consecrated by the Bishop of Lichfield on 10th

October 1844. Built in the Gothic style with rather striking pinnacles, some of the original stone used was quarried in nearby Codnor Denby Lane as well as from further afield at Little Eaton. The bell was brought from Eastwood Old Church and bears the inscription "God Save the Queen 1713". It is believed to have formerly been a ship's bell.

Codnor Historic Trivia: Castle and Coal

Codnor Castle was built by Henry de Grey in the 12th century, after the Codnor estate was granted to him by Richard I. The castle was then rebuilt in the early 14th century and further extended into the lower court in the 15th century – the dates of these three stages of construction being confirmed by a *Time Team* excavation in 2007. However, by 1727, the castle was in a ruinous state while today, it is designated as both a Scheduled Ancient Monument and a Building at Risk. As for the de Greys, they became a very powerful family and Henry de Grey's descendants included the long line of Lords Grey of Codnor, the Lords Grey of Ruthyn, Wilton and Rotherfield, Lady Jane Grey and the Earls of Stamford, and the extinct families of the Dukes of Suffolk and Kent. Richard de Grey was the first to settle at Codnor and he became an active Crown servant as governor of the Channel Islands, sheriff of various counties and a crusader to boot. He also remained loyal to King John at the time of Magna Carta (1215), with his uncle, Walter de Grey, the Archbishop of York, present at its signing. Lord John Grey then served Edward III during the 14th

St James' church, Codnor.

Codnor Castle, a Scheduled Ancient Monument with parts of the ruin dating to the 12th century.

century Scottish wars, commanding all the knights of Derbyshire while in 1415, Richard de Grey, 4th Baron of Codnor, led 222 men from Derbyshire into battle alongside Henry V at Agincourt. The Lancastrian Greys of Codnor then became involved in a bloody 15th century dispute with the Yorkist Vernons of Haddon Hall before the de Grey line finally became extinct in 1496. The estate then passed to the Zouche family of whom George Zouche was betrothed to Anne Gainsford, maid of honour to Anne Boleyn...and who lent Miss Gainsford a book called *The Obedience of a Christian Man* by William Tyndale. The book promoted the belief that Christians should be able to understand the Word of God without being dependent on corrupt religious leaders, and the story goes that George Zouche was caught reading the book by an appalled Cardinal Wolsey who promptly confiscated it. However, Anne Boleyn explained the incident to Henry VIII who demanded to see the book – and which thus seeded the idea that he *could* defy the Catholic Church, divorce Catherine of Aragon and marry Anne Boleyn, plus abandon the Catholic faith without abandoning God. And all, perhaps, because George Zouche of Codnor Castle was careless with his reading!

Both the de Grey and the Zouche family had extracted coal and ironstone from the surrounding parkland in the 15th and 16th centuries, while the first recorded charcoal blast furnace in Derbyshire was built at Loscoe at the southern end of Codnor in around 1582 by Sir John Zouche. However, the early mines were only capable of retrieving the coal and ironstone that was relatively close to the surface, but the late 18th century saw the coal and iron industries boom in the area as more advanced mining techniques emerged. The Butterley Company was set up as a combined coal and iron business a mile to the north-west of Codnor and they were soon investing huge amounts of money into mines that penetrated the deeper coal and ironstone seams. As a result, the company became the largest producer of coal and iron in the East Midlands, reaching the height of its success in the mid-19th century with its greatest ironwork

legacy being the 6,894 ton roof of St Pancras Station. For more on The Butterley Company, see pages 40-42. However, as ironstone seams became exhausted and new forms of steel became popular, both nationally and internationally, the Derbyshire ironworks began to decline. Codnor Park's blast furnaces were closed in 1902, while its forge was closed in 1965. Coal in Codnor only lasted a few years more with Ormonde Colliery closed in 1970. The mine had been sunk in 1906 by the Butterley Company, and first became operational in 1912. At its peak, it employed 1,230 men, while over its lifetime, 27,630,853 tonnes of coal were extracted there.

Codnor Quirk Alert:
Triplets, Phrenology and a Cutting Tale
On the 3rd July 2004 Emma Burns, aged seventeen, of Codnor became the youngest mother in Britain to give birth to triplets without IVF treatment.

Next, Codnor's "Professor" Joseph Millott Severn was a noted Victorian phrenologist – phrenology being a pseudo-science focused on measurements of the human skull, based on the concept that the brain is the organ of the mind, and that certain brain areas have localised, specific functions or modules. Severn interviewed and phrenologically examined many celebrities in his career, including David Lloyd George, Lord Beaverbrook, Sir Arthur Conan Doyle, Dr Sigmund Freud and Sir Ernest Shackleton. Severn also donated the four almshouses at the top of Nottingham Road along with his brothers, while he also penned the book *My Village Owd Codnor* in 1932.

Finally, three years ago, the "This is Derbyshire" website ran a story about the erection of the old Ormonde Colliery winding wheel in the centre of Codnor, which stands as a memorial to those who worked and died at the pit. An ex-miner contributes with a sobering story, recalling how, aged nineteen, he was sent into the tunnels to clear away rubble thrown out by a cutting machine at the coal face. It was only the next day when he was told that part of that "rubble" had included a fellow nineteen year-old miner!

The Butterley Company built these cottages for its workers at Golden Valley just north of Codnor.

Half of the pit winding wheel that used to serve Ormonde Colliery at Codnor.

NAME (STATUS):	**CRICH STAND** (Monument); **CRICH** (Village)
POPULATION:	2,821
DISTRICT:	Amber Valley
EARLIEST RECORD:	*Cryc*, 1009; *Crice*, 1086; *Cruc*, 1166; *Cruch*, c.1200; *Cruz*, 1229
MEANING:	Place at the mound or hill
DERIVATION:	From the Celtic word *crüg* (mound or hill)

The Red Lion, Crich Tramway Village.

Crich Pub: The Red Lion

Crich is home to The Cliff Inn, The Black Swan and The Kings Arms Inn. Meanwhile part of Royal Oak Cottages on The Common used to be The Royal Oak pub, with the rest of the buildings providing some of the best examples of former framework knitter houses. A similar cottage conversion applies to the former Rising Sun and The Bulls Head, while the Jovial Dutchman used to sit alongside the village's famous market cross until it, too, was closed in 2009. However, the pub featured here is The Red Lion. Originally a native of Stoke-on-Trent, it was reconstructed brick-by-brick in the early 1970s on the main street through Crich Tramway Village – this after the original site in Stoke was cleared to make way for the A500.

Crich Church: St Mary's and Crich Stand

St Mary's church is largely 14th century, but does retain a number of Norman relics including the font, the nave arcades and capitals. Built on top of a hill, the church can be seen for miles around, along with Crich Stand – the latter being an impressive 63ft lighthouse-like war memorial with a 40-ton stone dome. It was built in 1923 on top of a limestone outcrop called Crich Cliff, and was initially dedicated to the 11,409 members of the Sherwood Foresters, who died in World War I. Their colonel, Sir Horace Smith-Dorrien, is also commemorated on a plaque on the curved wall which sits just below the war memorial, and which includes his words to his men at Le Cateau in 1914: *"Gentlemen, we will stand and fight"*.

Crich Historic Trivia: Crich Stand and Crich Tramway Museum

In 1952, Crich Stand war memorial was further dedicated to the 1,520 men who died in the Second World War, while 1991 saw the addition of two bronze plaques that were placed either side of the tower doorway, the first remembering the death of all members of the Sherwood Foresters who gave their lives in service to their country between 1945 and 1970, and the second to those who have died since 1970 after which the regiment became known as The Worcestershire and Sherwood Foresters. A Service of Commemoration has been held at Crich Stand every first Sunday in July, since the memorial's erection in 1923.

St Mary's church, Crich.

The Queen's Golden Jubilee Beacon, erected in 2002 a few yards from its rather larger 1923 companion.

As for Crich Stand, it was constructed on the site of a previous tower that had also been named Crich Stand. That predecessor tower was built in 1851, and some of its stones were used in the construction of the present one. However, there were others before that one, including a wooden tower erected in 1760 to commemorate the accession of King George III. That tower only lasted for twenty-five years before being demolished but it was replaced by a conical limestone tower with a wooden top built by Francis Hurt in 1788. This tower, in turn, fell into disrepair before being replaced by the 1851 version, this one a circular tower made of local gritstone. So that makes at least four incarnations of a tower that we know about. But it is thought that an even older tower existed that was part of the beacon chain used in 1588 to warn of the approaching Spanish Armada, and was again used to celebrate victory two months later. Certainly, a beacon was lit there in 1988 to commemorate the 400th anniversary of the defeat of the Armada, while a new stone beacon was built in 2002 to commemorate the Queen's Golden Jubilee.

Just below Crich Stand is the National Tramway Museum, which is set in Crich Tramway Village – a period street with several re-built original buildings from all over the country. These include the facade of the former Assembly Rooms from Derby, the Red Lion Inn from Stoke-on-Trent and the fence and gates from the Fruit & Vegetable Market in the Bull Ring, Birmingham; the village also includes a cafe, an old-style sweetshop, and the museum's tram depots. As for the museum, it contains over 60 tramcars, with around 20 still active and which transport visitors through the village, a mile or so out into the countryside and then back again.

The trams are, of course, relics of a bygone age; beautifully restored vehicles rescued largely from around 20th century Britain as the tram networks closed,

although trams from Berlin, Den Haag, Johannesburg, Oporto, Prague and Sydney also make up the collection. The first tramcar had been purchased by a group of enthusiasts following the closure of Southampton Tramways in August 1948 and which still resides in the collection today. By 1955, the Tramway Museum Society was up and running and it first leased the Crich site in 1959 and later bought it, all the time bringing in a representative collection of tramcars for restoration – although the last tramway closure in the UK occurred only three years later when the Glasgow Corporation Tramway closed in 1962. The construction of the Crich Tramway Village commenced in 1967 in order to re-create an appropriate setting for the trams and the museum continued to add to its tram collection. In addition to the trams, the site also holds the largest tramway archives in the world containing some 8,000 books, 60,000 postcards and 70,000 photographs. As for the line on which the trams run, they follow part of the mineral railway line built by George Stephenson to link his limestone quarry (in which the Tramway Village now sits) with his limekilns alongside what was then the new North Midland Railway at Ambergate. The metre gauge line is believed to have been the first of its kind in the world.

Crich Quirk Alert: Cardale Chippie…and Prize-Winning Urinals!

Visitors to the village of Crich might be forgiven for mistaking it for Cardale from ITV's *Peak Practice*, starring Kevin Whateley and Amanda Burton – since that is where the 1990s series was filmed; in fact, the local fish and chip shop was even re-named as Cardale Chippie a few years ago. Meanwhile, one other addition to the Crich Tramway Museum not previously mentioned, is an original Victorian cast-iron urinal from Reading. But don't turn your nose up: it won the Virgin Trains Volunteers Award for restoration in 2004!

Crich Tramway Village. This is tram number 812, built in 1900 and a former worker on the Glasgow Corporation Tramway that finally closed in 1962. And yes, that is a London Police Box in the background – and which once stood on the North Circular Road in London and was operated by the Metropolitan Police. They tell me it is just the regular size inside…but when I touched it, I definitely detected some strange vibrations…

This is tram number 399, originally built to work the Leeds tramway in 1926. In the background are both Crich Stand and the Bowes-Lyon bridge. This cast-iron bridge was built in 1844 and installed at the Bowes-Lyon estate at Stagenhoe Park at Ware in Hertfordshire. The estate kindly donated the bridge to the Tramway Museum Society in 1971.

NAME (STATUS):	**CROMFORD** (Village)
POPULATION:	2,455
DISTRICT:	Derbyshire Dales
EARLIEST RECORD:	*Crunforde*, 1086 *(Domesday Book)*; *Crumford*, 1204; *Crumbeford*, 1251
MEANING:	Ford by the river-bend
DERIVATION:	From the Old English words *crumbe* (crooked, referring to a river-bend), and *ford* (ford)
FAMOUS RESIDENTS:	**Sir Richard Arkwright** (1732-1792), industrialist. **George Turner** (1841-1910), English landscape artist. **Alison Uttley** (1884-1976), prolific children's author.

The Greyhound Hotel, Cromford.

Cromford Pub: The Greyhound Hotel

The Greyhound Hotel was built in 1778 by Sir Richard Arkwright and was initially intended for use by businessmen visiting the Cromford mills. The Georgian coaching inn was named after the black greyhound on the family crest of Phillip Gell, owner of Hopton Hall and the land on which the hotel was built. The hotel's most famous tale tells of how Georgina Duchess of Devonshire famously met with Richard Arkwright Jnr in the bar to discuss a loan to pay off her gambling debts. Meanwhile, today, the Greyhound Hotel is referred to locally as the "Black Dog".

Cromford Church: St Mary's

St Mary's church was initially built as a private family chapel, begun in 1786 by Sir Richard Arkwright, and completed by his son, Richard Arkwright Jnr, in 1797 – by which time it had been authorised for public worship within the parish of Wirksworth. The gothic tower and porch were added in the 1850s by the well-respected architect, H. I. Stevens of Derby.

Cromford Historic Trivia: Mills and Canals

Although already covered in detail in the *Conventional Derbyshire* section, it is worth reiterating that Arkwright's mill became the world's first water-powered cotton-spinning mill in 1771 thus earning Cromford the title of "Crucible of the Industrial Revolution". By 1775, Arkwright had mechanised the process and his water-frame was soon duplicated throughout the country while he also built further mills at Cromford, plus others at Bakewell, Wirksworth and Cressbrook. By the 1790s, his mill complex at Cromford was employing 800 operatives, many of whom enjoyed good working conditions and superior mill-worker

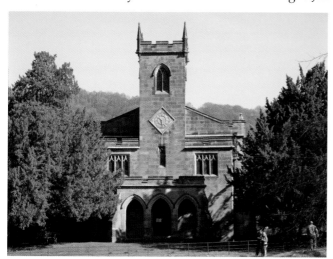

St Mary's church, Cromford.

In the background is Arkwright's famous First Mill, built in 1771, while in the foreground is the head race and wheel pit constructed in 1776-77 as part of the Second Mill development.

cottages such as those that Arkwright built on North Street. He also formed friendly societies, and built a Sunday school while he had the splendid Willersley Castle built for himself. Arkwright remains to this day, Derbyshire's wealthiest resident amassing a fortune of around half a million pounds, which translates into two hundred million pounds, today – but his achievement of mass production of cheap clothing for the masses made him worth every penny.

Alas, Arkwright died at the height of his success in 1792, but his Cromford mills continued in operation until around 1840 when the site lost its principal water supply. As for his historic First and Second Mills, both eventually fell victim to terrible fires. The Second Mill went first in 1890 when a catastrophic fire reduced the entire mill to a shell plus damaged one wing of the annex. Apart from the annex, all that remain today are the great wheel pit and the Second Mill's foundations. The First Mill fared slightly better, but a fire in 1929 still took out the top two floors reducing it to the three-storey building of today.

Cromford's medieval bridge from the southern side; these Gothic pointed arches date the bridge to around 1500.

Cromford's Victorian railway station, for which the southbound platform (on the right) appears on the front cover of Oasis's 1995 single, 'Some Might Say', while the waiting room won the 2009 Railway Heritage Trust Conservation Award.

Meanwhile, the Cromford Canal was constructed in 1789 by William Jessop and Benjamin Outram, with the northern wharf and terminus built in Arkwright's back garden! The canal ran for 14.5 miles from Cromford to the Erewash Canal at Langley Mill and, with its later links to Manchester via the High Peak Railway, Cromford thus had direct access to both eastern and western coastal ports. As for the canal's exports, these included limestone and timber while imports included coal, food and luxury goods. What is today referred to as the Gothic Warehouse because of its embattled parapet, was built in 1794 as a trans-shipment shed, and by 1800, Nathaniel Wheatcroft & Son Ltd were the principal canal carriers – and their name and trade is still imprinted above the Gothic Warehouse entrance.

Cromford Quirk Alert: The Bridge of Sides, and Silence…Some Might Say…

For many centuries, Cromford was a lead-mining village. However, the lead trade resulted in a somewhat ironical reverse for the area during the medieval period, as a bridge was constructed over the River Derwent at Cromford and became a crucial part of the Wirksworth to Chesterfield route by which lead was transported. Unfortunately, this route saw neighbouring Wirksworth gradually lose its status as the commercial centre of the lead trade to Chesterfield. As for the medieval bridge, it went on to spawn a local legend about two squabbling artists. The story goes that both had painted the bridge, but one showed it with three pointed arches and the other with three rounded arches and so both accused the other of not actually painting it *in situ*. Of course, they were both correct for the arches are rounded on the northern side and pointed on the southern side, with the pointed side still comprising some of the oldest bridge-work in Derbyshire, thanks to it being part of the original packhorse footbridge; indeed, the Gothic arches date the southern side of the bridge to around 1500. Built at around the same time alongside the bridge on the south-western bank of the river, was a chantry chapel. It was common medieval practise to build chapels alongside bridges as a place where travellers could say their prayers for a safe journey and to make a contribution to the upkeep of the bridge. Alas, like so many others of its type, the chapel was destroyed in 1547 following Edward VI's dissolution of chantries and guild chapels although its ruins remain. As for the bridge's rounded arches, they appeared in the 18th century when the road was widened on the upstream side.

Finally, the red brick building in the west yard of the Arkwright mill complex was used as a laundry during the late 19th century and was run by the resident launderess, Silence Allen. But was that the name she was christened with, a later nickname…or had she maybe taken a vow of silence for some unfathomable, laundry-related reason. Answers on a postcard please; no verbal responses permitted!

Threes-Up!

	BRAMLEY	CLIFF	COMMON SIDE
STATUS:	Hamlet	Hamlet	Part of a village
POPULATION:	c.30	c.40	c.100
DISTRICT:	North East Derbyshire	High Peak	North East Derbyshire
EARLIEST RECORD:	*Bromleye*, 1239	*Unknown*	*Unknown*
MEANING:	Woodland clearing where broom grows	Place at the cliff or bank	On the side of the village where the common is
DERIVATION:	From the Old English words *brōm* (broom) and *lēah*, (wood, wood-land clearing or glade)	From the Old English word *clif* (cliff, steep slope or river-bank)	The name is probably a modern derivation

Threes Up Trivia!

Bramley is located a mile or so to the west of the town of Eckington and just south of the border with South Yorkshire. The place is tiny, essentially a cluster of houses at the northern end of Marsh Lane, but which includes the Bramley Park Residential Park Home Site and which is run by the National Association of Park Home Residents. However, the "place" called Bramley does still feature on old maps, such as Thomas Burdett's map of Derbyshire from 1767, which places it alongside Bramley Moor – the same area represented by the photograph shown below.

Meanwhile, **Cliff** is a linear settlement located in four distinct housing batches on Swallow House Lane that climbs steeply out of the north-west of Hayfield. The first batch is a row of stone houses that appear on the right with splendid views beginning to emerge over towards the Kinder plateau to the east and the Sett valley to the south. A little further on, and another fine cluster of houses appear with Cliff Villas and Middlecliffe Cottage among those on the right and Lower Cliffe Farm on the left, the latter of which announces itself as being established in 1713 A.D. Then there is another gap up to the next cluster of houses, with the top-most part of the settlement represented by Upper Cliffe Farm.

The Trout Inn, Common Side – and formerly known as the Tickled Trout!

As for **Common Side**, there are at least two in Derbyshire, including the southern part of Heanor between Heanor Gate and Marlpool, and the southern part of Barlow, just north-west of Chesterfield while there's also a Commonside on the A52 just north-west of Brailsford. Of these, the Barlow-based Common Side is home to a Commonside Road that runs up the hill and out of the back of the settlement in a south-westerly direction. The place is also the location of a Caravan and Camping site, a series of fishing ponds, a trout farm and the appropriately named Trout Inn – although the pub used to be known as the Tickled Trout, named after the art of rubbing the underbelly of a trout to coax it into a trance-like state! The "art" was mainly practised by poachers and is currently illegal in Britain – mainly on account of the fact that once in a trance, the fish is grabbed and dashed to death on a rock! Known as guddling in Scotland and noodling in the USA, the technique is mentioned in Shakespeare's *Twelfth Night*, as well as in works by Mark Twain and Roald Dahl.

The area defined as Bramley Moor on Thomas Burdett's 1767 map of Derbyshire.

The first group of stone houses at Cliff as you climb up Swallow House Lane.

NAME (STATUS):	**CROSS O' TH' HANDS** (Village)
POPULATION:	c.30
DISTRICT:	Derbyshire Dales
EARLIEST RECORD:	*Unknown*
MEANING:	See *Historic Trivia*, below

The Primitive Methodist chapel, Cross o' th' Hands. Rumour has it, that if you watch those windows for long enough, you'll see them blink!

Cross O' Th' Hands Church:
Methodist Chapel

Cross o' th' Hands doesn't have an old church, but it is home to a Primitive Methodist chapel, founded in 1903 and which still holds services every Sunday evening, despite its remoteness.

Cross O' Th' Hands Historic Trivia:
Crossroads or Crossed Fists?

Around half way between Belper and Ashbourne on the east-to-west aligned A517 the road is crossed by a pretty country road running south-to-north from Derby to Wirksworth. Taking the northern route at this cross-roads down Hillcliff Lane, the road falls away dramatically, offering spectacular views over the Ecclesbourne valley which is dominated on the right-hand side by Alport Heights and Bole Hill. However, if you took the opposite Derby-bound Intakes Lane, you would be in the delightful little hamlet of Cross o' th' Hands – a place that some will have you believe is named after these very crossroads. The more likely theory, though, is that the settlement is named after its original public house which, in turn, is thought to be named after the staging of bare-knuckle fist fights at a nearby gravel pit in the 19th century – with contestants crossing their hands (or rather their fists) during each bout, in time-honoured tradition.

Cross O' Th' Hands Quirk Alert:
Nailers and Guitouki's

Cross o' th' Hands also lends its name to a popular, Derby-based folk band who are perhaps unique in having amongst their instrument collection, the world's only "guitouki", a combination of guitar and bouzouki crafted by band member John Adams. Amongst their repertoire of songs is *The Nailers Song*, based on a prize-fighter from Belper, a town famous for its nail industry. And rather neatly, the band-name features in the lyrics:

Bare knuckle fighting it is our leisure,
It is our sport and it is our pleasure,
At Cross 'o th' Hands, lads we've got their measure,
And the constable's far away.

Cross o' th' Hands, thought to be named after bare-knuckle fist-fighting.

Heading northwards towards the crossroads that could also be the source of the hamlet's name.

NAME (STATUS):	**CURBAR** (Village)
POPULATION:	c.500
DISTRICT:	Derbyshire Dales
EARLIEST RECORD:	*Cordeburg*, 1203; *Cordesburwe*, 1285; *Quordborough*, 1346; *Cordborgh*, 1356; *Corburg*, 1365; *Coresburgh*, 1423; *Corber*, 1577
MEANING:	Stronghold of a man called Corda
DERIVATION:	From the Old English personal name, *Corda*, plus the Old English word *burh* (stronghold/fortified place)

Curbar Pub: The Bridge Inn

The Bridge Inn was built in the 17th century on the banks of the River Derwent, and today, it sits alongside the later 18th century bridge and directly opposite All Saints' church. Offering log burning fires for the winter and a large riverside garden for the summer, The Bridge Inn is a popular stop for tourists and walkers throughout the year. Up until 1920, it had been under the ownership of the Duke of Rutland, lord of the manor and principal landowner in the area, whilst since then, there have only been five further landlords. Meanwhile, the oak beams in the bar are unusually decorated with hundreds of foreign currency bank notes, while there is also a large collection of antique fire-fighting equipment on display, too!

Curbar Church: All Saints (*see Calver*)

Curbar Historic Trivia: Pinfolds and Plague

Although not able to boast the lead and cotton history of its neighbour, Calver, the village of Curbar does have some intriguing relics. One is a circular pinfold or stock compound, where stray animals were kept until claimed by their owners. Then there is the covered well

The Bridge Inn, Curbar.

The circular pinfold where stray Curbar animals were kept.

In the centre of Curbar is this horse trough, some old millstones and the old well.

View from Curbar Edge looking north-west.

Calver Mill in the foreground, with Curbar Edge behind.

and circular trough alongside a village lock-up with a conical roof with a couple of millstones embedded in the pavement in between.

Curbar also suffered from the Great Plague in the 1630s, pre-dating the more famous plague in Eyam by around 30 years. The gravestones of the Cundy family who lived at Grislowfield farm, Curbar, can be found on the moors above the village, along with a man called Sheldon – all victims of the plague. Then there are also a number of tombs just below the Wesleyan Reform chapel, which are dated 1632; the chapel itself was built in 1862 from stone quarried locally and is located in the upper reaches of the village.

Curbar Quirk Alert: X Marks the Spider
It is claimed that Bar Road in Curbar has the highest average house value in Derbyshire. It is also part of an old Roman Road which, in turn, became part of the local packhorse route. It crosses the River Derwent at Calver Bridge, moves into Curbar and continues upward beyond the village, passing through Curbar Gap at the top of a majestic escarpment behind the village that is known as Curbar Edge. This route was also part of one of the "salt routes" from Cheshire to Chesterfield – and hence the Saltergate area of the latter. As for Curbar Edge, this remains a popular rock-climbing escarpment offering some of the hardest grit-stone rock climbing in Derbyshire. However, if you stand on that outcrop and look due west you will note that the two villages of Curbar and Calver are part of a perceptible X shape, with Calver Mill sitting at the centre like a giant stone spider!

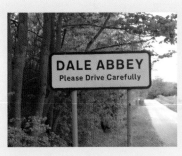

NAME (STATUS):	**DALE ABBEY** (Village)
POPULATION:	c.200
DISTRICT:	Erewash
EARLIEST RECORD:	*Depedala*, 1158; *La Dale*, 1242
MEANING:	The deep dale
DERIVATION:	From the Old English word *dæl* (valley). The "Abbey" affix dates from the early 13th century.
FAMOUS RESIDENTS:	**Rev. Joseph Hollingworth**, Methodist Minister;

Dale Abbey Pub: The Carpenters Arms

The Carpenters Arms was established in the 1880s by the Hollingworth's of Dale, although the family were originally from Breadsall where they were also publicans of the Old Hall Inn. The family had also been publicans of the much older Bluebell Inn at Dale Abbey, and which at that time was adjoined to All Saints' church. Nevertheless, when the Methodist movement came to Dale Abbey in 1771, the Hollingworth's became very much involved, and when Rev. J. Taylor formed a Methodist Society in 1786, William Hollingworth became one of its first members. His grandson, the Rev. Joseph Hollingworth was to later become one of the more notable Methodist priests to circuit the Midlands between 1802 and 1836 while more recently, one of their direct descendants – the Rev. Peter John Hollingworth AC, OBE – was Archbishop of Brisbane from 1989 to 2001, the 23rd Governor-General of Australia from 2001 to 2003 and 1991's Australian of the Year. As for Dale Abbey Methodist church, that was opened in 1902 on the site of a former Wesleyan chapel. Meanwhile, perched on a hill to the west of Dale Abbey is the Cat and Fiddle – not a pub but a windmill! Built in 1788, it is one of only two working

The Carpenters Arms, Dale Abbey.

windmills in Derbyshire and the only surviving wooden post mill.

Dale Abbey Church: All Saints

All Saint's church is thought to date to around 1150. At only 26ft by 25ft, it is thought to be the smallest church in the country still in regular use, although its aisle makes it slightly larger than Stockwood in Dorset and Culbone in Somerset. Despite its size, though, All Saints is reputed to house the largest chalice in England, dated 1701 and measuring 9 inches high and 15 inches round. More particularly (and again, despite its size), All Saints is thought to be *two* churches merged into one (see *Quirk Alert* for more). However, the church's quirkiest feature is the fact that it shares a roof with a neighbouring farmhouse and has served as both farm and church over the years while the non-church side has also been an abbey infirmary and even a pub at one stage! Admittedly difficult to envisage, but the western side became The Bluebell Inn after the 1539 Act of Dissolution and the story goes that the clergy used to dress in the bar which doubled up as the vestry and then entered the chapel through a now blocked doorway. Today, the house is owned

All Saint's church, Dale Abbey, the smallest church in England still in regular use, and the only church that shares its roof with a farmhouse!

The Cat and Fiddle windmill, the only surviving post mill in Derbyshire.

privately while the church continues as such, having retained its box pews, gallery and pulpit, plus some late 13th century wall paintings.

Dale Abbey Historic Trivia:
The Abbey at Dale

The place became known as Dale Abbey from the 13th century thanks to the medium-sized abbey built there by the Premonstratensians or White Canons between 1200 and 1250. However, this was not the first attempt to establish a religious institution here as some Augustinians from Calke were invited to establish a priory here in the 1150s. They remained for thirty years before Henry II sent them back to Calke for breaching the laws of his Forest of East Derbyshire. Two more attempts failed until William FitzRanulph, an important royal official, successfully founded the abbey in Stanley Park in 1200, locating it adjacent to the former monastic settlement at Depedale, while also persuading William de Grendon to donate both Depedale and Boyah. An abbot and nine canons duly arrived from England's senior Premonstratensian house at Newhouse in January 1200 and permanent buildings were completed four years later. Over the next three centuries, the abbey grew in importance and wealth, acquiring numerous local granges and quarries, but that all ended with the 1539 Act of Dissolution, after which the furnishings and fittings were either gradually sold off or stripped out and installed in other churches. Nearby Morley church became home to some of the 15th century stained and painted glass and is acknowledged as the best collection of medieval glass in Derbyshire. Morley church also acquired some of the abbey's floor tiles and an entire porch-way, while other elements ended up at Radbourne church, Chaddesden church and the Moravian Settlement at Ockbrook…but at least the font eventually found its way back to All Saints' church at Dale Abbey in 1884! Today, just the one remaining arch from the east chancel window dominates the abbey's former site, although other remains of the building can be found somewhat quirkily built into houses around the village such as part of the kitchen, the refectory wall and a gateway. Excavations have also unearthed part of the nave, the choir, the 100ft transepts and two chapels.

Dale Abbey Quirk Alert: A Hermit's Tale

It was when the place was still called *Depedala* that Dale Abbey's most famous resident came to stay. For it was sometime between 1130 and 1140 that a baker from Derby, having allegedly had a vision in which he was told to leave his work and become a hermit in *Depedale*, cut his home out of the sandstone cliff in the woodland above Dale Abbey and proceeded to live life as a recluse. What is known as the Hermit's Cave survives to this day, and is well-preserved, measuring 6 yards by 3 with a doorway, two windows, a peephole and a niche for a light. It was originally two compartments: a dwelling place and an oratory but the dividing structure between them has long since gone. The hermit's story does have a happy ending though, for when Norman nobleman Ralph Fitz-Geremund was hunting in the woods and found the hermit, he was so touched by his poverty that he gave him not only the site of the hermitage but a tithe of his mill at Borrowash, too. The story goes that the hermit used the money to build a more pretentious oratory and a cottage in which to end his days – and therefore lends some credibility to the legend that All Saints' church was originally *two* churches merged into one, with the south aisle on the site of the hermit's second oratory, and the nave and chancel part of the chapel extension built by a titled lady known as the Gome of the Dale. This also accounts for the church's quirky shared roof with the neighbouring farmhouse. Alas, my research failed to turn up any information on the status of a Gome. Then again, perhaps the lady in question had a white beard, wore a red hat and suffered from an inability to pronounce her n's…

The only in-situ remains of Dale's 12th century abbey are this 40ft high, 16ft wide east chancel window.

The Hermit's Cave, Dale Abbey, cut out of sandstone rock in the 12th century by a Derby baker!

NAME (STATUS):	**DERBY** (City)
POPULATION:	258,643
DISTRICT:	City of Derby
EARLIEST RECORD:	*Deoraby*, 917; *Deorby*, 959; *Derby*, 1086 *(Domesday Book)*
MEANING:	Settlement where deer are kept
DERIVATION:	From the Old Scandinavian words *djúr* (deer) and *bý* (settlement)
Famous Residents:	Too many to mention. Wikipedia lists 59 for Derby (http://en.wikipedia.org/wiki/Derby).

Derby Pub: The Seven Stars

The Seven Stars dates from around 1660, although it has an even earlier foundation. However, it is not certain when the building was converted into a pub, nor when it became known as the Seven Stars, either. That said, it remains little altered to this day, despite the extensive road alterations that have recently taken place all around it. One of its quirkier stories is that when the old porcelain works used to stand nearby, customers were supplied with china tankards from which to drink their beer instead of glasses. Alas, the works closed in 1935 and there are no tankards left today, with many having been taken as souvenirs.

The Seven Stars, Derby.

Derby Church: All Saints

Derby All Saints' church has also been known as Derby Cathedral since 1927. All Saints was one of two Anglo-Saxon minster churches of Derby founded in the 8th century, the other being St Alkmund's whose 19th century successor was demolished in the late 1960s to make way for the Inner Ring Road. The current incarnation of All Saints was largely built in the 13th century with the west tower added in 1532 and the nave and chancel rebuilt in the 1720s. Derby also has three other significant churches with the predecessors of St Peter's and St Werburgh's founded in the 10th century while St Mary's was built in 1839.

Derby Historic Trivia: Rich and Varied

Derby has a rich history dating back to Roman times when the camp of *Derventio* was founded alongside the River Derwent. Much of the city's interesting history has already been covered in the *Conventional Derbyshire* section. So in a break with protocol, Derby gets its very own chronology…

Derby Chronology

DATE   DERBY-RELATED EVENT

c.60 AD The Romans build a fort on the site of Belper Road, to the west of the River Derwent.

c.80 AD The Romans build *Derventio* on the eastern side of the Derwent around modern-day Chester Green.

Derby All Saints' church, aka Derby Cathedral since 1927.

St Mary's Bridge, originally built in 1275, but re-built in 1794.

c.2ndC	The area just east of *Derventio* is home to pottery kilns and a cemetery.
c.7thC	The Anglo-Saxons found Northworthy to the south of the current city.
c.8thC	The Anglo-Saxon minster church of All Saints and a second church are built in Derby.
c.800	Second church re-named as St Alkmund's and the saint's body interred here.
871	The body of the Mercian ealdorman, Æthelwulf, is also buried at St Alkmund's.
873	The Danes invade, sack Northworthy and found *Deoraby* to the north of Northworthy.
878	Derbyshire becomes part of the Danelaw and *Deoraby* becomes its capital and one of the Five Boroughs.
917	The Saxons under Lady Æthelflæd re-capture Derby.
c.10thC	Derby expands south of the Markeaton Brook and the churches of St Werburgh and St Peter are founded.
1086	Derby appears in the *Domesday Book* (as *Derby*) with a population of c.2,000.
1137	The hospital of St Helen is founded on the northern outskirts of the borough.
1146	The Augustinian monastery at Darley Abbey is founded.
1154	Derby is given a market charter by Henry II.
1159	Darley Abbey takes ownership of St Michael's, St Peter's and St Werburgh's.
1238	The Black Friars establish a Dominican priory on the site of the present-day Friary Hotel.
c.1275	The first St Mary's Bridge is built, and is the only crossing of the Derwent into Derby.
1348	On the eve of the Black Death, Derby has a population of c.3,500. This rapidly declines.
c.1450	St Mary's chapel is built on St Mary's Bridge.
1532	The new west tower of Derby All Saints is completed.
1554	Derby Grammar School is re-founded.
1558	Derby's population is still only 2,000-2,500.
c.1570s	Derby becomes a major export point for the county's lead and wool industries.
1580	The Dolphin Inn on Iron Gate is first licensed as an inn.
1588	The Padley Martyrs are hung drawn and quartered in Derby on a charge of high treason.
1597	Bess of Hardwick founds some almshouses close to All Saints' church.
1608	Bess of Hardwick is buried at All Saints' church in Derby.
1610	Derby is still contained within the confluence of the Markeaton Brook and the Derwent.
1636	Derby suffers an outbreak of plague.
1642	The English Civil War breaks out, and Derby is garrisoned for Parliament by Sir John Gell.
1660	The Shire Hall in St Mary's Gate is completed.
1665	Derby is struck by plague again.

1680	The Seven Stars public house is built.
1692	George Sorocold designs and implements a piped water system in Derby that survives until 1841.
1702	Thomas Cotchett builds the first silk mill in Derby, designed by George Sorocold.
1710	Derby's population has risen to around 4,000.
1718	John Lombe opens another silk mill on the site of Thomas Cotchett's former mill.
1720	An Act of Parliament makes the Derwent navigable between Derby and the River Trent.
1723-25	The nave and chancel at All Saints' church are completely rebuilt and are divided by Robert Bakewell's wrought-iron screen.
1745	Bonnie Prince Charlie reaches Derby, but turns back for Scotland. Derby's streets are now lit by oil lamps.
1755	Derby's original Assembly Rooms are opened as a ballroom, supper room, cards room, etc.
1756	John Heath enters partnership with Andrew Planché and William Duesbury to manufacture porcelain.
1759	Jedediah Strutt develops the "Derby Rib", to manufacture ribbed stockings. The mechanical production of gloves, shirts, drawers and caps soon follow.
1768	An Improvement Commission is formed to clean, pave and light the streets of Derby.
1770	William Duesbury takes over sole control of the Derby porcelain works.
1773	George III visits Derby and agrees that a picture of a crown should appear on Duesbury's china; Crown Derby is born.
1785	Jedediah Strutt erects a second silk mill at Morledge.
1789	Derby has 12 silk spinning mills employing 1,200 people.
1792	William Strutt builds a six-storey calico mill.
1794	St Mary's Bridge is rebuilt, but retains one original arch on which the medieval chapel was built.
1801	With 10,832 inhabitants, Derby is the 36th largest town in England.
1810	An infirmary is built in Derby on London Road.
1817	Jeremiah Brandreth executed for high treason outside Derby Gaol for his part in the Pentrich Revolution.
1821	The streets of Derby are lit by gas.
1839	St Mary's church is built and the Derby workhouse is opened on Osmaston Road. Also opened is the Midland Counties Railway between Derby, Leicester and Nottingham, engineered by George and Robert Stephenson. This includes the construction of the world's first ever railway roundhouse.
1840	The Midland Railway comes to Derby and the largest railway works in Europe are built

in Litchurch. The Midland Hotel is also built. Derby is now home to 17 mills, while Joseph Strutt gives the Arboretum to the town as a gift, and which is England's first public park.

1841 The Guildhall is remodelled after a disastrous fire.

1843 The New County Gaol is built on Vernon Street.

1846 St Alkmund's church is demolished and built anew.

1848 The Old Crown Derby China Factory moves to King Street in Derby, while Andrew Handysides takes over the Britannia Foundry on the banks of the Derwent.

1850 Bishop John Lonsdale founds a female teacher training college. Exeter Bridge is built.

1851 Derby's population is 32,741. Locomotives are first built in Derby.

1852 The Markeaton Brook is culverted.

1867 Michael Bass founds Bass Recreation Ground.

1868 Andrew Handysides builds his brass foundry.

1870 Derbyshire County Cricket Club founded at the Racecourse.

1871 Derby Carriage and Wagon works is built.

1872 The Derby Friargate Line is built by the Great Northern Railway, connecting Burton with Nottingham.

1873 A public swimming pool is built.

1877 A hospital for sick children is built. The Derby Workhouse moves from Osmaston Road to Uttoxeter Road, and the Derby Crown Porcelain Company buy the original workhouse premises.

1877 Derby is extended south to include "Railway Derby". Andrew Handysides builds a malleable cast iron factory.

1878 Derby School of Arts opens.

1879 A public library and museum is built.

1880 Horse drawn trams run through the streets.

1884 Derby County Football Club is founded as an offshoot of Derbyshire County Cricket Club. They initially play their games at the Racecourse Ground.

1886 Derby Grand Theatre is opened. The Racecourse hosts the first FA Cup final outside of London where Blackburn Rovers beat West Bromwich Albion 2-0 in an FA Cup final replay.

1889 The County Borough of Derby is created.

1890 Queen Victoria bestows her royal seal of approval upon Crown Derby and also grants the company the title of The Royal Crown Derby Porcelain Company.

1891-94 The infirmary on London Road is rebuilt becoming the Derbyshire Royal Infirmary.

1894 Derby's streets are lit by electricity for the first time.

1895 Derby County move to the Baseball Ground.

1896 Derby County finish the season as Football League runners up.

1898 Thomas Barton starts public bus services in Derby. Derby County reach the FA Cup final but lose 3-1 to Nottingham Forest.

1899 Derby County reach the FA Cup final again, but lose again – this time 4-1 to Sheffield United.

1901 Derby's population is 69,266.

1904 The first electric trams run in Derby.

1907 Rolls-Royce opens a factory to the south of the city where cars and aircraft will be made.

1910 The first museum in Derby opens.

1913 Trent Motor Traction Co. commences several bus services to and from Derby.

1916 A German airship bombs Derby killing 5 people.

1916-19 The chemicals company, British Celanese, construct their main manufacturing facility at Spondon.

1924 A War Memorial is erected in Derby.

1927 The diocese of Derby is formed and All Saints' church receives cathedral status.

1929 The City Hospital is built.

1930 The last electric tram runs. Derby County finish the season as Football League runners up. Rolls-Royce commences work on the Merlin engine.

1931 Markeaton Park opens to the public.

1933 A new bus station opens.

1934 The River Gardens open. Derby expands south-west, absorbing Sinfin.

1936 Derby County once again finish the season as Football League runners up.

1939-41 The Council House is built in front of the River Gardens.

1939-45 Seventy four people in Derby are killed by German bombing and 350 wounded.

1940s Rolls-Royce commences development of the world's first turbofan engine.

1946 Derby County win the FA Cup, defeating Charlton Athletic 4-1.

1950s A large council estate is built at Mackworth.

1963 The original Derby Assembly Rooms are largely destroyed by fire.

1967 St Alkmund's church is demolished to make way for the Inner Ring Road.

1968 Derby is extended into the rural districts of Belper, Repton and South East Derbyshire. The town's population increases to c.220,000.

1969-71 The inner ring road is built.

1971 The c.800 A.D. sarcophagus of St Alkmund is discovered during excavations of St Alkmund's church. Rolls-Royce suffers financial collapse and many workers are made redundant. The company is nationalised.

1972 Derby County become Football League Champions for the first time. A fourth incarnation of St Alkmund's church is built, further up Kedleston Road with a blue spire.

1974   The Industrial Museum opens.

1974   The County Borough of Derby is abolished and replaced by the Non-Metropolitan District of Derby.

1975   The Eagle Centre is built and Derby Playhouse opens.

1975   Derby County become Football League Champions for the second time.

1976   Derby is twinned with Osnabruck.

1977   The Assembly Rooms open and Derby is made a city in the Queen's Silver Jubilee year.

1987   Rolls-Royce becomes a private company again.

1988   British Rail Engineering Ltd acquires Derby Locomotive Works and proceeds to strip its assets and gradually demolish the works.

1989   Rolls-Royce merges with Northern Engineering Industries. The company still controls 25% of the world market for civil aviation engines.

1997   Derby is made a Unitary Authority. Derby County move to a new 33,000 all-seater stadium at Pride Park.

2005   Derby's population is recorded at 233,750.

2007   Derby's new Westfield shopping centre is opened

2011   Derby train-maker, Bombardier, loses a multi-million pound deal which the government awards to the German company, Siemens.

2013   Derby's population is now 258,643.

Derby Quirk Alert:
Entrails and a Blue Lady!

The Dolphin Inn was founded in 1580 and is therefore Derby's oldest pub. However, it is also the most haunted! The most gruesome of its legends is that of a young 18th century doctor who was lodging there in the days when part of the building was a lodging house. The story goes that the doctor had the body of a young woman secretly delivered by body-snatchers in the dead of night. He took the body into the cellar and began to dissect her, opening up her stomach and pulling out her entrails – at which point the woman was said to have awoken, leapt up from the table and ran round the cellar screaming hysterically, dragging her entrails behind her before finally succumbing to loss of blood. Splattered in viscera, the traumatised young doctor was driven out of his mind while his hair was alleged to have turned white. His well-to-do family then covered up the incident and put him in a lunatic asylum. However, the ghost of the girl is still said to scream in the dead of night!

Another story involves an apparition seen by a number of people in the 1950s, of a man in Highland regalia, armed with a sword, running through the passage carrying a woman on his back! Then there is the Blue Lady, wife of the landlord and reputed to have had an affair with Dick Turpin. The husband cottoned on when he noticed his wife wearing a new blue dress allegedly given to her by Turpin. Shortly afterwards she disappeared, never to be seen again. Some say she eloped with her lover, but a more probable explanation is that she was murdered by her husband and her body concealed somewhere inside the Dolphin!

The Midland Hotel, built alongside Derby Railway Station in 1840.

The Dolphin Inn, founded in 1580.

NAME (STATUS):	**DORE** (Village)
POPULATION:	7,078
DISTRICT:	City of Sheffield
EARLIEST RECORD:	*Dor,* 942; *Dore,* 1086 (*Domesday* Book – and also noted as being part of the Derbyshire wapentake of Scarsdale)
MEANING:	Place at the gate or narrow pass
DERIVATION:	From the Old English word *dor* (door, as in the opening to a narrow pass)
FAMOUS RESIDENTS:	Former England football and cricket captains, **Bryan Robson, Emlyn Hughes** and **Michael Vaughan**. Former footballers **Chris Waddle, Gary Megson,** and football manager **Dave Bassett**.

Dore Pub: The Dore Moor Inn

When turnpike roads became popular in the 18th and 19th centuries, there was a need for watering holes on the routes, usually in the form of coaching inns. One of these was the Devonshire Inn, built in 1816 on the Sheffield to Chapel-en-le-Frith road (today's A625), and on what is today called Hathersage Road at the north-western tip of Dore. Its location brought in so many travellers looking to rest their horses that extensive stabling had to be added to the west of the inn. However, the inn was renamed as The Dore Moor Inn in 1827 and has remained that ever since.

Dore Church: Christ Church

Dore didn't become a parish in its own right until 1844 which ties in with Christ Church being a relatively new church. Constructed in 1829 for £1,000, its graveyard then had to cater for the deceased residents of both Dore and Totley, as the latter didn't acquire a church until much later. Somewhat quirkily, though, the two communities were separated in death on either side of the churchyard! Much earlier in around 1175, land to the east of Dore was granted by Robert FitzRanulph de Alfreton, the Lord of Edwalton, to establish a house of Premonstratensian canons, and this became Beauchief Abbey in 1183. The area thus became more prosperous, with the monks keeping sheep on the moors, and grinding corn at mills on the River Sheaf – although Dore was expected to pay tithes to the monks of Beauchief. The abbey eventually succumbed to Henry VIII's Act of Dissolution in 1536.

Dore Historic Trivia: Saxons and Boundaries

Dore was the ancient gateway or the pass between the two Anglo-Saxon kingdoms of Deira (later absorbed into Northumbria) and Mercia. The earliest written record of Dore comes from the *Anglo-Saxon Chronicle* and refers to 829 when King Ecgbert of Wessex, who had just conquered Mercia, led his army to Dore to receive the submission of King Eanred of Northumbria. It reads: *"And Ecgbert led an army to Dore against the Northumbrians and they offered him obedience and concord and thereupon they separated."* As a result, Ecgbert became the first Anglo-Saxon king to establish over-lordship over *all* of Anglo-Saxon England. The *Chronicle* thus records Ecgbert as: *"Our Lord of the whole English speaking race, from the Channel to the Firth of Forth."*

A gritstone monolith commemorating this significant event was erected on the village green in 1968 by the Dore Village Society, as the meeting was thought to have taken place at Kings Croft next to the green. The monolith comprises a black granite plaque in the shape of a Saxon shield, and is decorated with a Wyvern, the war emblem of Wessex. Of course, by the 11th century, the boundary between the two kingdoms, as marked by the Limb Brook (where *Limb* means limit or boundary), had been re-used to define the border between Yorkshire and Derbyshire (and did so until 1934), as

Christ Church, Dore, built in 1829.

The plaque on Dore village green commemorating the submission of Northumbria to Wessex in 829.

well as defining the boundary between the provinces of York and Canterbury. As for the 942 reference to *Dor*, this one records another Anglo-Saxon victory when Edmund, son of Edward the Elder, conquered the Danes of Mercia "as far as where Dore divides".

Moving forward to the period between 1650 and 1750, this was the era before turnpike roads were created to accommodate wheeled vehicles and so the main method for transport was by packhorse. Routes and bridges were often built by private individuals or at parish expense and a fine example of a packhorse bridge survives over the Burbage Brook at Carl Wark. This sturdy bridge that was built without parapets was the joint responsibility of the inhabitants of Dore and Hathersage for the brook marked their boundary although the route was eventually superseded by the 18th century turnpike route which then became the A625. At that time, Dore was only a collection of build-ings dotted about and linked by muddy tracks. However, this all changed following the Dore Enclosure Act in 1822. The Duke of Devonshire, who had acquired the Manor of Dore in 1742, applied with other landowners for the enclosure of common land and the resulting straight roads and boundaries can still be seen today.

Finally, on the northern border of the Dore parish is Abbeydale, the birthplace of crucible steel as invented by Benjamin Huntsman in 1742. However, despite the resulting heavy industrialisation on its doorstep, it was the arrival of the railways in the mid-19th century which finally shaped the Dore of today as owners and managers of Sheffield factories realised they could live in comfort outside the smoke of the city, and travel in by rail from the newly built Dore and Totley Station. A new 'Dore Road' was also built by the Duke of Devonshire connecting Dore to the new station and Victorian villas began to spring up along it bringing new prosperity to the area. It was only the creation of Sheffield's green belt in the mid-20th century that called a halt to Sheffield's expansion towards Dore.

Dore Quirk Alert: County Cricket, England Captain's Galore…and Polecats!

Dore's local cricket ground is known as Abbeydale Park, and it has been a home venue for both Derbyshire and Yorkshire County Cricket Clubs over the years. This is because Dore was annexed by Sheffield from Derbyshire in 1934 along with Totley, Bradway and several other North Derbyshire villages – although Derbyshire were still playing first-class matches at Abbeydale Park in 1946 and 1947, while Yorkshire didn't play there until the period between 1974 and 1996. The ground was also home to Sheffield F.C., the oldest football club in the world, who played there from 1921 until 1988.

Sticking with modern sport, Dore is one of Sheffield's wealthiest suburbs, and has thus become home to a number of high-profile sportsmen, including former England football and cricket captains Emlyn Hughes, Bryan Robson and Michael Vaughan. The latter would clearly have had a short walk to home games at Abbeydale Park, while the ground is now home to the Michael Vaughan Cricket Academy that has brought through such modern stars as England batsman Joe Root. As for those famous sporting Dore inhabitants, their ranks also include former Sheffield Wednesday player and manager, Gary Megson, former Sheffield Wednesday and England international, Chris Waddle, and former Sheffield United manager, Dave Bassett. And sticking with the village's attraction of high-profile celebrities, the MP for Dore and Totley is none other than Liberal Democrat leader and Deputy Prime Minister, Nick Clegg. However, a special mention for Liverpool and England captain, Emlyn Hughes, is in order, for he became a much-loved football pundit following his retirement from the game in the 1980s, as well as becoming one of the most memorable captains on BBC's *A Question of Sport*. Sadly, he died from a brain tumour in 2004, aged only fifty-seven.

Finally, if you're wondering about the polecats, well, the 1835 Constable's Accounts for Dore and Totley show that 51 of them were caught between 1832 and 1835! Was it worth the wait?

This 17th century packhorse bridge over the Burbage Brook also marked the boundary between the Derbyshire parishes of Dore and Hathersage.

Abbeydale Park, home to both Derbyshire and Yorkshire First Class cricket over the years.

NAME (STATUS):	**DOVE** (River)
DISTRICT:	High Peak, Derbyshire Dales, South Derbyshire
EARLIEST RECORD:	*Dufan*, late 10th century; *Duvesdale*, 1289
MEANING:	Unknown
DERIVATION:	From the Celtic word *dubh* (black or dark)
FAMOUS RESIDENTS:	**Izaak Walton** (1593-1683), writer. **Charles Cotton** (1630-1687), writer.

River Dove Geographic and Historic Trivia:

The River Dove is 45 miles long and forms the majority of Derbyshire's border with Staffordshire. The source of the Dove is at Dove Head on Axe Edge Moor, with the distinctive Axe Edge lying to the north-west and Chrome Hill to the south-east. Indeed the Dove has a pronounced valley within half a mile of its source where it plunges steeply downwards. Then, as the river flows in a south-easterly direction delineating Derbyshire from Staffordshire, it begins to widen at Hollinsclough before flowing past the Derbyshire reef knoll quartet (the remains of ancient coral reefs) of Hollins Hill, Chrome Hill, Parkhouse Hill and Hitter Hill that lie on its northern bank. It then passes Glutton Bridge, Crowdecote and the remains of the 11th century Norman motte-and-bailey castle at Pilsbury before passing within a mile of the pretty village of Hartington, famous for cheese-making and always a tourist hot-spot. The village also serves as the perfect base for walking the central section of the Dove, for south of the village the valley begins to cut through a series of stunning limestone gorges starting with Beresford Dale and followed by Wolfscote Dale, Milldale and ultimately Dovedale. With its narrow gorge, striking rock pillars, famous stepping stones and the steep Thorpe Cloud rearing up behind them, Dovedale is undoubtedly the jewel in the crown, and attracts more than a million visitors every year.

Unsurprisingly, much of the countryside from Beresford Dale to Dovedale is owned by the National Trust, with Dovedale acquired first in 1934, and Wolfscote Dale in 1948. Dovedale was also declared a National Nature Reserve in 2006, while its ash woods were also designated as a Site of Special Scientific Interest as they are one of the few surviving woodlands of their type in the country. The whole area from Beresford Dale to Dovedale is also associated with Izaak Walton and the River Dove provided the inspiration for his 17th century classic book *The Compleat Angler*. Walton was also friends with Charles Cotton of Beresford Hall, a poet and writer who contributed to Walton's great book, and who in 1674 built a Fishing Temple which still stands in a corner of private grounds by the river at the entrance to Beresford Dale, and which is a shrine to all anglers.

Just south of Dovedale, the Dove is joined by the River Manifold before separating Mappleton from Okeover – site of a New Year's Day bridge jump and race to the Okeover Arms. From there, the Dove passes a mile or so to the west of Ashbourne before flowing through the border villages of Church Mayfield, Lower Ellastone and Rocester, eventually arriving in the low-lands of Southern Derbyshire. Having generally flowed in a southerly direction since Pilsbury Castle, the Dove then takes a south-easterly turn just after Doveridge before eventually flowing into the River Trent at Newton Solney. As for Doveridge, the place takes its name from the Grade II-listed, six-arched bridge over the River Dove just to the north-west of the village. The bridge – which is also a Scheduled Ancient Monument – was built in the 15th century of sandstone, with two rounded

Beresford Dale.

Wolfscote Dale.

central arches and four pointed outer arches. Both the current bridge and its medieval predecessor were known as Dove Bridge, and hence the name of the nearby village with recordings dating back to 1086 (*Dubrige*) and 1252 (*Duvebruge*).

In terms of River Dove trivia, early Mesolithic or Middle Stone Age flint tools have been found in the Dove valley, such as axes, barbed spears and harpoons, indicating that man lived in the caves along the valley between 8,000BC and 4,500BC. Moving forward considerably to Anglo-Saxon times, and it is likely that the villages of Pilsbury, Norbury and Sudbury were all constructed on the River Dove as fortifications to guard passage over the river – with the "bury" suffix deriving from the Old English word *burh*, meaning "fortified place or stronghold". And then from medieval times onwards, the outstanding grazing pasture with its rich alluvial soil that is to be found along the valley of the southern Dove began to be exploited, and dairy cattle became prevalent. Cheese-making began to flourish, particularly in the 17th century when London cheese-mongers established a factory at Uttoxeter while cheese chambers became a feature of local farmhouses.

A fisherman in Dovedale.

The famous stepping stones at Dovedale with Thorpe Cloud behind.

Close-up of the Dovedale stepping stones.

The Grade II-listed, six-arched bridge over the River Dove just north-west of Doveridge.

Threes-Up!

	CREWTON	DIMPLE	FALLINGE
STATUS:	Suburb	Suburb	Hamlet
POPULATION:	c.4000	c.1000	c.10
DISTRICT:	City of Derby	Derbyshire Dales	Derbyshire Dales
MEANING:	Probably "farmstead owned by the Crewe family"	Possibly referring to a geographic feature	Possibly "woodland clearing" or "fallow land"
DERIVATION:	From the family name Crewe, plus the Old English word *tŭn* (farmstead or enclosure)	In this case, a dimple in the landscape on the side of a hill	From either the Old English *felling* (woodland clearing) or *felging* (fallow land)

Threes Up Trivia!

Crewton is a suburb of Derby sandwiched in between Alvaston, Allenton, Osmaston and Litchurch. The area is largely comprised of parallel streets of terraced Victorian housing, and includes The Mission Church which was built on Brighton Road in 1891. The church was the gift of Mrs Robotham of Nunsfield House, Boulton Lane, and who was a long standing patroness of the parish. From 1951 The Mission Church became known as St Peter's church before closing in 1991. However, the building still survives today and is still in use as a place of worship. As for Crewton, it dates back many centuries before the 19th century and was named after the local Crewe family.

Meanwhile, **Dimple** lies on the north-western outskirts of Matlock and is named after Dimple Road which runs all the way up the hill from the A6/Bakewell Road. It runs past Dimple House and Dimple Crescent, before turning in a north-easterly direction, eventually joining Smedley Street, high on the hill-side above the River Derwent where you will also find the Derbyshire County Council offices – and which were once the location of the famous

Alvaston Methodist church on Brighton Road, Crewton. But is this the former Mission church built in 1891 or is that the New Testament Church of God at the other end of Brighton Road? Answers on a postcard please!

hydro spa set up by John Smedley. There is also a Dimple Lane in Crich set into an appropriate dimple on the village's east-facing hillside.

Four miles south-east of Bakewell is **Fallinge** – a controversial inclusion in the Shire-Ode thanks to its questionable pronunciation! As for the place, it is basically comprised of Fallinge Farm just off to the right of the B6012 between Rowsley and Beeley, plus a gritstone edge called Fallinge Edge (*shown below*) which runs in a vaguely south-west to north-easterly direction, again between Rowsley and Beeley, albeit a couple of miles to the east. Close to Fallinge Farm you will find Burntwood Quarry and Smeltingmill Wood, each giving an indicator of the area's industrial past – although trees and foliage now largely hide any landscape scars. Much older than these are the small funerary cairns located on Fallinge Edge, and although some of the stones may have been purloined from this ancient cemetery over the centuries, it is still recognisable as an ancient site. Finally, you will also find a trig point on top of Fallinge Edge from where you can enjoy spectacular views.

The Roundhouse on Brighton Road, Crewton.

Cotton grass on Fallinge Moor in July. This is the view to the south-west.

View north-west across Fallinge Moor towards Fallinge Edge.

NAME (STATUS):	**FERNILEE** (Village)
POPULATION:	c.50
DISTRICT:	High Peak
EARLIEST RECORD:	*Ferneleia*, 1108; *Ferneley*, late 12th century
MEANING:	Woodland clearing where ferns grow
DERIVATION:	From the Old English words *fearn* (fern or bracken) and *lēah* (wood, woodland clearing or glade)

Fernilee Pub: The Shady Oak

The Shady Oak Inn is located on the A5004 that passes through the linear village of Fernilee. The inn was opened in 1841 to cater for workers and passengers on the Cromford and High Peak Railway, along with employees of a nearby gunpowder works. And for the record, its first publican back in 1830 was a twenty-year-old blacksmith called Hugh Oldham!

Fernilee Historic Trivia: Railways, Gunpowder and Reservoirs

The High Peak Railway was one of the very earliest, and was built in 1830 to link the Cromford Canal with the Peak Forest Canal via the canal basin at Whaley Bridge, thus allowing onward journey by barge to Manchester and Liverpool. Unsurprisingly, the majority of the cargo was minerals and aggregates mined in central Derbyshire, and the section through the Goyt valley and alongside Fernilee was in operation from 1831 to 1892.

Meanwhile, a nearby former gunpowder factory was thought to date back to the 16th century and supplied ammunition to Sir Francis Drake during his battle with the Spanish Armada. However, although being very active during World War I, it closed soon after – which was just as well, as within twenty-years its remains had been submerged

The Shady Oak, Fernilee.

following the construction of Fernilee Reservoir in 1938. Situated in the Goyt valley alongside the village that it takes its name from, Fernilee Reservoir was built by the Stockport Water Corporation at a cost of £480,000, although it is currently owned and operated by United Utilities. The reservoir provides drinking water for the town of Stockport and its surrounding areas, and it holds 4,940 million litres of water. Its neighbour to the south, Errwood Reservoir, was completed much later in 1967, and although it holds slightly less water (4,215 million litres), inflation saw that the construction cost had risen to £1.5 million. The two reservoirs are separated by a substantial bank with Fernilee much the lower-lying of the two.

Fernilee Quirk Alert: Half In, Half Out

Despite its tiny size, Fernilee sits half in, half out of the Peak District, with the southern half taking the honour of National Park membership. The line is delineated by the Peak District National Park millstone which sits in between the Shady Oak Inn to the north and Fernilee's main line of houses to the south. This odd quirk is down to the National Park's shape, which saw a slice taken out of its western flank when created in 1951, thanks to heavy industry – particularly quarrying – as it was deemed to despoil the landscape.

Fernilee Reservoir.

This millstone sits on the A5004 in the centre of Fernilee, meaning that only half of the village is in the Peak District National Park!

NAME (STATUS):	**FLAGG** (Village)
POPULATION:	163
DISTRICT:	Derbyshire Dales
EARLIEST RECORD:	*Flagun* (1086); *Flagge*, (1284); *Flagh* (1315)
MEANING:	Place where turfs are cut
DERIVATION:	From the Old Scandinavian word *flag* (turf or a sod of earth) in its plural form of *flagum*

Flagg Pub: The Bull i' th' Thorn

The Bull i' th' Thorn is situated at around 1,000ft on the western edge of Flagg Moor. It also lies on the A515 between Ashbourne and Buxton alongside the minor road that heads north-eastwards towards the village of Flagg. The inn dates back to at least 1472 when it was known as just "The Bull". Situated on the old Roman road from Little Chester to Buxton, the inn became a natural resting place for travellers, particularly during the 18th and 19th centuries when it became a prominent coaching inn on the Derby to Manchester route.

The Bull i' th' Thorn, Flagg.

Flagg Historic Trivia: Derbyshire's Grand National

Flagg is situated on the site of an old Viking settlement, probably established due to its rich veins of lead ore. It is also famous for turf cutting, which allegedly gives Flagg its name. More recent fame, though, is due to its cross-country horse races that are known locally as Derbyshire's Grand National, and which have been held almost every Easter Tuesday on Flagg Moor since 1892 – the exception being the war years and 2001 and 2003 due to Foot and Mouth disease. However, the race was also cancelled in 2012, due to unusually dry weather throughout February and March and which therefore made it impossible to maintain the "good to firm" going to ensure safe racing. Ironically, it rained almost every day for the next six months after that!

As for the races, they are now the only remaining point-to-point horse races in the UK that take place over natural hunting country, including dry stone walls, some of which date back to the 16th century. The races – which are also the highest horse races in the UK at around 1,000ft above sea level – generally start in the village of Flagg and run up to the local racecourse. However, the most popular race is the unique Hunt Members' race which starts in the open countryside between the villages of Flagg and Pomeroy and covers three miles and four furlongs before also finishing on the racecourse.

Flagg races are very popular and attract over a hundred entries, with some of the horses going on to major success. This includes Gunner Welburn who won the 1999 Members Race at Flagg, before going on to finish fourth in the Grand National of 2003. Another regular at the Flagg Moor races is the famous trainer Ginger McCain, and one of his former horses, The Tallet, won the Members Race in both 2005 and 2006. Meanwhile, the Maiden Race winner has traditionally received the Croxden Cup. However, it disappeared after it was presented to the winner in 1975, only to be unearthed years later by a demolition company's excavator – at which point it was returned to its rightful home. As for the race's most famous jockey, that has to be King Edward VIII who is rumoured to have ridden in the race when he was still the Prince of Wales!

Flagg Quirk Alert: The Haunted Human Skull

The Elizabethan Manor House known as Flagg Hall contains an alleged haunted human skull. It resides on a staircase in the hall and legend has it that evil will befall anyone who removes or attempts to remove it from its place. Several attempts have been made to do so, but all resulted in strange events and thus the skull has stayed put. One such attempt was made to bury the skull at Chelmorton, but when the funeral cortege neared the village, the horses refused to proceed and despite encouragement from the coachman, they reared and stamped so much that both cortege and skull returned to the Hall.

Flagg Hall – location of the famous haunted human skull!

NAME (STATUS):	**FOREMARK** (Hamlet, Hall, Reservoir)
POPULATION:	c.100
DISTRICT:	Derbyshire Dales
EARLIEST RECORD:	*Fornewerche*, 1086 *(Domesday Book)*; *Fornewerk*, 1242
MEANING:	Old fortification
DERIVATION:	From the Old Scandinavian words *forn* and *verk*
FAMOUS PEOPLE:	Sir Francis Burdett (1770-1844, Reformist Politician

Foremark Churches:
St Saviours and Anchor Church

Historically, Foremark was a part of the Repton parish, and included a chapelry affiliated to the minster church of St Wystan's at the old Mercian capital of Repton. Consequently, Foremark's church of St Saviour was not built until 1662, when it was erected and consecrated by Sir Francis Burdett, the 2nd Baronet of Bramcote. However, Foremark is also the location of a much older "church" courtesy of Burton upon Trent's obscurely-named patron saint, Modwen. According to legend, Modwen was a 7th century nun from Dundalk who set off on a pilgrimage to Rome, but stopped off at Burton and founded a religious community there beside the Trent. During this time, she allegedly met with a hermit called Hardulche who was living a life of austerity nearby in a cell hewn out of a rock face. This is now thought to be Anchor Church at Foremark.

St Saviour's church, Foremark, which is situated in the grounds of Foremarke Hall.

Foremark Historic Trivia:
The Burdetts and Foremarke Hall

In 1619, Thomas Burdett – the local squire of Foremark and former sheriff of Derbyshire from 1610-11 – was created Baronet of Bramcote. A century and a half later, Foremarke Hall was built in Palladian and neo-Classical style between 1759 and 1761 for Sir Robert Burdett. However, it was Sir Robert's grandson, Sir Francis Burdett (1770-1844) who achieved the most fame. Having married Sophia Coutts in 1793, the daughter of the wealthy banker Thomas Coutts, Sir Francis went on to become a reforming Tory politician, protesting at the Peterloo massacre of 1819 and strongly advocating the abolition of flogging in the army, while it was Sir Francis's pressurising that helped to bring about some of the early prison reforms. Amongst his high-profile sympathisers was Sir Francis Chantrey, arguably England's finest ever sculptor and also born

Probably the location of the ancient "Anchor Church", home to a 7th century hermit known as Hardulche.

in Derbyshire at Jordanthorpe. Earlier in 1808, Chantrey had exhibited six of his works at the Royal Academy, one of which was a bust of Sir Francis Burdett. When Burdett died in 1844, he also left his daughter, Baroness Burdett-Coutts, as the richest lady in the country. As for Foremarke Hall, it was used as a military hospital in World War I and as an officer training centre in World War II while the surrounding fields were set up as a decoy town in a starfish configuration to distract German bombers en-route to bomb Derby. After the war, the Grade I-listed building was leased by Repton Preparatory School in 1947. It was then purchased in 1967, and it is still in use as a prep school today for girls and boys of ages three to thirteen.

Foremark Quirk Alert: White Letters

A new addition to the Foremark clan arrived in the 1970s in the shape of Foremark Reservoir, both a reservoir and a 230-acre nature reserve open to the public for walking, fishing, bird watching and horse riding. It is fed by the Rivers Trent and Dove and is reputed to be home to 27 different varieties of butterfly including rare varieties such as the Large Skipper, the Speckled Wood, the Small Copper, the Holly Blue, the Brown Argus… and the White-letter Hairstreak – so-named because of the letter "W" that is formed by white lines on the underside of its hindwings.

Foremark Reservoir. Those trees in the foreground may well be home to a White-letter Hairstreak!

NAME (STATUS):	**GLUTTON BRIDGE** (Hamlet)
POPULATION:	c.30
DISTRICT:	Derbyshire Dales
EARLIEST RECORD:	*Glotunhous*, 1358
MEANING:	Possibly "farmstead by the bright or shining stream"
DERIVATION:	Possibly from the Old Scandinavian word *glus(s)*, (bright or shining) and the Old English word *tūn* (farmstead). NB: Higher up the road from Glutton Bridge, the place is announced simply as Glutton. The "Bridge" affix would have been applied later when the first bridge over the River Dove was built here (derived from the Old English word *brycg*).

Glutton Bridge Pub: The Quiet Woman

Glutton Bridge doesn't have a pub, but it's certainly worth highlighting the quirky pub in Earl Sterndale half a mile to the north-east. The Quiet Woman is thought to be over 400 years old and was run by the Heathcote family for over 300 of those years. The name refers to an over-talkative woman who was decapitated as a consequence and is one of three in the UK, while there are

Said to represent an over-talkative woman who was decapitated as a result, this pub sign bears a controversial one-liner!

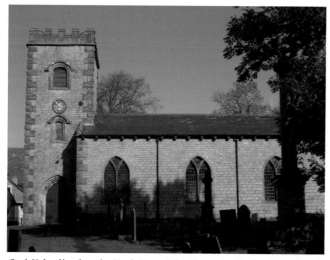

St Michael's church, Earl Sterndale, the only Derbyshire church badly damaged by German bombs in World War II.

variations on this theme throughout Europe, too. Other pubs carry the rhyme: "Here is a woman who lost her head, she's quiet now – you see, she's dead". This particular version in Earl Sterndale has the words "Soft words turneth away wrath", above both the pub sign and the placard on the pub wall!

Glutton Bridge Church: St Michael's

St Michael's church is also in Earl Sterndale and dates back to Norman times when it was a chapelry of Hartington. However, after falling into disrepair in the 18th century, it was rebuilt in 1828 only to become the sole Derbyshire church to be struck by German bombs during World War II (see *Quirk Alert* for more). It is likely that the bombs were meant to strike a high explosives dump in a quarry near Buxton. The church was rebuilt ten years later in 1951.

Glutton Bridge Historic Trivia:
Caving Haven

In terms of place-name origin, the former part of the name "Glutton" is not clear, although Glusburn in North Yorkshire and Glympton in Oxfordshire both derive the former part of their name from Old Norse *glus(s)*, meaning "bright or shining". So Glutton probably means "farmstead by the bright or shining stream" – the stream being the Dove, of course. That said, another story suggests the place was named after Bonnie Prince Charlie's men who stole cattle from nearby Cronkstone Grange and then gorged themselves on the animals during a huge feast at Glutton. If there is any truth in that story, though, it is likely that the soldiers just thought it amusing to feast at a place called Glutton; they certainly didn't name the place as it is referred to as *Glotunhous* way back in 1358 at a point when it was one of the many bercaries or sheep farms created by the Duchy of Lancaster in their Upper Dove estates. As an etymological aside, an even earlier Pipe Roll of 1201 is thought to contain the first ever recording of the name Glutton, when a Nottinghamshire chap by the name of Simon Le Glutun is listed. Further research turned up another old reference to the name, stating that "the origin of Glutun would seem to be a nickname appertaining to personal eating habits,"… which sort of

View from the bottom of Glutton Bridge towards Parkhouse Hill on the right and Chrome Hill on the left. The latter is the site of the famous double sunset.

suggests that Mr Simon probably liked his food!

As for Glutton Bridge today, it is home to the British Caving Library which is funded by the British Caving Association (BCA) and the British Cave Research Association (BCRA). Some of the library's books date back 100 years and include expedition reports, maps, charts and surveys, while the library is also home to around 500 journals.

Glutton Bridge Quirk Alert:
The Double Sunset and a Very Wise Man

Glutton Bridge is one of the few locations in the country where you can see the legendary double sunset on the 20th, 21st and 22nd June – weather permitting, of course. The sun sets on the summit of Chrome Hill to the west of Glutton Bridge, but then reappears in its entirety from behind the hill's steep northern slope to provide a second sunset. Spectators for this event meet annually at around 8:15 pm at Glutton Bridge's phone box and post box.

Finally, the bombing of the aforementioned St Michael's church inspired local humourist, Tom Wise, to write these words:

> They bombed our church them Germans did,
> In nineteen forty one,
> And left it there without a lid,
> Exposed to wind and sun,
> And when at last the war was o'er,
> And Hitler was the loser,
> We knelt, praying as of yore,
> Thanked God they missed the boozer!

The famous double sunset is best viewed on the evenings of 20, 21 and 22 June when the sun sets behind Chrome Hill only to reappear in its entirety from behind the hill's steep northern face to provide a second sunset. This was the sequence on 21/06/2013.

NAME (STATUS):	**HATTON** (Village)
POPULATION:	2,690
DISTRICT:	South Derbyshire
EARLIEST RECORD:	*Hatune*, 1086 *(Domesday Book)*; *Hetton*, 1230
MEANING:	Farmstead on a heath
DERIVATION:	From the Old English words *hæth* (heath, heather, or uncultivated land) and *tūn* (enclosure or farmstead)
Famous Residents:	**John Berry**, designer of the Esso tiger and writer of many children's Ladybird Books. **Roger Davies,** former Derby County and Club Bruges footballer, and who won League Championships with both clubs as well as being Belgium Player of the Year 1977.

Hatton Pub: The Castle Hotel

The Castle Hotel is a free house that sits on the north bank of the River Dove, just in front of the village's 19th century bridge and which enjoys impressive views towards Tutbury Castle.

Hatton Church: All Saints

All Saints church, Hatton, is a former mission church on Station Road that was built at the end of the 19th century.

The Castle Hotel, Hatton.

Hatton Historic Trivia: Fleams and Dolce Gusto

The Grade II-listed bridge over the River Dove that separates Hatton from Tutbury and Derbyshire from Staffordshire, was constructed in 1815 at a total cost of £8,000. Abutting its central arch is a man-made island formed when a fleam was dug out to run alongside the Staffordshire side of the island in order to power a 19th century cotton mill in Tutbury. During the island's excavation in 1831, approximately 300,000 Anglo-Saxon coins were unearthed on the Hatton side of the riverbank. Meanwhile today, what is known locally as Dougie's Island has become a dedicated nature reserve and contains bird and bat boxes while it is also home to otters, too.

Between the 17th and 19th centuries, the Lower Dove became a hot-bed of dairy farming and cheese-making, and it was for this reason that Nestlé built a factory at Hatton in 1901. Initially, they processed milk from local farms and until the late 1970s the factory had its own private siding which gave access to milk trains. However, in the 1930s, Nestlé also started producing coffee and ever since then, the factory has remained a major employer in the area. Today the factory continues to be a major coffee producer, and it is the sole UK facility producing the Dolce Gusto range. It also produces the famous Nescafé brand, too – although that is not exclusive to Hatton as it is also made in the company's London factory at Hayes. The factory also announced in November 2011 that it was investing £110 million to extend the plant with twelve new high-speed production lines that will make coffee pods for sale in the UK and 38 other countries. This was expected to treble production and lead to the creation of 300 new jobs.

Hatton Quirk Alert: Salt Box Café

Hatton is also home to the Salt Box Café which has won awards as the best transport café in the UK. Located on the A511, it was also placed 8th in the *Independent* newspaper's 2006 list of the UK's 50 best cafés, thanks to its "huge lashings of splendid grub aimed at truckers and pensioners alike", and "easily the best chips in the county". No connection inferred, but Hatton was also home to the inspirational Jody Bunting, who between 2001 and 2004 lost 275lbs (over 19 stones) in weight, dropping from 31 stone to a trim 12 stone.

The bridge over the River Dove that separates Hatton from Tutbury, and Derbyshire from Staffordshire.

The Nestlé coffee factory at Hatton, first established in 1901, and today's sole producer of Dolce Gusto coffee in the UK.

Threes-Up!

	FORD	HALFWAY	HAZELWOOD
STATUS:	Hamlet	Suburb	Village
POPULATION:	c.30	c.4,000	310
DISTRICT:	North East Derbyshire	City of Sheffield	Amber Valley
EARLIEST RECORD:	Unknown	Unknown	*Haselwode*, 1306
MEANING:	Place at the ford or river-crossing	See *Threes-Up Trivia*	Place at the hazel wood
DERIVATION:	From the Old English word *ford* (ford or river-crossing)	See *Threes-Up Trivia*	From the Old English words *hæsel* (hazel) and *wudu* (wood)

Threes Up Trivia!

The hamlet of **Ford** lies within a mile of Birleyhay and Bramley and this trio of Shire-Ode hamlets are also located just to the north-west of Eckington, and close to Derbyshire's border with South Yorkshire. In fact, Ford lies almost *on* the border, and was presumably named after a ford which crosses the brook known as The Moss that part-marks the boundary between the historic counties of Derbyshire and Yorkshire – although a bridge now takes Ford Lane across The Moss and up the hill towards Ridgeway.

Meanwhile, **Halfway** is a south-eastern suburb of Sheffield, but was only annexed from Derbyshire in 1967. Halfway is also something of a misnomer, these days, as it is actually the south-eastern terminus for the Sheffield Supertram service *(see above centre)*. However, its original meaning was quite literal, as it marked the half-way point on the stagecoach route between Chesterfield and Rotherham. That said, there is an amusing online Sheffield Forum that discusses the meaning of Halfway. Several "halfway" alternatives are proposed including between Sheffield and Clowne, Beighton and Eckington, and Worksop and Sheffield, but my favourite was offered by some wag who pointed out that Halfway is also half way between the North Pole and Timbuktu! Nevertheless, Halfway was indeed named after an 18th century inn called the Halfway Inn that was built to capture trade at the half-way point on the Chesterfield to Rotherham road. Difficult to believe now, but during the 17th and 18th centuries, Chesterfield and Rotherham were towns of much greater significance than Sheffield. Today, Halfway is the location of a housing estate laid out such that no house looks directly onto another with curving, meandering walkways and a complex network of through routes to Halfway Drive, the suburb's main thoroughfare.

As for **Hazelwood**, the village runs in a largely linear fashion up along Hazelwood Hill and then down Hob Hill while at their crossroads you will find the church of St John the Evangelist. Built in 1846, it was almost totally destroyed by fire in 1902 caused by sparks from the original coal-fired heaters, but was rebuilt within a year. Hazelwood was also the home of author Edith Maude Hull (pen-name E.M. Hull), who lived at The Knowle in Hazelwood following her marriage and up until her death in 1947. And it was here in 1921 that she wrote the international best-seller, *The Sheik*, and followed this up with *Son of the Sheik*. Both novels were then adapted for the big screen and starred Rudolph Valentino. In fact, *The Son of the Sheik* (1926) was Valentino's final film before his premature death in the same year from severe pleuritis. He was aged just thirty-one.

St John the Evangelist church, Hazelwood.

NAME (STATUS):	**HEANOR** (Town)
POPULATION:	22,620
DISTRICT:	Amber Valley
EARLIEST RECORD:	*Hainoure*, 1086 *(Domesday Book)*; *Henovre*, 1236
MEANING:	Place at the high ridge
DERIVATION:	From the Old English *hēan* or *hēah* (high) and *ofer* (flat-topped ridge)
FAMOUS RESIDENTS:	**Henry Garnet** (1555-1606), Jesuit priest. **Samuel Watson** (1663-1715), craftsman. **John Hieron** (d.1682), nonconformist. **William Howitt** (1792-1879) prolific author, many titles co-written with his wife, Mary (née Botham). **Edward Smith** (1819-1874), medical author. **Billy Bestwick** (1875-1938), cricketer.

Heanor Pub: The Red Lion

The present incarnation of the Red Lion was built at the turn of the 20th century where Derby Road joined Market Street. It replaced an earlier Red Lion on the same site which, in turn, had given its name to the now demolished Red Lion Square in front of the building and which, at the end of the 19th century, had been the focal point of the town. Prior to that, Heanor had been a small hill-top settlement with a small market, but this was all transformed largely thanks to the growth of coal mining and iron manufacture in the 19th century. A new market place was then laid out further up the hill in 1894, replacing the original Red Lion Square.

Heanor Church: St Lawrence

St Lawrence's church was largely rebuilt in 1868, and only the 15th century tower now remains of the original. The rebuild therefore occurred a year after the Town Hall was built and a few years before the new market place was laid out in 1894 across the road from the church.

St Lawrence's Church, Heanor.

Heanor Historic Trivia: Equivocation and Coal

Heanor's most famous son was Henry Garnet, born in the town in 1555. Educated at Winchester College, he moved to London in 1571 to work for a legal publisher. However, in 1575, he travelled to Portugal where he joined the Society of Jesus, was then ordained in Rome in around 1582 after which he became a Professor of Hebrew, lecturing also on metaphysics and mathematics. He then returned to England in 1586 as part of the Jesuit mission, knowing that Jesuits had been banished from England the year before, and if discovered risked the charge of high treason. Nevertheless, Garnet soon became Jesuit Superior and established a secret press while he also interceded in religious disputes. He was undoubtedly a peaceful man and preferred a passive approach to Catholic persecution. Unfortunately, in the summer of 1605, he learned of the existence of Robert Catesby's Gunpowder Plot, but as the information was received under the seal of the confessional, he felt that Canon Law prevented him from speaking out. Instead, he wrote to his superiors in Rome and urged them to

Heanor Town Hall, built in 1867.

warn English Catholics against the use of force. Of course, the plot failed and, as a result of his knowledge of it, Garnet was eventually arrested in January 1606, taken to London and interrogated by the Privy Council. Imprisoned in the Tower of London, his conversations with fellow prisoners were eavesdropped, and letters to friends were intercepted. Criticised for his use of equivocation, he was sentenced to be hanged, drawn and quartered. He was executed on 3rd May 1606, the only "mercy" being that having been hung and thrown off the ladder by the executioner, many in the crowd pulled on his legs to spare him the worst parts of his grim sentence.

Coal-wise, the first pit was recorded at Heanor in 1692, but it wasn't until the 19th century that the coal industry exploded in the Heanor area, mainly when the railways arrived in the 1840s to facilitate exports, with Heanor being on both the Midland Railway line and a branch line of the Great Northern Railway from Ilkeston. Heanor's population thus increased from 3,058 in 1841 to 12,418 in 1901, although mining communities were later tempted into Nottinghamshire in the 1920s thanks to the opening of new, deeper pits. All that remains of the industry today, though, is the Loscoe Colliery pit winding wheel and which stands as a monument to its former miners on High Street. The pit had thrived in the 19th and early 20th century, particularly after affiliation to the Butterley Company in 1856, but was eventually closed in 1933. As for those 19th century railways, their construction at Heanor led to the famous discovery of a hoard of 800 Roman coins found in a vase!

Heanor is bordered to the south and west by Shipley Country Park and this vast green space consists of most of the former estate of the Miller-Mundy family who lived at Shipley Hall from the 17th century until the

The HQ on Heanor Gate Road of Matthew Walker Christmas Puddings, the oldest Christmas pudding maker in the world.

The outline of the ground floor rooms of Shipley Hall have been retained, but the building itself was demolished in 1943 due to subsidence.

1920s. It was during the tenure of Edward Mundy (who was also High Sheriff of Derbyshire in 1731), and that of his son, Edward Miller-Mundy (who became MP for South Derbyshire), that the first Shipley coal extraction began. This was then followed by the construction of the Nutbrook Canal in 1796 in order to transport coal to the Erewash Canal, and then the construction of the reservoirs at Mapperley and Shipley to feed the canal. The ever-increasing income from the family coal business led to extensive development of the estate and the Hall was rebuilt in 1799. Then came the railways, and by the time that Alfred Edward Miller-Mundy was running the show in the late 19th century, the colliery employed 1800 colliers and excavated around 420,000 tons of coal a year. Alfred Edward, who was regarded as an excellent employer with a hands-on approach, also moved in high circles and was the only host of an official royal visit to Shipley Hall when the Prince of Wales, later destined to become King Edward VII, visited. Alas, by the time Godfrey Miller-Mundy inherited the estate in 1920, death duties were biting and he had to sell the estate to the Shipley Colliery Company. Subsequent mining under the hall caused subsidence, and it had to be demolished in 1943.

Finally, in June 1921, legendary Derbyshire bowler Billy Bestwick took career-best figures of 10-40 which, at age forty-six, makes him the oldest first-class player to have achieved a ten-wicket haul in one match. However, born the son of a Heanor miner, his wild temperament and reckless behaviour earned him the title of "the bad boy of cricket." Also renowned for his alcoholism, he killed a man in a fight in 1907 after a night's drinking, although the inquest at the pub the next day brought in a verdict of "justifiable homicide".

Heanor Quirk Alert: Puddings and Loaves

Heanor is home to Matthew Walker Christmas Puddings, the oldest Christmas pudding maker in the world and thought to be the only factory in the world producing *just* Christmas puddings. Matthew Walker, the son of a Derbyshire farmer, first opened a small factory in Exeter Street, Derby, in 1899, with his product based on his mother's 19th century recipe although it wasn't until 1967 that the company opened their purpose-built factory in Heanor. Today, Matthew Walker employs c.120 staff producing c.20 million puddings a year which is around 40% of the world's Christmas puddings! Meanwhile, 1980 saw the first Great Christmas Pudding Race in Covent Garden, with teams balancing Matthew Walker Christmas Puddings on trays around an obstacle course to raise money for Cancer Research.

And now from puddings to loaves...for Heanor is also home to John Evans, the World Head Balancing Champion. Head balancing feats involve balancing a 352lb mini, 96 milk crates, 62 Guinness Record books, 11 beer barrels and 101 bricks. Then in 2008 he broke the world record for balancing loaves on his head – 300 to be precise, and a clear case of using your loaf to transport loaves!

NAME (STATUS):	**HOPE** (Village)
POPULATION:	900
DISTRICT:	High Peak
EARLIEST RECORD:	*Hope*, 926; *Hope*, 1086 *(Domesday Book)*
MEANING:	Small enclosed valley, or enclosed plot of land
DERIVATION:	From the Old English word *hop* (small enclosed valley, or enclosure in marsh or moor).

Hope Pubs: Old Hall, The Cheshire Cheese Inn, The Woodroffe Arms

Hope has a number of pubs. The Old Hall on the A6187 used to be Hope Hall, the former home of the Balguy family. Its grounds originally covered the cattle market area and it was the squire, John Balguy, who in 1715 obtained a charter for a weekly market. Meanwhile, the Cheshire Cheese Inn on

The Cheshire Cheese Inn so-named as it was an overnight stop on the old trade route from Cheshire.

Edale Road at the northern tip of Hope was so-named because it was an overnight stop on the old trade route from Cheshire – and payment for lodging was actually paid in cheese. However, located at the junction of Castleton Road and Pindale Road and opposite the old Blacksmiths Cottages, is the pub which offers the oldest Hope history. This is the Woodroffe Arms and it was built on land belonging to the historic Woodroffe family who had fought at Agincourt and obtained a Grant of Arms, taking their place in the Roll of the County Gentry of Derbyshire. They were also the King's Foresters of The Peak, with the family name deriving from the title of Wood-Reeve, while they also held the office of Parish Clerk, which passed from father to son continuously for over 200 years from 1628 to 1855.

Hope Church: St Peter's

St Peter's church was built in the 14th century but its predecessor was one of Derbyshire's nine c.8th century Anglo-Saxon minsters (mother churches). The churchyard is also home to an ancient Anglo-Saxon cross which is carved with knot-work and foliage and dates from somewhere between the 9th and 11th centuries; intriguingly, it had also remained hidden in one of the walls of the local school between the English Civil War and 1858. Alongside it today, is a guide post from c.1709 which was found in 2000 and placed here in September 2003 by the Hope Historical Society. As for Norman evidence, the only survivor is the church's font – although it has been theorised that it might even pre-date 1066.

Hope Historic Trivia: Battles, Forests… and Cement!

In 626, legend has it that a key battle was fought to the north of Hope known as the Battle of Win Hill and Lose Hill – and thus the names of the two iconic peaks that rear up behind Hope. The legend suggests that Prince Cwichelm and his father, King Cynegils of Wessex, possibly with the aid of King Penda of Mercia, gathered their forces on Lose Hill and marched on the Northumbrians and King Edwin to their east whose forces were based on Win Hill. Despite their superior numbers, though, Wessex was defeated by the Northumbrians building a wall and rolling boulders

St Peter's church, Hope.

Anglo-Saxon cross in St Peter's churchyard.

Lose Hill, as seen from the west from the trig point on Mam Tor.

Lose Hill viewed from the slopes of Win Hill.

One thing that is "contested" between the neighbouring villages of Bradwell and Hope is the generic name of the nearby cement works which opened in 1929, right in the middle of what would become the Peak District National Park in a further twenty-two years' time. The works is usually said to be located half way between the two settlements, with houses built for workers in both villages during the company's early years. Geographically, the works is slightly nearer to Bradwell, but its intensive freight is shipped out to Hope Station via its own dedicated railway, so both villages could lay claim if they so wished – which is why it can be variously referred to as either Hope Cement Works or Bradwell Cement Works. What is for sure, though, is that situated between large, easily quarried deposits of limestone to the south and west, and of shale to the north and east, the site was ideal. And to its credit, the firm has cooperated with the National Park Authority over the years in order to minimise the visual impact of its quarrying works by appropriate landscaping and tree planting, while it also takes various measures to reduce dust and emissions, too. You can't hide that enormous chimney, mind!

Hope Quirk Alert: Stoned Madwomen

The strangest name in the Hope parish must be Madwoman's Stones – a rocky outcrop on top of bleak moorland where the Hope parish meets the Edale parish. It is thought they were used as boundary markers and the name may have something to do with the annual tour of duty by local clergy where they would stop at points around the parish's perimeter and bless the land, thus deterring evil spirits and encouraging bumper crops. Quite how this spot relates to a mad woman is not clear, although anyone living in such an inhospitable place would surely have their sanity questioned. Much easier to understand is the Hope Cross, an ancient guide post and parish boundary marker situated behind Win Hill towards the end of the western finger of Ladybower Reservoir. The present guide post is dated 1737, but it almost certainly replaced a much older predecessor.

down upon them. However, as none of the Anglo-Saxon chronicles record this battle, the legend remains a legend!

In medieval times, Hope lent its name to one of the three administrative wards of the Royal Forest of the High Peak (*Fforesta de Alto Pecco*), created in the 12th century by the hunting-mad Norman royalty and nobility. They also created Chapel-en-le-Frith (the "Chapel in the Forest") and built St Thomas Becket church there in 1225 to save locals the long journey to Hope St Peter's – although the latter does still today contain a number of memorials displaying the axes, horns and other symbols of Forest officials. Also present in Hope in 1293 was the Crown's stud with a breeding stallion and 21 mares while shortly after that, the Woodroffe's took over the post of wood-reeve in the Forest of High Peak for many generations.

The Hope Cross marks part of the ancient Hope parish boundary.

Before abandoning Hope, though, Arthur Mee's 1937 volume of *The King's England, Derbyshire* includes a similar play on words, referring to a number of nonagenarians that he spoke to during his research. He therefore suggests that: *"Where Hope there is life, long life."* Remarkably, these folks would have been born in the 1840s, and so in two short literary *hops* (if you catch my etymological drift), Arthur and I link back to the very beginning of the Victorian era.

NAME (STATUS):	**HOPTON** (Village)
POPULATION:	c.100
DISTRICT:	Derbyshire Dales
EARLIEST RECORD:	*Opetune*, 1086 *(Domesday Book)*; *Hopton*, 1251
MEANING:	Farmstead in a small enclosed valley
Derivation:	From the Old English words *hop* (small enclosed valley) and *tūn* (farmstead).
FAMOUS RESIDENTS:	**Sir John Gell**[1] (1593-1671), Parliamentary Colonel. **John Gell**[1] (1613-1689), MP for Derbyshire. **Philip Gell** (1651-1719), MP for Derbyshire and founder of the Hopton almshouses. **Philip Eyre Gell**[1] (1723-1795), builder of the Via Gellia. **Admiral John Gell** (1740-1806), famous Royal Navy Commander. **Philip Gell** (1775-1842), MP for Malmesbury. **Sir William Gell** (1777-1836), archaeologist and illustrator. **Philip Lyttelton Gell**, Editor of Oxford University Press. **Philip Houthem Gell** (1914-2001), esteemed immunologist. [1]Appointed High Sheriff of Derbyshire.

The Miners Arms, Carsington.

St Margaret's church, Carsington.

Hopton Pub: The Miners Arms

Hopton itself has neither a pub nor a church but can lay claim to both through its twin – the adjoining village of Carsington. The Miners Arms dates from the 16th century, although the 21st century sees it offering cycle hire for the many tracks around the area, including the ten mile circumnavigation of Carsington Water.

Hopton Church: St Margaret's

Hopton/Carsington's church is the tiny St Margaret's, measuring only 50ft long by 20ft wide. It does, however, retain elements dating back to the 14th century while it also contains many references to the Gells of neighbouring Hopton Hall, with all of their women from 1452 to 1862 represented in one window and all of their men since 1404 in another.

Hopton Historic Trivia:
The Gells, Tunnels and Steep Inclines

Although a farmstead in Anglo-Saxon times and later a manor and seat of the de Hopton family in Norman times, the manor of Hopton eventually came to the Gell

family when it was acquired in 1553 by Ralph Gell (1491–1564). However, the most famous of the Gell owners was Sir John Gell (1593-1671), who was also created 1st Baronet in 1642 on the eve of the English Civil War. He was born into a wealthy family that owned the lead tithes in the mines of Bakewell, Hope, Tideswell and nearby Wirksworth. Between 1624 and 1634 he was a captain in the militia, but it was during the 1630s that he earned favour with King Charles I, ruthlessly collecting rents and dues for the crown, and which resulted in him being appointed High Sheriff of Derbyshire in 1635 and ultimately resulted in his baronetcy reward in 1642. Ironically, though, when the English Civil War broke out, Gell became a leading Parliamentary Colonel and raised a regiment to garrison Derby; it would appear that, as a Presbyterian, he was opposed to both the king's attempts to reform the church and to his political absolutism. Gell thus commissioned a number of prominent Derbyshire landowners to serve under him who, in turn, recruited troops locally, albeit often by coercion. Nevertheless, Gell managed to maintain the county's allegiance to Parliament throughout the First

English Civil War (1642 – 1646), with units of his regiment also seeing action in the neighbouring counties of Cheshire, Staffordshire and Nottinghamshire. During this time, Gell was also appointed Governor of Derby in 1643, but he eventually fell out with Parliament and actually requested a pardon from the king.

In 1650, though, he was tried and found guilty of "misprision of treason" thanks to his alleged knowledge of a royalist plot but which he didn't reveal to the authorities. He was sentenced to life imprisonment and confiscation of his estates although the authorities failed on the latter count since John Gell the younger was able to prove that the estate had transferred to him prior to his father's trial and sentence. John Gell Senior was imprisoned in the Tower of London but released in 1653 on grounds of ill health and was eventually pardoned by Charles II at the Restoration in 1660, plus given an appointment at the royal court. In time, many of Sir John Gell's descendants went onto great things, too (see *Famous Residents*). The Gell line finally became extinct when the last daughter and heiress, married William Pole Thornhill MP, on whose death the estate passed to his kinsman Henry Pole, later known as Henry Chandos-Pole-Gell – and yet another High Sheriff of Derbyshire in 1886.

The year 1831 saw the opening of the High Peak Railway which includes the 113-yard Hopton Tunnel as well as the Hopton Incline, an infamous part of the line where trains were initially pulled up the 1 in 14 incline by a stationary beam engine. However, the stretch of line between Middleton Top and Parsley Hay was later modified to be adhesion-worked by locomotives. The Hopton Incline thus became the steepest incline in the country where trains pulled themselves up without

Hopton Hall's crinkle-crankle wall.

assistance – literally "under their own steam" – although trains did have to be frequently split and pulled up a few wagons at a time.

Hopton Quirk Alert: Crinkle-Crankle

Hopton Hall was built in the 16th century by Thomas Gell as a two-storey, three-bay manor house. It was extended and remodelled by Philip Gell, the 3rd Baronet in the late 18th century and the north entrance front now has three storeys and seven bays, flanked by tower wings with pyramidal roofs. Alas, in the 20th century, the Hopton estate of some 3,700 acres was broken up with a major part sold to Severn-Trent water authority for the creation of Carsington Reservoir in the early 1990s. However, as well as its spectacular display of snowdrops every February, another survivor of Hopton Hall is its crinkle-crankle wall. The wall runs along the estate's northern boundary, and is based on an 18th century concept of building brick walls in ribbon-like patterns, thus lending strength to the structure and allowing the wall to stand without buttresses. Some of these walls had alcoves used for growing and ripening fruit, a process helped by circulating warm air from a stove through vents in the brickwork; Hopton's wall has a summer-house built into the middle of it instead. It is thought that the beech-hedged Serpentine Walk at Chatsworth was inspired by Hopton's crinkle-crankle wall.

Part of Hopton Hall.

NAME (STATUS):	**KINDER** (Estate, Hill, Plateau, Reservoir, River, Village [now de-populated])
POPULATION:	A couple of farms!
DISTRICT:	High Peak
EARLIEST RECORD:	*Chendre, 1086 (Domesday Book); Kynder, 1285*
MEANING:	Unknown, but probably Celtic and probably relates to a hill
DERIVATION:	Regarding Kinder Scout, the "Scout" affix is likely to relate to the Old Scandinavian word *skuti* (overhanging rock – presumably the one at Kinder Downfall)

Kinder Geographic Trivia: Crags, Groughs, Bogs…

Kinder Scout in north-western Derbyshire is the highest point in the Peak District, standing at 2,088ft above sea level, although this "highest point" is actually part of a 15 square-mile plateau rather than a distinct peak. That plateau – which is largely covered by peat bogs intersected by channels known as groughs – rises steeply from the surrounding ground. At the southern edge of the plateau there are several crags, the western flank sees the Kinder River flow straight off the edge in a spectacular waterfall called Kinder Downfall and the northern side sees another long series of rocky outcrops. Meanwhile, the eastern edge of the plateau sees the level gradually lower and taper to a narrow neck of high ground which connects Kinder to Win Hill. As for Kinder Downfall, it forms the tallest waterfall in the Peak District, and the 100ft fall blows back on itself when faced with a strong westerly wind. In cold winters the waterfall also freezes and provides local mountaineers with an icy challenge that can be climbed with ice axes, ropes and crampons.

Kinder Downfall lies on the Kinder River which, in turn, flows into Kinder Reservoir, while completing the Kinder family we have Kinder Low which at 2,077ft lies just to the south of Kinder Scout. Below here is the Edale Cross which marks the former junction of the three wards of the Forest of the Peak: Glossop and Longdendale, Hopedale, and Campana. The first cross on the site may have been set up in 1157 by the Abbots of Basingwerk Abbey to mark the southern boundary of their land, while the date of the current cross is thought to be medieval and was re-erected in 1810 by a number of local farmers.

Kinder Historic Trivia: The Mass Trespass

The Kinder plateau is most famous for being the location of the "mass trespass" in April 1932. This act of wilful trespass by c.500 ramblers was intended to highlight the questionable law of the time that denied walkers in England or Wales, access to areas of open

The plaque in Bowden Bridge car park that commemorates the mass trespass onto Kinder Scout.

country. There were some scuffles with police and some of the protestors were imprisoned. However, the mass trespass resulted in law changes that would allow all citizens access to public footpaths, regardless of whether they crossed private land, and eventually culminated in the Countryside and Rights of Way Act 2000, which legislates for rights to walk on mapped access land. Indeed, introducing the Act was a key promise in the 1997 New Labour manifesto and was followed up in 2003 when the "right to roam" on uncultivated land was made law, too. In reality, of course, the Kinder region and the high moorland areas around it have been designated as "Open Country" for many decades. Meanwhile, a plaque in the Bowden Bridge car-park from where the protestors set off commemorates the mass trespass while the car park also has a bench that is carved with the words: *As I trudge through the peat at a pace so slow, There is time to remember the debt we owe, To the "Kinder Trespass" and the rights they did seek, Allowing us freely to ramble the Dark Peak.*

The ancient Edale Cross is protected under the Ancient Monument Act 1913-53. It marks the former junction of the three wards of the Forest of the Peak.

View from the very top of Kinder Downfall and the beginnings of the Kinder River. If you're ever up here and have food, watch out for aggressive sheep!

The trig point at Kinder Low (633m/2077ft), looking south-eastwards towards Rushup Edge and Mam Tor.

Slightly off to the right of Kinder Low is Noe Stool, seen here in the foreground and looking eastwards towards Pym Chair.

View from Kinder Downfall, looking south-west over Kinder Reservoir. At 100ft (30m), Kinder Downfall is the tallest waterfall in the Peak District.

Looking back across Kinder Reservoir towards Kinder Downfall.

Threes-Up!

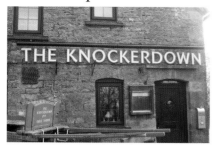

	KNOCKERDOWN	LITTLEMOOR	OKER
STATUS:	Hamlet	Village	Hamlet
POPULATION:	c.20	c.100	c.30
DISTRICT:	Derbyshire Dales	North East Derbyshire	Derbyshire Dales
MEANING:	Probably "hillock on a hill"	Place on the little moor	Probably "hill of conflict"
DERIVATION:	From the Celtic word *cnocc* (hillock) and the Old English word *dŭn* (hill)	From the Old English words *lȳtel* (little) and *mōr*, (moor, marshy ground, barren upland)	Thought to be a shortened corruption of the Roman name *Occursus*, which means "hill of conflict"

Threes Up Trivia!

Knockerdown is the tiniest of hamlets and sits in an elevated position a short walk above the western shore of Carsington Water. The place consists of The Knockerdown Inn – which has its own campsite – and Knockerdown Farm, the latter of which comprises the Knockerdown Farm holiday cottages, along with leisure and spa facilities.

Meanwhile, **Littlemoor** is a small village located a mile or so to the east of Ashover. Stunning views can be seen to the east, running all the way down from the north-east to the south, with obvious landmarks including Bolsover Castle, Chesterfield's crooked spire, Hardwick Hall and Ogston Reservoir. However, on a clear day you can see as far as South Yorkshire to the north, Lincolnshire to the east and Leicestershire to the south.

Finally, **Oker** is a tiny linear village which sits above the western bank of the River Derwent facing Matlock. The place-name is thought to be a shortened corruption of the Roman name *Occursus*, which means "hill of conflict", and today's village is thought to be on the site of an ancient un-trenched hill fort built by the Roman Legions, who had ousted the previously incumbent lead-mining Britons. Many centuries later, the summit of Oker Hill became famous for the story of the two Shore brothers Peter and Will. Peter decided to make his fortune overseas, but before he departed, he and his brother each planted a sycamore tree on Oker Hill. The story goes that they intended to use the wood from the trees for their coffins. Alas, Peter died shortly after his departure, while his tree also died, too. So moved by this story was he, that the great William Wordsworth wrote a beautiful sonnet in their memory.

Carsington Water from Knockerdown.

NAME (STATUS):	**LEA** (Village)
POPULATION:	1,106 (Parish of Dethick, Lea and Holloway)
DISTRICT:	Amber Valley
EARLIEST RECORD:	*Lede*, 1086 *(Domesday Book)*; *Lea*, c.1155; *Lee*, 1326
MEANING:	Place at the wood or woodland clearing
DERIVATION:	From the Old English word *lēah* (wood, woodland clearing or glade)
FAMOUS RESIDENTS:	**Peter Nightingale** (1737-1803), lead merchant/financier. **John Smedley**, founder of Lea Mills and John Smedley Ltd. **John Smedley Jnr** (1803-1874) manufacturer. **Florence Nightingale** (1820-1910), nurse, writer, statistician. **John Marsden Smedley** (1867-1959) founder of Lea Green and Lea Gardens.

Lea Pub: The Jug and Glass Inn

The Jug and Glass Inn was built in 1782 somewhat inevitably by the Nightingales – a family whose stamp is all over the history of the village – but more on them shortly. More recently, though, the pub had the honour of being named one of the *Daily Telegraph's* Pubs of the Week in 2009.

Lea Church: Christ Church

As the above Lea welcome sign demonstrates, Lea's parish church sits just behind the western approach to the village. However, although Christ Church is the parish church of Dethick, Lea and Holloway, it is formally recog-

The Jug and Glass Inn, Lea.

nised as being in Holloway – despite the evidence of the above photo! What is undisputable, though, is that Lea Chapel *is* in Lea. Built in 1671, it is one of the oldest non-conformist chapels in the country and was endowed for the use of Protestant Dissenters in 1735 by Thomas Nightingale. It sits at the top of Lea Main Road, just above Lea Green – the latter having been initially developed by John Marsden-Smedley in 1895 but which today is locally famous as a learning and personal development centre.

Lea Historic Trivia: Florence and the Machines

This section is all about Florence Nightingale and the cotton-spinning machines invented by Richard Arkwright a mile or so down the road in Cromford. And as it happens, there is a direct connection between the Lady with the Lamp and Arkwright's cotton-spinning water-frames – because Florence's paternal grandmother was the niece of Peter Nightingale, the wealthy lead merchant who in 1776 had heavily financed Arkwright's Great Second Mill at Cromford. He also provided Rock House for Arkwright overlooking his mill along with cottages for his workers. Then eight years later in 1784, Peter Nightingale along with businessman John Smedley, also founded a cotton-spinning factory at Lea Bridge and which became known as Lea Mills. Unsurprisingly, Lea Mills was based on the design of Arkwright's ground-breaking mills down the road, with this one using water from Lea Brook to power the large wheel. Lea Mills initially specialised in the production of muslin and spinning cotton to send out to local cottages equipped with hand frame looms,

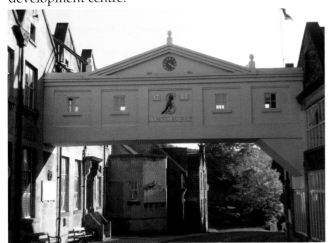

The crest of John Smedley Ltd on the corridor that links the company's buildings on either side of the road through Lea Bridge.

Lea Hurst, built in 1825 and the summer retreat of Florence Nightingale and family.

but towards the end of the 18th century, the company had extended its activities to include knitting and hosiery manufacture. By this stage, John Smedley was running the business alone although the Nightingale family retained an interest in the property. However, it was Smedley's son, also John Smedley (1803-1874), who exceeded his father's fame. He took over the running of the mill in 1825 and expanded operations to produce a wide range of finished garments, rather than simply manufacturing cloth; this included Long Johns, named after Smedley himself. He invested his wealth by building his world-famed hydrotherapy spa at Matlock followed by the rather ostentatious Riber Castle. As for John Smedley Ltd, it is still going strong today, still trading as John Smedley Ltd, and is still run by the original John Smedley's descendants. It is also the oldest original mill in the world that is still active – which also makes it the oldest manufacturing business in the world, too.

Statue of Florence Nightingale outside the former Derby Royal Infirmary on London Road, Derby.

As for Florence Nightingale, although born in Italy in 1820, she and her family spent most of their summers at Lea Hurst, which had previously belonged to the aforementioned Peter Nightingale. This "small house with only 15 bedrooms," was how a young Florence described it, thus hinting at her birth into a rich, upper-class and well-connected British family! Of course, she went on to become arguably Derbyshire's most famous daughter, becoming most celebrated for her role as a pioneering nurse, but also as a writer and statistician, too. However, she became most famous for her nursing during the Crimean War, where she tended to wounded soldiers and became known as "The Lady with the Lamp" thanks to her habit of making rounds at night. It was asserted by the *Dictionary of National Biography* in 1911 that Florence Nightingale reduced the death rate amongst British troops in the Crimea from 42% to 2% either by making improvements in hygiene herself or by calling for the Sanitary Commission which arrived in March 1855 and effected immediate improvements to living conditions. These improvements soon also benefited the sanitary design of hospitals at home, while a Nightingale Fund was set up towards the end of the Crimean War to pay for the training of nurses. By 1859 the fund had raised £45,000 and with this, Florence set up the Nightingale Training School at St Thomas' Hospital in London in July 1860, and which is still to this day called the Florence Nightingale School of Nursing and Midwifery as part of King's College London. Florence also greatly improved medical care and public health services in India considerably reducing mortality among soldiers while in 1870 she mentored Linda Richards, "America's first trained nurse". By 1883, she had been awarded the Royal Red Cross by Queen Victoria while in 1904 she was appointed a Lady of Grace of the Order of St John. Then in 1907, she became the first woman to be awarded the Order of Merit and the following year was awarded the Honorary Freedom of the City of London. Today, the Nightingale Pledge is still taken by new nurses, while her birthday is celebrated annually as International Nurses Day.

Finally, we return to the Smedleys, for in 1895, it was John Marsden Smedley who converted Lea Green farm into the splendid mansion that is owned by Derbyshire County Council today, and which is one of the country's leading outdoor learning and personal development centres. It was also John Marsden-Smedley who created the spectacular Lea Gardens. By 1935, paths had been laid and verandas built to complement Marsden-Smedley's eventual collection of 350 varieties of rhododendron and azalea on the two acre site, including less-hardy varieties that were only supposed to survive in west coastal regions. The gardens have been open to the public since 1960.

Lea Gardens home to the 350 varieties of rhododendron and azalea collected and nurtured here by John Marsden-Smedley.

Lea Quirk Alert: Polar Areas and Coxcombs

One lesser known fact about Florence Nightingale is that she became a pioneer in the visual presentation of information and statistical graphics. She is credited with developing a variant of the pie chart known as the polar area diagram, or occasionally the Nightingale Rose Diagram, equivalent to a modern circular histogram, with this one used in order to illustrate seasonal sources of patient mortality in military field hospitals. She called a compilation of such diagrams a "coxcomb", and used these to present reports on the nature and magnitude of the conditions of medical care in the Crimean War to MPs and civil servants. In 1859 she was elected the first female member of the Royal Statistical Society and later became an honorary member of the American Statistical Association, too.

NAME (STATUS):	**LITTLE EATON** (Village)
POPULATION:	2,060
DISTRICT:	Erewash
EARLIEST RECORD:	*Detton*, 1086 (*Domesday Book*); *Little Eton*; 1392; *Lytyll Eton*, 1502
MEANING:	Farmstead on a spur of land or dry ground in marsh, or well-watered land
DERIVATION:	From the Old English word *ēg* (island, land partly surrounded by water, dry ground in marsh, well-watered land) and *tūn* (farmstead). The "Little" affix differentiates the village from Long Eaton (*Aitune*, 1086; *Long Eyton*, 1288). In Little Eaton's case, the spur of land probably relates to a river-bend on the Derwent.
FAMOUS RESIDENTS:	**T.P. Cameron Wilson** (1888-1918), poet and novelist.

Little Eaton Pub: The Queen's Head

There are three pubs in Little Eaton: the New Inn, the Bell and Harp and the Queen's Head. Situated on Alfreton Road, the Queen's Head is a historic Grade II-listed coaching inn dating back to 1835. It was originally named the Delvers Inn after the delvers who worked in the local quarries, but was later named the King's Head in the early 20th century; it then became the Queen's Head following Queen Elizabeth II's coronation in 1953.

Little Eaton Church: St Paul's

Little Eaton's church is dedicated to St Paul – although apparently, before it was rebuilt in 1791, it used to be a blacksmith's shop! But moving forwards to the early 20th century, and the son of the vicar of St Paul's was Theodore Percival Cameron Wilson, a poet and novelist best known for his poignant war-time poem *Magpies in Picardy*. A teacher at prep school, his first novel, *The Friendly Enemy*, was published in 1913, but the war intervened before his writing career could flourish. Alas, having achieved the rank of captain, he was killed by a stray bullet in March 1918. Ironically, Wilson loathed war and his poems were full of his love for the countryside, particularly his vicarage garden of which he wrote so poignantly before his departure for war:

"Never again a thrush in the lilac at six o'clock, a bee droning up the sunlit silences, a poplar pointing against the stars, the village voices and cries, the faint scent of wet lavender in the night." However, his bravery throughout the conflict was unflinching and indeed, the day before his own death, he rescued one of his men left wounded on barbed wire and in the face of machine-gun fire, he brought him safely back. A wooden cross in the church-yard offers the poignant words: *His grave is unknown* while his name appears on the list of those remembered from World War I inside the church lych-gate.

Little Eaton Historic Trivia: Gangways and Paper

In the 19th century, Little Eaton was a hive of activity with coal mining, quarrying and malting the main industries, while corn mills flourished on its stretch of the Derwent. Prior to 1793, pack horses had been used to export goods to Derby, but in that year the Derby Canal was extended to Little Eaton, making it 14 miles long from its new terminus all the way back to the Trent and Mersey Canal at Swarkestone. A narrow gauge industrial wagon-way called the Little Eaton Gangway was then constructed to link the canal wharf terminus at Little Eaton with the collieries and pottery at Denby. It

The Queen's Head, Little Eaton.

St Paul's church, Little Eaton. To the left is the lych-gate where the name of the famous wartime poet, T.P. Cameron Wilson is one of many remembered.

was so-called as it used six to eight wagons, each of which carried a load of between 1.65 and 1.87 tons and which were drawn by four horses that were known as a gang. The bodies of the wagons were then loaded onto the barges by a crane at the canal wharf at Little Eaton after which they were towed by horses down to Derby for onward distribution through England's canal network or by road. The process therefore perhaps became the first instance of containerisation anywhere in the world.

One of the original stone sleepers taken from the Little Eaton Gangway and built into the wall at the foot of Morley Lane.

Arkwright's cotton spinning mills. In time, the water wheels were replaced by two turbines, while steam power was introduced to the site in around 1890, this also being the time that the large brick chimney was built, and which still dominates this particular part of the Derwent valley today. Alas, the chimney also brought about the demise of the paper mill, for in 1906, a neighbour successfully sued the company on grounds of smoke and pollution and in 1908 the mill was forced to close. Other businesses such as lace-making and glove-making used the site until the 1960s after which the mill became derelict. However, in 1990 it was converted into a private residence. Also surviving into the 21st century is a terrace of fourteen cottages on the hill to the east of the mill and which are known as Blue Mountain Cottages. These were built for employees of the paper mill between 1820 and 1850.

Both canal and wagon-way were constructed by the famous pairing of Benjamin Outram and William Jessop; in fact, the Gangway was also known as Outram's Railroad although it was Jessop who had first proposed it in 1792. The Gangway was authorised by the Derby Canal Act of 1793 and was opened in 1795. It finally closed in 1908. Today, although the tracks were removed in 1926, some of the stone sleepers were built into the high wall at the junction of Morley Lane and Alfreton Road. Meanwhile what is known as the Clock House still survives, too, this being the original canal wharf office and which sits very close to today's multi-million pound development site known as Outram's Wharf.

At the northern edge of Little Eaton is Peckwash Mill. Initially a corn mill dating back to the 13th century, it became one of the largest paper mills in the world in the mid-19th century and brought much prosperity to the area. Its conversion from corn mill to paper mill was masterminded by corn miller Thomas Tempest in around 1800 and his design was similar to Richard

Little Eaton Quirk Alert:
The Famous Bacon Box

Alice Grace was a popular character who was born in Little Eaton in 1867 but following the death of her parents and her inability to keep up the rent payments, she was evicted from her cottage. She became known as the "Little Eaton Hermit", living for twenty years in sheds, barns and disused buildings, but culminating in her famous bacon box home – a box generously donated by a local butcher and which had previously housed pigs on their way to the slaughterhouse! Alice's touching story is also told in a song called *Alice in the Bacon Box*, written by Derbyshire singer-songwriter Lucy Ward.

The old station house on a now-closed stretch of railway which followed the same path as the Little Eaton Gangway.

The Clock House, the former Derby Canal wharf office.

NAME (STATUS):	**LITTLEOVER** (Village/Suburb)
POPULATION:	14,370
DISTRICT:	City of Derby
EARLIEST RECORD:	*Parva Ufre*, 1086 *(Domesday Book)*
MEANING:	The little place at the ridge
DERIVATION:	From the Latin *parva* (little) and the Old English word *ofer* (flat-topped ridge, hill or promontory). The "Little" affix distinguishes Littleover from Mickleover *(Magna Ufre)*.
FAMOUS RESIDENTS:	**Judith Hann** (b.1942), TV presenter. **Fiona May** (b.1969), athlete and double world long jump champion. **Kelli Young** (b.1981), singer with Liberty X. **Lee Camp** (b.1984), footballer with Derby County, QPR, Nottingham Forest and Bournemouth. **Michael Socha** (b.1987), actor.

Littleover Pub: The Half Moon and The White Swan

The Half Moon pub is recorded as being one of two inns in the village in 1577. It began life as a farm and alehouse and in the 18th Century served as a coaching inn for

The White Swan, Littleover.

which the stables still survive. Also surviving from 1577 is the White Swan. Situated opposite St Peter's church, the pub along with the church marked the centre of Littleover for many centuries and was home to a square where fairs, feasts and markets were held and proclamations were declared, while dancing and revelry would take place on public holidays such as Plough Monday and St Peter's Day.

Littleover Church: St Peter's

Although St Peter's church was heavily restored in the 19th century, it still retains a Norman doorway and a large Norman font while the windows in the chancel and south aisle are still 14th century. The chancel is also home to a monument to 17th century Sir Richard Harpur and his wife. Meanwhile, given the derivation of the place-name, it shouldn't come as a surprise to learn that St Peter's church at Littleover (the little place at the ridge) was a chapelry of Mickleover (the large place at the ridge) until St Peter's acquired independence in 1866.

Littleover Historic Trivia: High Sheriffs and Thegns

The Harpur family date back to the Norman Conquest and the family claim to have supplied more High Sheriffs for Derbyshire than any other house in the county. Before the Harpur's were lords of the manor, though, the Anglo-Saxon King Æthelred had given both Mickleover and Littleover to a high-ranking Mercian thegn called Morcar in 1011. However, by the time of Edward the Confessor (1042-66), Littleover belonged to the king, along with Mickleover.

Littleover Quirk Alert: Suburban Absorption

The *village* of Littleover maintained independence from Derby until 1968, although the process of absorption had begun in 1890 following The Derby Corporation Act, which added a part of the parish of Littleover to that of St Werburgh's in Derby. A further Act of 1927 saw more of Littleover and parts of Mickleover incorporated into the Borough of Derby, before it all finally succumbed along with other outlying areas in 1968. And remarkably, this one act in 1968 was instrumental in seeing Derby's population rise by a staggering 87,170 (to 219,578) between the censuses of 1961 and 1971.

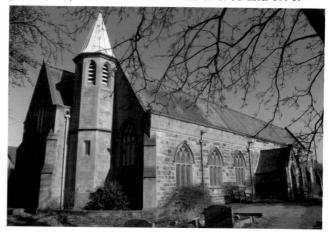

St Peter's church, Littleover.

Littleover Cottage in The Hollow, dates from the 16th century.

Melbourne: Queen of the South

NAME (STATUS):	**MELBOURNE** (Town)
POPULATION:	5,092
DISTRICT:	South Derbyshire
EARLIEST RECORD:	*Mileburne*, 1086 *(Domesday Book)*
MEANING:	Mill stream
DERIVATION:	From the Old English words *myln* (mill) and *burna* (stream)
FAMOUS RESIDENTS:	**William Lamb** (1779-1848), Lord Melbourne, British Prime Minister 1834 and 1835-41. **Thomas Cook** (1808-1892) Travel Agent.

Melbourne Pub: The Lamb Inn

The Lamb Inn is named after William Lamb, also known as Lord Melbourne of Melbourne Hall and British Prime Minister, 1834 and 1835-41. The inn sign boasts a portrait of Lord Melbourne which was painted during his tenure as Prime Minister. As for the man himself, he was the 2nd Viscount Melbourne and his tenure as Prime Minister also ensured that his home town would give its name to a fledgling Australian town in the state of Victoria in March 1837. Back then, the Derbyshire Melbourne had the larger population of the two; they now differ by around four million! As for Lord Melbourne, he became particularly well-known for his close political mentoring of Queen Victoria on her ascent to the throne in 1837, aged only eighteen. Alas, before that, he had acquired unwanted fame in 1812 as the husband of Lady Caroline Lamb (née Ponsonby), who had a very public affair with Lord Byron and indeed was the person who coined that famous phrase: "mad, bad and dangerous to know".

Melbourne Church: St Michael and St Mary

Built on the site of its Anglo-Saxon predecessor in c.1125, when Henry I was lord of the manor, St Michael and St Mary is one of the finest Norman churches in Britain. It is also something of an enigma. For starters it doesn't have a churchyard, plus it was originally dedicated solely to St Mary. However, these oddities *can* be explained, since Melbourne's original parish church was known as St Michael and stood further north at the end of Castle Street. Alas, it was partly demolished during the Reformation and St Mary's thus became the parish church under a joint dedication – although St Michael's graveyard continued to be used as the parish burial ground until 1860. But that doesn't explain why such a spectacular building was built so close to a parish church. A long-established theory derives from the fact that Henry I granted the tithes and ecclesiastical dues of Melbourne and its chapelries to Adelulf, the first bishop of Carlisle, when his see was founded in 1133. It was therefore thought that the church was built to suit the status of a bishop, while it also served as a secure base for Adelulf who resided rather too close to the raiding Scots for comfort! More recent research, however, suggests that Adelulf didn't actually flee south but remained in Carlisle and became a Scottish bishop. That would then favour the alternative theory that Henry I had St Mary's built as a royal church and therefore the rare two-storey feature of the west gallery was perhaps a royal pew and its upper chancel was for the King's private use.

Regardless of the reason for its special purpose, the grandness of St Michael and St Mary is perhaps at its most apparent when viewed from the *inside*, and which is recognised as one of the finest Norman interiors in

Melbourne Pool, re-modelled and landscaped by William Lamb between 1841 and 1847.

The market place in Melbourne town centre.

St Michael and St Mary's church from the north.
Inset: *John Nost's lead sculpture, built in 1705 and known as the Vase of the Seasons. Each side depicts a different season.*

Melbourne Hall built in 1628 for Sir John Coke.

The Old Mill, perhaps built on the site of the original after which Melbourne is named.

A cruck-framed cottage on High Street, Melbourne, that dates from the 15ᵗʰ or 16ᵗʰ century.

Inset: *Melbourne's parish church, St Michael and St Mary, built in the early 12ᵗʰ century and one of the finest Norman churches in the land.*
Above: *A knockout Norman nave! This is the view from the nave through the base of the tower towards the chancel.*

England. This includes 125 Norman arches with those in the nave the most striking. Here, there are five bays on each side, with chevrons resting on huge 15 foot pillars, each over 12 feet round. Then above these arches are further smaller arches known as triforium arcades, and which open onto the high-set clerestory windows. Again, the majority of these are the Norman originals, including all of the north side and one bay on the south side; the rest are 13th century. Then we have the three tiers of Norman arcading in the central tower, including the capitals of two of its huge pillars which are nationally acclaimed courtesy of their intricate Norman carvings. Also appearing on the north-west tower pier is an extremely rare 14th century wall painting of a horned devil with outstretched wings above either gossiping or quarrelling women with smaller devils on their backs. The principal devil is also holding a scroll bearing the legend IC EST CELIA DEABOL, a meaning which escapes scholars today but is thought to refer to vanity.

Melbourne Historic Trivia: From Thomas Coke to Thomas Cook

By the early 14th century, the royal manor of Melbourne had passed to Thomas, Earl of Lancaster, and it was he who built what was reputed to be a magnificent new castle between 1311 and 1322, and which was probably built on the site of its Norman predecessor. However, it was pulled down in the early 17th century and all that remains today is a high wall covered in ivy. What we do know, though, is that the castle was extensively repaired between 1483 and 1485, and was still going strong in 1562 when an illustration was made of it as part of an Elizabethan survey. The castle remained a royal property until James I sold it to the Earl of Nottingham, who eventually demolished it.

In terms of medieval architecture, not a great deal remains in Melbourne, as many houses were replaced by stone or brick buildings in the 18th and 19th centuries. However, a cruck-framed house can still be found on Melbourne's High Street while other timber-framed houses survive such as the marvellous 16th century thatched farmhouse located at the junction of Castle Street and Potter Street. Today, it forms just one large house, but certainly in 1824 it was divided into seven cottages by the Melbourne Hall estate. As for Melbourne Hall itself, it was built in 1628 on the site of the medieval bishop's residence for Sir John Coke, a

secretary of state in Charles I's parliament. But it was his son, the Rt. Hon. Thomas Coke, architect and Vice Chamberlain to Queen Anne, who laid out the Hall's nationally acclaimed gardens between 1696 and 1706. The gardens include John Nost's "Vase of the Seasons", one of the finest examples of Baroque lead sculpture in an English garden, as well as Robert Bakewell's fine wrought iron arbour, built in 1711 and known today as "The Birdcage".

Robert Bakewell's wrought iron arbour, constructed in 1711 and which soon became known as the "The Birdcage".

As well as William Lamb, Melbourne's other famous son is Thomas Cook, born at 9 Quick Close on 22nd November 1808. An apprentice cabinet maker at fourteen, by eighteen he was doing the village rounds as an evangelist, before becoming a Baptist minister two years later. In 1832 he left Melbourne for Market Harborough, but he always retained a great affection for his place of birth, later donating the Thomas Cook Memorial Cottages for those in need. By 1841, he had organised the first ever public excursion using the recently opened Midland Counties Railway in order to take a group of 570 temperance campaigners from Leicester to a rally at Loughborough 12 miles away. Over the following three years, Cook arranged a succession of trips in the Midlands, but then in 1845, he undertook his first commercial venture, organising a trip from Leicester to Liverpool, providing tickets at 15 shillings for first-class passengers and 10 shillings for second class. He also investigated the route and published a handbook of the journey and this 60-page booklet was therefore a forerunner of the modern holiday brochure. By 1851, Cook was arranging for 165,000 people to attend the Great Exhibition in London and thereafter, his business went rapidly global.

Melbourne Quirk Alert: Double Top

As already stated, William Lamb (aka Lord Melbourne) was a former British Prime Minister. However, Melbourne has strong links to a *second* British Prime Minister, through William Lamb's sister, Emily. Originally married to the 5th Earl Cowper, when the latter died, Emily Lamb re-married – to none other than Lord Palmerston (1784-1865), British Prime Minister from 1855-1858 and 1859-1865. Double top indeed! However, by this stage, the Lambs had already relinquished control of Melbourne Hall to the Cowper's because Emily's brother, the third and last Viscount Melbourne (1782-1853), died childless.

NAME (STATUS):	**OAKOVER** (Road); **OKEOVER** (Hamlet, Estate, Parish, Pub)
POPULATION:	Road, c.150; Hamlet, c.30
DISTRICT:	City of Derby (Road); East Staffordshire (Hamlet, Estate, Parish); Derbyshire Dales (Pub)
EARLIEST RECORD:	*Acovre*, 1086
MEANING:	Ridge where oak trees grow
DERIVATION:	From the Old English words *āc* (oak-tree) and *ofer* (flat-topped ridge, hill or promontory)

Okeover Pub:
The Okeover Arms

Okeover/Oakover was the last of a trio of ridge-based ofers used in verse 2 of the Shire-Ode – and for which I have to ofer up a confession! Growing up on a road close to Ashover Road, Birchover Way and Oakover Drive, I'd assumed that all three were legitimate Derbyshire places, with a vague perception that

The Okeover Arms, Mappleton.

Oakover was located somewhere just south of Ashbourne. So perhaps I was confusing it with both Osmaston and the Staffordshire hamlet of Okeover that borders Derbyshire just north of Ashbourne. Thankfully, the Okeover Arms is located a few yards over the River Dove in the Derbyshire village of Mappleton; a legitimate bit of Okeover in Derbyshire, after all!

Okeover Church: All Saints; St Mary's

Although only an estate, Okeover Hall does have its own church, known as All Saints, which dates from the 14th century when it was built alongside a former manor house on the same site as the present hall. However, the nearest parish church is St Mary's, a few yards over the border in Derbyshire at Mappleton. This unusual 18th century church has a dome rather than a tower or steeple, and was built on the site of a 13th century predecessor.

St Mary's church, Mappleton, with its unusual dome.

Okeover Historic Trivia:
Okeover Hall

The village of Okeover was the estate to Okeover Hall which, in turn, is the seat of the Okeover family who have been in residence since the reign of William II (1087-1100). The current building is Grade II listed with the oldest part dating back to 1745-46, which was also when both church and house were pillaged by Jacobite soldiers marching south with Bonnie Prince Charlie in late 1745.

Okeover Quirk Alert:
Tombstoning in Brigadoon

In 1887, Maud Okeover, of Okeover Hall, married Sir Andrew Barclay Walker, a successful brewer of Gateacre, Liverpool and who in 1884 had purchased…wait for it…Osmaston Manor! So perhaps this hard link between Okeover and Osmaston somehow resulted in the birth of this mythical Brigadoonesque place in my mind! Anyway, Walker acquired Okeover in 1888, but assumed the name of Walker-Okeover while his grandson, the 3rd Baronet, demolished Osmaston Manor in 1964, and moved the family seat back to Okeover. However, several members of the Okeover family have served not just as High Sheriffs of Staffordshire over the centuries, but as High Sheriffs of Derbyshire, too! The linkage is just too strong to deny!

Finally, Okeover is located a stone's-throw over the Staffordshire border, just beyond the bridge over the River Dove. When I visited Okeover in May 2012, the bridge was playing host to a group of tombstoning teenagers! I then later read that the bridge is part of a traditional, annual race on New Year's Day, involving the river, a boat and a 30 foot plunge from the top of that very same bridge into the icy River Dove, followed by a

run across the field to the Okeover Arms where the contestants imbibe of a well-earned pint or three! So perhaps I caught them in training!

The tombstoning bridge at Okeover/ Mappleton … minus the tombstoners!

NAME (STATUS):	**OAKS GREEN** (Hamlet)
POPULATION:	c.10
DISTRICT:	Derbyshire Dales
MEANING:	Probably "green where oak trees grow"
DERIVATION:	From the OE words *āc* (oak) and *grēne* (green-coloured, grassy place or village green)

Oaks Green: Geographic Trivia

Oaks Green is located in south-west Derbyshire a mile or so north-west of Sudbury, and must be a candidate for one of Derbyshire's tiniest places. At first glance from the A515, it only appears to include Oaks Green East Farm and the Meynell Hunt Kennels. However, if you join the A515 from the A50 heading northbound for Ashbourne and then take a first left towards Somersal Herbert, you will soon find on your right-hand side a row of pretty houses. See *Quirk Alert* for more.

Oaks Green Pub:
The Vernon Arms at Sudbury

The nearest pub to the hamlet of Oaks Green is the Vernon Arms, located a mile to the south-east in the village of Sudbury. It was built as a coaching inn in the late 17th century and is named after the local Lords of the Manor who lived at Sudbury Hall. The Vernons inherited the estate in the early 16th century when the heiress Helen Montgomery married Sir John Vernon (d.1545), a younger son of Henry Vernon of Haddon Hall. The Sudbury Estate remains in the hands of Vernon descendants to this day.

Oaks Green Church:
St Peter's at Somersal Herbert

As already mentioned above, Oaks Green is a tiny hamlet, so it will come as no surprise to find that it doesn't possess its own church. The nearest is St Peter's church, a mile or so to the north-west at Somersal Herbert – the churchyard of which contains a rather fine 15th century cross and which is also a Scheduled Ancient Monument.

Oaks Green Historic Trivia:
Medieval Families

Also in nearby Somersal Herbert is Somersal Herbert Hall (see *Conventional Derbyshire, pages 20-21*). What this means is that Oaks Green is wedged in between two of the most significant medieval landowners in Derbyshire's history: the Fitzherberts at Somersal Herbert and the Vernons at Sudbury – although Oaks Green is part of the estate of the latter.

Oaks Green Quirk Alert:
Place With No Name and Tippling Posties

As stated above, Oaks Green pretty much comprises one row of houses, and one of the residents was kind

These houses are pretty much the sum total of Oaks Green. I was reliably informed by a very pleasant resident that the colour of the doors is Sudbury Green, and that no one else is allowed to paint a door that colour other than a representative of the Sudbury estate!

The Vernon Arms, Sudbury.

enough to furnish me with bags of interesting information about the hamlet, plus digging out some very old books and maps that confirmed that Oaks Green existed in the 19th century, too. However, there is no Oaks Green welcome sign either side of these houses and, worse still for the occupants, mail-wise, the *road* doesn't have a name either. The only evidence for the motorist that the place exists is the walking and cycling path sign which is located down in Sudbury village and which directs you north under the A50.

All of which must make receiving mail a bit of a lottery at Oaks Green – unless you're related to the postmaster – which, as chance has it, the resident was!

Apparently, generations of this particular family have lived in the area, including Fred Allen, the local postmaster who used to deliver mail by bicycle, as the settlements in the area were small and pretty well spaced out. The problem was, that the residents were so friendly, that every house insisted that Fred should join them in a glass of this, that and the other and the poor chap became renowned for having the odd mishap with his bike – and which sometimes involved having a little kip in a ditch somewhere around the Oaks Green area! I then learned that Oaks Green is part of the Sudbury Hall estate, and since the houses are part of that estate, they are not for sale and have to remain rented; indeed, the occupants of these houses still pay their water rate money direct to the Lords of the Manor at Sudbury Hall. Cash in hand, I believe!

Finally, Oaks Green is also located around 8-miles due south of Okeover and given the lack of place-name welcome signs and roads without names it could almost pass for a *second* Derbyshire Oak-related Brigadoon!

St Peter's church, Somersal Herbert.

Sudbury Hall, built in the 1660s by George Vernon. The Vernons have owned Oaks Green ever since.

NAME (STATUS):	**OAKWOOD** (Suburb)
POPULATION:	13,450
DISTRICT:	City of Derby
EARLIEST RECORD:	Late 20th century (modern housing estate)
MEANING:	Wood where oak trees grow
DERIVATION:	See *Name Derivation* section below

Oakwood: Name Derivation

Oakwood was built mainly in the 1980s on the site of ancient oak woodland, and which used to be known as Chaddesden Common prior to Oakwood's birth. The original oak wood has been preserved as Chaddesden Wood Nature Reserve and remains the only ancient oak woodland in the city of Derby. As for Oakwood today, not only is it a modern housing estate that covers a large slice of Derby's north-eastern suburbs, but it is also one of Europe's largest housing estates, too.

Oakwood Pub: The Oak and Acorn

The oak theme continues with Oakwood's main pub, The Oak and Acorn. Situated in the centre of the suburb, the pub is as modern as the 1980s-built community that it serves. As for Oakwood's other pubs, they are all situated on its outskirts (see *Quirk Alert* for more).

Oakwood Church: The Church on Oakwood

As Oakwood is relatively new, it doesn't possess an old church. However, it does have a modern church called "The Church on Oakwood" which was officially dedicated in May 1993 by the Anglican Bishop of Derby, the Roman Catholic Bishop of Nottingham, the Moderator of the East Midlands United Reformed Church and the Chairman of the Nottingham and Derby District of the Methodist Church. The reason for this long list is because it is one of very few Ecumenical churches in the country comprising a partnership between four different Christian faiths that recognise it is their similarities that are of far greater significance than their differences.

Oakwood Historic Trivia: Academy Awards

Having been built mainly in the 1980s, Oakwood's history is somewhat limited. However, in 2003, Derby County's Football Academy was built on the north-eastern fringe of Oakwood. Known as Moor Farm, it cost £5m, covers 50 acres and features six full-sized training pitches plus an indoor pitch. The build of the site was initially controversial as it was deemed it would create an eyesore on open countryside. However, true to their promise, Derby County developed a site that blended into the countryside with low-lying buildings and minimal impact on the surrounding flora and fauna. Since its inception, the academy has produced a number of notable internationals including England midfielder Tom Huddlestone, while many of Derby's

Derby County's Moor Farm Football Academy on Morley Road, Oakwood.

current squad are academy graduates, including Mason Bennett who set the club record for youngest first team appearance when he made his full debut in October 2011 at the age of fifteen years and ninety-nine days.

Oakwood Quirk Alert: Rhomboid Geography

As mentioned above, apart from The Oak and Acorn, all other Oakwood pubs are situated on the suburb's outskirts in locations previously associated with other areas of Derby. Examples include The Windmill Inn, which is located on Breadsall Hill Top at the north-western edge of the suburb and thus traditionally associated with the village of Breadsall. Then there is The King's Corner *(top left)*, located at the north-eastern tip of the suburb and which several decades ago was in no-mans-land between Breadsall, Morley and Locko Park, while The Paddock is situated at the south-western tip of the suburb and which was traditionally seen as a Chaddesden pub. All that is missing to make a unique rhombus of pubs is another at the south-eastern corner of the suburb where Morley Road joins Chaddesden Lane. That said, at the bottom of Chaddesden Lane is The Toby Carvery (formerly The Beau Brummel), although this pub was, is and presumably always will be an integral part of Chaddesden.

Above and below: *Path through the centre of Oakwood's historic oak wood.*

NAME (STATUS):	**PEAK FOREST** (Village)
POPULATION:	307
DISTRICT:	High Peak
EARLIEST RECORD:	*Peake Forest*, 1577
MEANING:	Forest in the peaks
DERIVATION:	From the 13th century medieval hunting forest, which is first referred to in 1223 as *foresta de Pecco*. Here, the word "Peak" derives from the Old English word *pēac* (a peak or pointed hill), and "Forest" derives from the Middle English word *forest*.

Peak Forest Pub: The Devonshire Arms

The Devonshire Arms was originally a 17th century coaching inn on the Chesterfield to Chapel-en-le-Frith route, now known as the A623. The pub was named after the local Dukes of Devonshire who resided (and still reside) at nearby Chatsworth House.

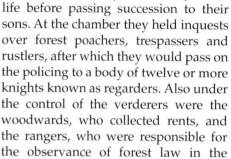

The Devonshire Arms, Peak Forest.

Peak Forest Church: Charles, King and Martyr

The unusually named Charles, King and Martyr Church was built close to the location of a former chapel that had been allocated a mysterious "peculiar jurisdiction" (see *Quirk Alert* for more). The original church was built in 1657, its name betraying local Royalist leanings to the king who had been executed eight years earlier. It was built on the instruction of Christian, Countess of Devonshire who intended it to be a private chapel within the Royal Forest and not under standard ecclesiastical jurisdiction. The church was then re-built in its current form in 1876-77 as a gift from the 7th Duke of Devonshire.

Peak Forest Historic Trivia: Forest Courts

At the western end of Peak Forest, Chamber Farm marks the spot of a former medieval hunting lodge that was known as the "chamber in the forest", where minor courts were held for the Campana ward (one of three wards in the Forest of the Peak). These were run by four verderers who were answerable only to the bailiff of the Forest of the Peak, and who usually held their jobs for life before passing succession to their sons. At the chamber they held inquests over forest poachers, trespassers and rustlers, after which they would pass on the policing to a body of twelve or more knights known as regarders. Also under the control of the verderers were the woodwards, who collected rents, and the rangers, who were responsible for the observance of forest law in the remoter parts of the forest. From the 14th century onwards, though, the laws were slackened and the royal hunting parties became less popular. The land gradually fell into private ownership and by the end of the 15th century not much of the former Forest of the Peak remained. Then in the 16th century an enclosed park of about 4 square miles was created. The ranger built a house there and further dwellings followed...and thus the settlement of Peak Forest was born. Meanwhile, Chamber Farm was rebuilt in the 17th century.

Peak Forest Quirk Alert: Derbyshire's Gretna Green

In 1665, the minister at Charles, King and Martyr was given the power to prove wills and to grant marriage licences without reading the banns, this thanks to his title of "Principal Official and Judge in Spiritualities in the Peculiar Court of Peak Forest" (let's just call him The Minister). His powers probably stemmed from the aforementioned chapel with the "peculiar jurisdiction", but he could certainly marry couples on the spot, without parents' consent; nobody asked their ages or where they came from, and thus Peak Forest became the Gretna Green of Derbyshire. Word spread around the country, and lovers made difficult journeys across the hills and moors to get there, sometimes with relatives in hot pursuit; in fact, it was not unknown for runaways to get The Minister out of bed, and race him through the ceremony in his night shirt! By 1728 so many runaways were wed at Peak Forest that a second register began for 'foreign marriages'. In 1753 the Marriage Act should have put an end to the solemnising of elopers, but the last runaway couple married there was as late as 1938!

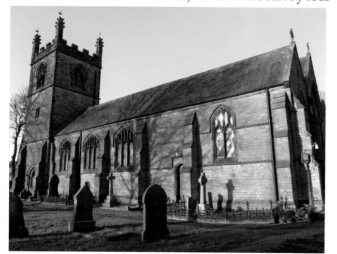

The church of Charles, King and Martyr, at Peak Forest.

Threes-Up!

	PRESS	SCOTCHES	SLACK
STATUS:	Hamlet	Suburb	Hamlet
POPULATION:	c.30	c.200	c.10
DISTRICT:	North East Derbyshire	Amber Valley	North East Derbyshire
MEANING:	The origin, meaning and meaning derivation of all three places is unknown – but *see Threes-Up Trivia* for an educated guess on all counts!		

Threes Up Trivia!

The name **Press** is most likely to derive from the Old English word *prēost*, meaning "priest" – although where that connection would come from is not clear. The only other potential candidate for the name's origin is a long shot – for given the hamlet's location in north-eastern Derbyshire, it is unlikely that it would derive from the Welsh word *pres* or *prys* meaning "brushwood or thicket" – but given the heavily wooded nature of this particular area you never know!

As for **Scotches**, Ordnance Survey maps name this area of north-western Belper singularly – although it rather conveniently contains a road called *The* Scotches, too. But geographically, the area

known as "Scotches" covers the hill behind the town's historic mill complex, and is dotted with former mill cottages built by the philanthropic mill-owning Strutt family – who also built mill cottages in Long Row and The Clusters which lie to the south of the mill complex.

As for how and why the place was named, perhaps it does have something to do with the malt whisky that is made in Scotland after all! Certainly, in the late 18th century, commercial distilleries began introducing whisky made from wheat and rye and branded it as Scotch Whisky, so the timing would be perfect; so perhaps, like Brad in our Shire-Ode, the mill workers of Scotches had a particular penchant for the tipple, too!

Meanwhile, **Slack** is located a mile or so to the west of Ashover on the A632 between Matlock and Chesterfield. Again, its origins are uncertain but, given the topography of the land there, and the fact that the place is located in the eastern half of Derbyshire and therefore in strong Viking territory, it could feasibly derive from the Old Scandinavian word *slakki*, meaning "a shallow valley". Today, Slack is an even tinier hamlet than Press, comprising solely of Slack Lane where you will only find Slack Lane Farm.

The tiny hamlet of Press.

Row of former mill cottages on The Scotches.

NAME (STATUS):	**PYE BRIDGE** (Village)
POPULATION:	c.500
DISTRICT:	Amber Valley
MEANING AND DERIVATION:	*See Quirk Alert*

Pye Bridge Pub: The Dog and Doublet

The Dog and Doublet Inn has been located at Pye Bridge since at least 1857, as it is listed in White's *Directory of Derbyshire* for that year; for completeness, the landlord was John Peck! However, in those days, Pye Bridge was little more than a railway station.

Pye Bridge Historic Trivia: Triangulation

Pye Bridge sits on the B600 roughly half way between Somercotes in Derbyshire and Selston in Nottinghamshire. Its most historic feature is the Ambergate to Pye Bridge railway line that was a short east-west line linking the Midland Main Line with the Erewash Valley Line. The line was opened by the Midland Railway in 1875 and ran from the Midland Main Line north of Ambergate at Crich Junction and proceeded through Sawmills, Butterley and Swanwick before connecting to the Erewash Valley Line via a triangular junction known as Riddings Junction, with Pye Bridge Station on the Erewash Valley Line sitting just to the north-east of this triangle. Passenger services were withdrawn on 16th June 1947, just before the line passed into British Rail ownership, after which the Beeching Axe was wielded and freight service was also eventually withdrawn in 1968. However, although disused by regular railway operators these days, the line has been partially restored by the Midland Steam Railway between Hammersmith and Ironville, while on the western section the A610 has been built on a similar alignment. Ironically, when you enter Pye Bridge today from the east, you cross into Derbyshire at the point that the main railway to the north crosses over the B600 via a bridge. Interestingly, a 19th century reference refers to Pye Bridge railway station sitting just south of the forking of the Erewash Valley Railway to Chesterfield and Mansfield. Today, exactly the same configuration applies.

Pye Bridge Quirk Alert: Gnat Pie

In terms of place-name origins, either the railway bridge or a predecessor bridge may well account for half of the name. As for other English places beginning with Pye, they usually derive from the Old English word *pīe* which means "gnats or other insects". For example, the West Sussex village of Pyecombe means "valley infested with gnats or other insects". Similarly, the Devon village of Pyworthy means "enclosure infested with gnats or

other insects". So somewhat ironically, Pye Bridge has recently been the location of a locally reviled and smelly incinerator at Pye Bridge Industrial Estate. Its gas field eventually became depleted, but the company's considerations for a new gasification incinerator have led locals to campaign long and hard against its introduction, particularly as independent researchers on incineration and toxicology have recently raised concerns about the health effects of emissions from such devices.

The Dog and Doublet, Pye Bridge.

Heading out of Pye Bridge along the B600 and into Nottinghamshire.

NAME (STATUS):	**SAWLEY** (Village)
POPULATION:	6,500
DISTRICT:	Erewash
EARLIEST RECORD:	*Salle*, 1086 (*Domesday Book*); *Sallawa*, 1166; *Sallowe*, 1242
MEANING:	Hill or mound where sallow trees grow
DERIVATION:	From the Old English words *salh* (sallow or willow-tree) and *hlāw* (tumulus, mound or hill)
FAMOUS RESIDENTS:	**William Booth** (d.1464), Archbishop of York (1452-1464). **Lawrence Booth** (1420-1480), Archbishop of York (1476-1480). **John Clifford** (1836-1923), nonconformist minister, propagandist, writer, Liberal politician and greatest Free Churchman of his day.

Sawley Pub: The Trent Lock

Two of Sawley's pubs tie in very nicely with the Historic Trivia: The Harrington Arms, which was an 18th century coaching inn, and The Trent Lock. Formerly The Navigation Inn, The Trent Lock now takes its name from the point where the Rivers Trent and Soar meet with the beginning of the Erewash Canal. The lock also sits on the border of Leicestershire, Nottinghamshire and Derbyshire.

The Trent Lock, Sawley.

Sawley Church: All Saints

Despite Sawley being named after sallow trees, it is two beautiful rows of lime trees (24 in total) that line the approach to Sawley All Saints. As for the church, it still has traces of Saxon and Norman architecture, with the oldest element the round chancel arch that dates from Saxon times although other herringbone-patterns elsewhere suggest pre-Conquest masonry, too. The splendid north doorway, most of the windows and the nave are all 14th century, while the clerestory and spire are 15th century.

Sawley Historic Trivia: Confluences

Built in 1790, the Harrington Bridge made Sawley very important as it commanded the first river crossing of the River Trent in the area south of Nottingham. It also put the local ferry out of business, 150 yards upstream!

Sawley also lies one mile west of Trent Lock where the Erewash Canal flows down from the north to join the River Trent, while almost opposite this junction the River Soar flows up from the south to join the Trent, too. Meanwhile another mile to the south-west of Sawley is the mouth of the River Derwent where it flows into the River Trent and which is also the starting point of the Trent and Mersey Canal. And sticking with the water theme, Sawley Marina is located on a navigational cut of the River Trent and is the largest Inland Marina in the UK, with a water space of 23 acres. On site you will find the chandlery and stores with over 4,000 square feet dedicated to the sale of over 10,000 items of boating merchandise, along with The Dolls House Workshop, a one-stop shop for all things dolls house – even wallpaper!

Sawley Quirk Alert: Stinky Foals

William Owen's 1770 *Book of Fairs* declares that Sawley holds an annual Fair for Foals! Meanwhile, a more recent alliteration is the Sawley Stink – a pungent smell caused by the dumping of waste on nearby farmland. Fortunately, a local group conducted a successful campaign in 2009 to put an end to the process! So that's people power putting paid to the Pye Bridge Pong and the Sawley Stink in successive sections!

The final lock of the Erewash Canal before it joins the River Trent.

Sawley Marina.

NAME (STATUS):	**SHIRLEY** (Village)
POPULATION:	254
DISTRICT:	Derbyshire Dales
EARLIEST RECORD:	*Sirelei*, 1086 *(Domesday Book)*; *Schyrelayg*, 1230; *Schirleg*, 1247
MEANING:	Either "bright or shire woodland clearing" or "woodland clearing where the shire meeting is held"
DERIVATION:	From the Old English words *scīr* (shire, district or bright/clear) and *lēah* (wood, woodland clearing or glade)
FAMOUS RESIDENTS:	**John Cowper Powys** (1872-1963), author. **Theodore Cowper-Powys** (1875-1953), author.

Shirley Pub: The Saracens Head

The Saracen's Head dates from 1791 but was built on the site of a previous pub of the same name. This, in turn, was named after the exploits of one Sewallis de Shirley who accompanied William de Ferrers under Richard I on the Third Crusade to the Holy Land (1189-1192). The name originates from the commemorative coat of arms of the Shirley family marking service in the Crusades. Meanwhile, the current pub was built from bricks made by the nearby Shirley Common Brickyard.

Shirley Church: St Michael's

Shirley's church is called St Michael's, and although the tower is 19th century (1861) along with the north aisle (1842) and the arcade leading to it, the rest of the church is mainly 14th century, while the font is 15th century. The only Norman survivor is a stone in an outside wall that was once part of a tympanum above a doorway and which is crudely carved with animals and foliage. At the time that the tympanum in question graced the *door* in question, St Michael's church was owned by the 12th century Augustinian abbey at Darley Abbey.

Shirley Historic Trivia:
Sewallis and the Bonnie Prince

Although Henry de Ferrers held Shirley manor, he was probably overlord to a retained Saxon thegn called Sewallis – and it was this family who took the name de Shirley and settled in the area during the reign of Henry II (1154-1189), making it their principal seat in the early 13th century and remaining lords of the manor until the 19th century. The de Shirleys initially played an important role as knights and we've already mentioned Sewallis de Shirley's contribution to the Crusades in the *Shirley Pub* section. Meanwhile, the church is home to two 19th century memorials of the Shirley family one of whom, Sir Hugh Shirley, is immortalised by Shakespeare in *Henry IV* as "valiant Shirley", having been slain in the Battle of Shrewsbury of 1403. Twelve years later, his son, Sir Ralph Shirley was one of Henry V's commanders at the battle of Agincourt, while his son married Margaret the sister and sole heir of Thomas Staunton. They thus inherited the manor of Staunton Harold and this became the chief seat of the Shirleys in 1468.

The Saracen's Head, Shirley.

St Michael's church, Shirley.

Further relics of medieval times can be found at a farmhouse near the church, built on the site of Shirley Manor and later Shirley Hall, and which still has part of the old homestead preserved in a gable and some oak panelling. It also has the remains of the ancient moat which today is a real rarity. After the Shirley's vacated the Hall, the Goodall family, well-known local farmers in the area, occupied it for the next 450 years.

Finally, Bonnie Prince Charlie Walk passes through the Osmaston Manor Estate to the north-west of Shirley, and into Shirley along Park Lane. The Walk is so-named because the Young Pretender passed this way on his march south in 1745 and is said to have spent a night in the village. This beautiful estate, with its lake, trees and picturesque Saw Mill built in c.1845 and fed by a fast-flowing brook, was known as Shirley Park at the turn of the 20th century. The park is owned by the Okeover Estate which, in turn, owns the Osmaston Estate.

Shirley Quirk Alert: Vicars and Sensuality

The 19th century saw the creation of a brass cross to commemorate Canon Shirley of Christ Church, Oxford where he was buried in 1873 while an 1847 stone monument with three canopied niches commemorates Walter Augustus Shirley, a resident vicar who went on to become a bishop. Also in the 19th century the church was served by the Rev. Charles Francis Powys (1843–1923), cousin of the Shirley family, and father to a number of literary children, including John Cowper Powys. Born in Shirley in 1872, John Cowper Powys is therefore considered to be one of Derbyshire's most prolific authors – although the family did move to Somerset when John was seven, where his father was vicar of Montacute for thirty-two years. Nevertheless, John Cowper Powys went on to have 21 novels published (three posthumously), while he also wrote ten books on Philosophy, three collections of short stories, seven volumes of poetry, numerous essays and studies and has been subject of around twenty biographical and autobiographical works. However, although he was a famous lecturer and published a variety of both fiction and non-fiction regularly from 1915, it was not until he was in his early fifties, with the 1929 publication of *Wolf Solent* that he achieved critical and financial success as a novelist. *In Defence of Sensuality*, published at the end of the following year, was yet another best seller, while three more followed which, along with *Wolf Solent* became known as "the Wessex novels", these being: *A Glastonbury Romance* (1932), *Weymouth Sands* (1934) and *Maiden Castle* (1936). The settings and the style demonstrate his enthusiasm for Thomas Hardy and Walter Scott, although he was also seen as a modernist, with an affinity with Dostoyevsky, Nietzsche, Jung, Freud and D. H. Lawrence. John Powys also had an interesting personal life, becoming estranged from his Catholic wife, having numerous relationships with other women, particularly in the USA where he was also a great success, before settling down with Phyllis Playter in 1921. Four of his siblings also had much literary success, the most notable being another Shirley-born, Theodore Francis Powys, who wrote eight novels and fifteen collections of short stories.

Above and below: *The Saw Mill in Shirley Park, seen from both back and front. The mill lies on Bonnie Prince Charlie Walk.*

NAME (STATUS):	**STANLEY** (Village)
POPULATION:	2,091
DISTRICT:	Erewash
EARLIEST RECORD:	*Stanlei*, 1086 *(Domesday Book)*; *Stanlega*, 1169
MEANING:	Place at the stony woodland clearing
DERIVATION:	From the Old English words *stān* (stone, rock or boundary stone) and *lēah*, (wood, woodland clearing or glade)

Stanley Pub: The White Hart Inn

The White Hart Inn has been Stanley's only pub since the Bridge Inn was converted to a private residence in the 1990s. Situated a little further up the road on the opposite side, the Bridge Inn was actually converted by ex-work colleagues of mine, and who still appear on the picture on the sign that hangs outside the house! Conversely, the White Hart started out life as a row of cottages!

Stanley Church: St Andrew's

St Andrew's church was built in the late 12ᵗʰ century on the site of its Anglo-Saxon predecessor. However, although St Andrew's retains a few of its Norman features, such as the now blocked-up priest's doorway on the south side of the church, much of the building was restored in 1875 when it was also enlarged. Other ancient survivors are a small lancet window and some buttresses from the 13ᵗʰ century, the octagonal font and the east chancel window from the 14ᵗʰ century and the pulpit from the 17ᵗʰ century, while the church gates commemorate Queen Victoria's Golden Jubilee of 1887 with the year skilfully worked into the wrought iron. It is also rumoured that some stonework from Dale Abbey – to which the church had belonged up until the abbey's dissolution in 1539 – is also incorporated in the church. Meanwhile, the churchyard contains a memorial erected in 2004 to the six occupants who lost their lives when an experimental RAF Wellington Bomber, en route from Boscombe Down to Blackpool, disintegrated above Stanley in July 1942 with the debris falling to the ground near Quarry Farm. Finally, another church-related story from medieval times is that St Andrew's provided sanctuary for a murderer called William Welshman who could thus not be turned out of the building for 40 days.

Stanley Historic Trivia: Felix Kept On Walking

The chief grange of the nearby 13ᵗʰ century Dale Abbey was situated at Stanley. It was built shortly after 1291 and had a chapel of St Cross while a stone chamber was added when William Horsley was abbot of Dale Abbey (1332-1354). Stanley Grange Farm eventually became a Catholic school by the 17ᵗʰ century, but in a county with few Catholics, it was raided twice, first in 1637 after questions had been asked about it in the House of Commons and again by Parliamentary forces in 1642, and who were searching for Royalist arms during the First English Civil War.

Stanley is also inextricably linked with Felix Bus Services, a local bus service and tour operator, as Stanley was the main depot of the service right up until April 2012. It all began in 1921 when Norman Frost of Stanley bought a Crossley lorry from the War Department, and by 1924 he was operating a Derby to Ilkeston bus service via Chaddesden, Stanley and West Hallam, a route which remains part of their core service to this day. When asked to name one of his vehicles in 1924, Frost chose Felix based on a popular jazz song of the day called *Felix Kept On Walking*, and which was based on the cartoon cat. The vehicles were originally based on New Street in Stanley, where Frost's parents lived, but in 1937, a house and garage were built on Station Road, and became the firm's main depot. By

The White Hart, Stanley.

St Andrew's church, Stanley.

2002, Felix's fleet had peaked at 17, with all buses immediately recognisable thanks to their distinctive Black Cat logo. One of the fleet members was the football special run from Ilkeston to Pride Park Stadium on match days, and indeed Felix have been transporting supporters to Derby County home games almost as long as they have operated buses; an early vehicle order form showed three lines on the destination blind: "Derby", "Ilkeston" and "Baseball Ground".

Alas, despite having displayed the image of a cat for over eighty years, US company Felix the Cat Creations Inc., approached Felix Buses in 2005 and claimed it owned copyright for images of cats used next to the Felix name. A two-year license thus had to be purchased in order to continue using the cat image during which time Felix Buses introduced a redesigned cat image that didn't at all resemble Felix the Cat. However, the delightful Americans then asserted that they owned the rights to *any* feline image used with the name Felix and thus all cat images had to be removed from the fleet. Then in December 2011, the bus operations were sold to Midland General, the owners of Trent Barton, who also operate a Black Cat service between Ilkeston and Derby, along with the Ilkeston Flyer service. When this transfer took place, the bus services switched to using Trent's Meadow Road depot in Derby, bringing an end to c.ninety years of service from Stanley.

Stanley Quirk Alert: Stony Faces

In 1878, Stanley railway station was opened by the Great Northern Railway on what it called its "Derbyshire Extension" which ran from Burton to Nottingham. However, the station was soon re-named to "West Hallam for Dale Abbey" to avoid confusion with another Stanley Station in Yorkshire. In time, Sunday passenger services finished in 1939, and the line closed completely in 1964. However, the station has survived and is now known as the privately owned Station House. It is also a nice little garden centre today, offering plants and a large selection of stone garden ornaments, while the station house retains the original station clock, the old "WEST HALLAM FOR DALE ABBEY" sign above the door, and an original WEST HALLAM railway bench. Anyway, I recently bought from here a rather fine stone cast of an Easter Island statue for my brother-in-law as part of a long-running family joke. You had to be there, really, but we were once in a pub in Cornwall having the fourth pint of our "just the one before dinner", when the brother-in-law mentioned that he would "definitely be getting the Easter Island Treatment, now". Bang on cue, my sister opened the pub door and duly obliged. It was absolutely priceless! Plus she's still got no idea why I bought the present – until round about now, I guess!

Station House, West Hallam. I can recommend the Easter Island statues!

Threes-Up!

	THE BANKS	THE BRUSHES	THE FLOURISH
STATUS:	Hamlet	Suburb	Hamlet
POPULATION:	c.20	c.200	c.5
DISTRICT:	High Peak	Chesterfield	Erewash
MEANING:	See *Threes-Up Trivia*		

Threes Up Trivia!

The Banks is a private and rural area that is located a mile to the south of Mellor and a mile to the south-east of the Roman Lakes Leisure Park. Today, Roman Lakes is a popular recreational spot with its tea room a focal point. However, it also had a tea room in Victorian and Edwardian times when it was a popular destination for hundreds of visitors who came on the train to Marple and then walked up to the lakes where they would hire rowing boats and also enjoy a dance on the resident dance floor. Today, both The Banks and Mellor are part of the borough of Stockport in the ceremonial county of Greater Manchester, but both were part of Derbyshire until 1936 when they were transferred to the Marple Urban District in Cheshire. This means that The Banks has the rare distinction of having been part of *three* different English counties during the last eighty years.

Meanwhile, **The Brushes** is an area on the northern edge of Chesterfield to the north of Broomhill Road, so the chances are that the place-name relates to the broom (Old English *brōm*) growing on Broom Hill to the north of Broomhill Road. Furthermore, nearby there is a Broombank Road, Broombank Park and a Broom Business Park; a veritable collection of Brushes! Historically, though, there are internet references to a Johnson Street, The Brushes, Whittington, in 1910. However, older references to Johnson Street (in 1881, 1882 and 1891) place it in Whittington but *not* The Brushes – suggesting that it might have been a transient area of Whittington at *just* the start of the 20th century. What makes this theory feasible is the fact that the Census Street Index of 1891 for the Chesterfield Registration District, records a Johnson Street, whereas a modern street index of Chesterfield does not. But what is also vaguely amusing is that, in addition to the collection of "Broom streets" named above, the modern street index shows that the Chesterfield area is also home to a Broom Avenue, Broom Close, Broom Drive, Broom Gardens and Broomfield Avenue, while Broomhill Road is home to a Broomhouse nursing home. All in all, that's an awful lot of *brōm*!

As for **The Flourish**, I took slight poetic license to omit the word "The" before using the place-name in the Shire-Ode. But anyway, "The Flourish" is barely a hamlet, and primarily consists of Flourish Farm which today runs its own antiques business, too. It is situated on the A6096, lying roughly half way between Derby and Ilkeston and thus around 4 or 5 miles from each.

The road used to be an old coaching route between Derby and Ilkeston, and before the Second World War, Flourish Farm was in fact an inn called The Stanhope Arms. As a result of coach drivers calling in at the inn for food and drink, the place was deemed to have "flourished", and thus the name of "The Flourish" stuck.

Roman Lakes, a mile to the north-west of The Banks.

The Brushes, off Broomhill Road, Old Whittington.

Flourish Farm, a former coaching inn on what is now the A6096 between Derby and Ilkeston.

Threes-Up!

	THE FORTIES	**THE GUTTER**	**WASH**
STATUS:	Hamlet	No longer exists	Hamlet
POPULATION:	c.10	N/A	c.30
DISTRICT:	South Derbyshire	Amber Valley	High Peak
MEANING:	Named after Forties Lane	Unknown	See *Threes-Up Trivia*

Threes Up Trivia!

The Forties is barely a place in its own right, but it does appear as such in the *AA Close-Up Britain Road Atlas* where it is located just north of Smisby. However, it essentially appears to be comprised of just Forties Lane and Forties Farm.

Meanwhile, **The Gutter** is pinpointed on maps as an area to the south of the A609 in Belper where Nottingham Road becomes Kilbourne Road before climbing up to Openwoodgate. A report called "Urban Survey and Archaeological Assessment Report of Belper" also states that the area adjoining Whitemoor was called The Gutter in the 19th century. One reference states that: *"early pits were sunk at Belper Gutter and Belper Town"*, while *"a coal mine was worked at Whitemoor between 1863 and 1865"*. The document then talks about "Development at The Gutter", and as well as discussing 17th and 18th century enclosures there, it states that: *"A building is shown in this area on the 1698 plan, although it is difficult to identify its exact location…the present day Short Street was presumably formally laid out at that time, and by the end of the 19th century it was fronted by terraced housing. This has since disappeared."* The document then identifies a Wesleyan chapel built in 1816 (so presumably there was enough of a congregation to warrant its construction), an adjoining schoolroom built in 1870, plus a 19th century malthouse, a couple of smithies and another school built in 1877-

Forties Farm lies a mile north of Smisby.

1879 and which is still in use. The settlement was clearly separate from Belper but was absorbed around the turn of the 20th century. Meanwhile, an 1889 edition of the *Journal of the Derbyshire Archaeological and Natural History Society* confirms that a Pottery was established here in the late 18th century where "ordinary brown-ware" was produced by Messrs' Blood, Webster, and Simpson. It also states that: *"around the year 1800 the Pottery was removed to Denby, where Messrs' Bourne continue to carry on a large and lucrative business at the present time."* And of course, they continue to do so to this day, too, since that reference is to the hugely successful Denby Pottery that was founded in 1809 by Joseph Bourne, went on to acquire an international reputation and remains today one of the most renowned pottery manufacturers in the UK.

Finally, **Wash** lies a mile or so north of Chapel-en-le-Frith and is comprised of a delightful cluster of stone buildings alongside a lovely stream and with a nice old-fashioned red telephone box for company. As for the name, Wash, it may derive from the Old English word *wæsse*, meaning "riverside land liable to flood". Or, for once, it may mean what we'd expect it to mean – and thus derive from the Old English word *wæsce*, meaning "to wash" – in this case, perhaps sheep or clothes were washed in the stream located here.

The top of Short Street where it joins Kilbourne Road, and where The Gutter was centred in the 19th century.

The hamlet of Wash alongside the stream that may well contribute towards its name.

NAME (STATUS):	**WHATSTANDWELL** (Village)
POPULATION:	c.250
DISTRICT:	Amber Valley
EARLIEST RECORD:	*Wattestanwell ford, c.1390*
MEANING:	Walter Stonewell's ford
DERIVATION:	From the gentleman called Walter Stonewell, who owned the house next to the ford
FAMOUS RESIDENTS:	**Alison Hargreaves** (1963-1995), world record-breaking mountaineer. **Dame Ellen MacArthur** (b.1976), world record-breaking yachtswoman.

Whatstandwell Pub: The Derwent Arms

The Derwent Hotel is located on the eastern side of the bridge that takes the A6 over the River Derwent at Whatstandwell. The inn actually gets a mention in D. H. Lawrence's classic 1913 novel *Sons and Lovers* where it states: *"They went on, miles and miles, to Whatstandwell. All the food was eaten, everybody was hungry, and there was very little money to get home with. But they managed to procure a loaf and a currant-loaf, which they hacked to pieces with shut-knives, and ate sitting on the wall near the bridge, watching the bright Derwent rushing by, and the brakes from Matlock pulling up at the inn."*

The Derwent Hotel, Whatstandwell.

Whatstandwell Church: Methodist Chapels

Whatstandwell doesn't have a church of its own, and so the nearest parish church is St Mary's at Crich. However, it does have two former 19th century chapels. The first one appears on your left-hand side as you drive up the steep Hindersitch Lane, while the other – a former Methodist chapel – sits higher up the hillside on Top Lane.

Whatstandwell Historic Trivia: Walter's Bridge

Whatstandwell was named after Wat or Walter Stonewell, who "held of the convent" the house next to the ford, and later the bridge that John de Strepul built in 1393. This seems a more likely origin than the one offered by both of my late Grandads – both of whom were coincidentally called Walter – who believed that "Whatstandwell!" was the proud exclamation issued by the chief engineer on completion of the bridge over the River Derwent there! The bridge meant that the place was later referred to as Hottstandell Bridge on a 1791 map, although this was probably a literal spelling of the local dialect – as it appears as Whatstandwell Bridge on a mid-19th century Ordnance Survey map, this also being the name given to the railway station in the same century. As for the bridge today, it now carries heavy traffic on the A6 over the Derwent, while it also forms part of the second tier of an impressive parallel align-ment of river, road, railway and canal (in that order) up the eastern side of the Derwent valley.

Whatstandwell Quirk Alert: Modern Heroines

The following fact is not so much quirky as extraordinary, since the tiny village of Whatstandwell was home to not one, but two of Britain's greatest modern heroines. The most famous of the pair is record-breaking yachtswoman Dame Ellen MacArthur who was brought up in

The old chapel on Hindersitch Lane.

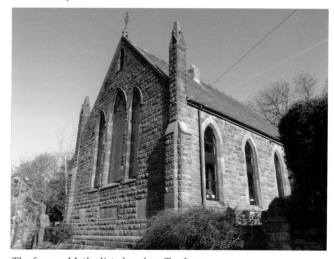

The former Methodist chapel on Top Lane.

Whatstandwell Station.

Whatstandwell – the much press-proclaimed irony being that the village is completely land-locked. Nevertheless, Ellen learned to sail at nearby Ogston Reservoir before embarking on a stunning career that has seen her become one of the greatest British sailors of all time. Her first world record came in June 2000, when she sailed the mono-hull *Kingfisher* from Plymouth, to Rhode Island in 14 days, 23 hours and 11 minutes and this remains the current record for a single-handed mono-hull, east-to-west Atlantic passage, and also the single-handed record for a woman in any vessel. However, Ellen first came to national and world prominence in 2001 when she came second in the Vendee Globe solo round-the-world sailing race in *Kingfisher*, and which is still the world record for a single-handed, non-stop, mono-hull circumnavigation by a woman. Then in June 2004, she sailed her trimaran from Lower New York Bay, to Lizard Point, Cornwall in 7 days, 3 hours, 50 minutes, setting a new world record for a transatlantic crossing by a woman. February 2005 then saw her greatest achievement when she became the fastest person ever to sail around the world single-handed, her 71 day effort beating the previous record by over a day. The next day, on 8th February, it was announced that she was to be appointed Dame Commander of the Order of the British Empire in recognition of her achievement, which at twenty-eight years old makes her the youngest ever recipient of this honour. Furthermore, this immediate recognition, rather than waiting for the New Year's or Birthday honours lists, was reminiscent of the knighthoods conferred upon Francis Drake and Francis Chichester upon arrival home after their respective circumnavigations in 1580 and 1967. Dame Ellen was also made an honorary Lieutenant Commander of the Royal Naval Reserve on the same day, while in France, where she is hailed as a heroine, she was awarded the French Légion d'Honneur by Nicolas Sarkozy in March 2008.

This bridge at Whatstandwell is the ultimate successor to the one built for Walter Stonewell in 1393 and after whom Whatstandwell is named.

Also hailing from Whatstandwell (but born in Mickleover) was Alison Hargreaves. Considered by many to be the finest woman alpinist in history, her achievements were considerable, having climbed solo up all of the great north faces of the Alps in a single season – a first for any climber. However, her greatest achievement came in May 1995 when she reached the summit of Mount Everest without the help of any Sherpas or bottled oxygen and, even more remarkably, having done so via the mountain's notorious north ridge from Tibet. Alas, it had been the first of a three summit challenge to climb Everest, K2 and Kanchenjunga, and it was the second of this trio of the world's highest mountains that was to claim her life, three months later. Along with three Spaniards, an American and a New Zealander, Alison reached the summit of K2 on 13th August. Tragically, the weather turned soon after they commenced their descent and all of them died in a violent storm. The next day, two Spanish climbers who had remained at Camp 4 were descending towards Camp 3 when they found blood-stained equipment belonging to Alison, as well as spotting a body in the distance. Suffering themselves from frostbite and exhaustion, they did not approach the body, so it was not positively identified, but they had little doubt that it was the extraordinary lady from Whatstandwell.

NAME (STATUS):	**WHITWELL** (Village)
POPULATION:	3,969
DISTRICT:	Bolsover
EARLIEST RECORD:	*Hwitewylle*, c.1002; *Witewelle*, 1086 *(Domesday Book)*
MEANING:	Place at the white spring, perhaps referring to clear or untainted water
DERIVATION:	From the Old English words *hwīt* (white) and *wella* (spring or stream)
FAMOUS RESIDENTS:	**Joe Davis** (1901-1978) multiple World Billiards and World Snooker Champion. **Les Jackson** (1921-2007), Derbyshire and England cricketer. **Chris Adams** (b.1970), Derbyshire and England cricketer. **Ian Bennett** (b.1971), footballer.

Whitwell Pub: The Boot and Shoe

Although by no means a large village, Whitwell actually possesses *six* public houses! That said, it once had as many as 11 meaning that, at that time, it held the record for most number of licensed premises per capita. Maybe the number of pubs has something to do with the number of top sportsmen this village has produced over the last 100 years or so (*see Historic Trivia*); there's certainly a chance that they all supped a pint at The Boot and Shoe some time, anyway!

Whitwell Church: St Lawrence's

St Lawrence's church at Whitwell is one of very few in Derbyshire that has a surviving Norman tower, while it also has a Norman nave, west doorway, clerestory and chancel arch. However, the rest of the chancel and transepts were redesigned in the first half of the 14th century when their windows were provided with geometrical tracery while the upper storey of the tower and bell chamber were added at around this time, too. Interestingly, the surviving Norman tower was rebuilt using some Anglo-Saxon stone, thereby hinting at an older, predecessor church; the font is also older than the church, being either Saxon or early Norman.

Whitwell Historic Trivia: Ancient Oak, Ancient Chapel and World-Class Sportsmen

The Anglo-Saxon Chronicle of 942, when outlining Derbyshire's boundaries, refers to the area between Whitwell Gap and the Old Shire Oak, where the latter is an ancient tree that marked the boundary between Derbyshire, Nottinghamshire and Yorkshire, some 4 miles to the north-east of the village. Meanwhile, nearby and still in the Whitwell parish is Steetley Chapel. The building is easily Derbyshire's best-preserved Norman chapel and it is home to the only Norman apse to survive in the county; indeed it is also one of England's finest small Norman churches, too. The style is mid-12th century, but not only is its dedication unknown, but its builders are uncertain too; it dates from Norman times but it is thought that the chisel work is very Saxon-orientated while the window balusters are also distinctly Saxon in style as is the pilaster work of the

St Lawrence's church, Whitwell, including its Norman tower and doorway.

apse exterior. Steetley itself is a deserted medieval village and the chapel stands alone in this far-flung corner of Derbyshire. It gradually became a ruin, but the chapel was painstakingly restored between 1876 and 1880 by the ecclesiastical architect, J. L. Pearson, who built a new roof and bellcote, plus an extravagant portal above the carved doorway to the nave.

Given the local geology, the inevitable Whitwell Colliery was sunk on Belph Moor in 1890 and was initially mined using the "hand-got" stall system. The Top Hard Seam provided the main source of supply for the first forty years but was exhausted by 1942, having produced nearly 4 million tons of coal between 1930 and 1942. The High Hazel Seam was worked from 1935 to 1976 while the Two Foot Seam was the last seam worked before the pit was closed in 1986 – by which stage it was making annual losses, with coal production allegedly costing £69 per ton against a selling price of £42.

Finally, the late, great Joe Davis was born on Welbeck Street, Whitwell, in 1901. Acknowledged as the greatest player of his era, Davis won ten World Billiards Championships as well as every snooker world title too. Meanwhile, his younger brother, Fred Davis, won eight World Snooker Championships between 1948 and 1956 and, perhaps more astonishingly, two World Billiard

Championships as well – astonishing as this occurred in 1980 and 1981 when aged sixty-six and sixty-seven, respectively. Sticking with Whitwellian sportsmen, Les Jackson played for Derbyshire between 1947 and 1963, and it was widely acknowledged that he should have won more than his meagre two England caps. Even stranger, is that those two test matches took place in 1949 and 1961 – the longest gap between tests of any English player with only two caps. More recently, Chris Adams is yet another Derbyshire cricketer not given the England recognition he richly deserved, winning only five caps. An aggressive right-handed batsman and occasional right-arm off-spin bowler, he played for Derbyshire between 1988 and 1997. He was also one of the greatest fielders of all-time, and certainly took the greatest catch that I've ever seen, at Chesterfield in a 1992 Sunday League game against Kent. He was sprinting towards the boundary, running straight towards me and my Grandad, with his back to the hoisted ball, and as it looped downwards over his head, he timed his look up to perfection and dived full length, pouching the ball without a fumble followed by a full length slide along the ground finishing just short of the boundary rope. In the same game, he had already hit an astonishing 141 not out, including 10 monstrous sixes, one of which I remember being caught by Devon Malcolm on the top tier of the pavilion! Adams later left Derbyshire for Sussex in 1997 where, as captain, he guided them to the County Championship titles in 2003, 2006 and 2007 – a quite astonishing feat. He was also one of five Wisden Cricketers of the Year in 2004, a feat matched by Les Jackson, in 1959.

Whitwell Quirk Alert: Naked Gremlins

Between 1969 and 1974, Whitwell Colliery was the location of the "Whitwell Phenomenon" known locally as "The Gremlins", whereby the conveyors would stop

The memorial cross, Whitwell, with the Boot and Shoe behind.

working for no obvious reason. First the high tension conveyor would stop, followed by the trunk conveyors, and all had to be restarted on manual control. Despite visits from senior engineers, managers, directors and maintenance men, no explanation was ever found – even though The Gremlins always seemed to take place on the day shift, beginning at 6.45 am, and seemed to disappear at around 12:45.

Finally, here is a tale from the writings of a certain Mr Forrest in 1755. He talks of having heard about the Naked Boys in Staveley one day, having just missed their 3-mile race. Surprised at the great crowds, the intense excitement and the fact that *"the earth was encrusted with thin ice and the northerly wind cut to the marrow"*, he is intrigued to hear that a similar race is to be run at Whitwell the following day. *"I made haste to arrive at the village…People came from as far afield as Sheffield, Derby, Mansfield, Chesterfield and Worksop. I was told the village of Whitwell has a population of some 700 souls, but here was another thousand added to the total. Six boys were taking part today, and I learned the same lad was running here, who had won on the previous day…his name was Flaxey Rotherham, a native of Whitwell. It had been freezing overnight, but no one paid the slightest attention to the freezing weather. At length, the contestants came into line, and a finer set of lads I had never before beheld. Their nakedness did not seem to embarrass in any way the many womenfolk, who were almost as numerous as the men; in fact they cheered as heartily as any of us. Flaxey went on to win the race, six strides ahead of his nearest rival and was paraded shoulder-high round the village."*

Six strides indeed!

Steetley Chapel is located at the north-eastern tip of Whitwell parish and is one of England's finest small Norman churches.

Threes-Up!

	WIGLEY	WOODSIDE (*2)	WOODVILLE
STATUS:	Hamlet	Hamlet (*2)	Village
POPULATION:	c.30	c.50	3,420
DISTRICT:	North East Derbyshire	Amber Valley/Bolsover	South Derbyshire
EARLIEST RECORD:	*Wiggelay*, 13th century	N/A	*Wooden-Box*, pre-1845
MEANING:	Wicga's woodland clearing	Place by the side of the wood	Place at the wooden toll booth
DERIVATION:	From the Old English personal name, *Wicga*, and the Old English word *lēah* (woodland clearing)	From the Old English words wudu (wood) and *sīde* (hill-side or land alongside a river or wood)	Named after the wooden toll booth on the toll road from Ashby-de-la-Zouch to Burton-upon-Trent

Threes Up Trivia!

Wigley is home to a pub called The Fox & Goose Inn which was built in the 15th century at the top of the westerly climb out of Chesterfield on what is the old London to Manchester road. It was used as a regular meeting place for the monks of Beauchief Abbey in the 15th century and it was the monks who also gave the pub its name, since Fox and Goose was the name of a board game that they played. Meanwhile, the hill upon which the inn was built is called Pudding Pie Hill since for several hundred years, local farmers spread burnt limestone on the farmland to add calcium to aid plant growth on the higher ground. This resulted in the hill emitting constant plumes of smoke and vapour, thereby giving the appearance of a giant steamed pudding! Of course, The Fox & Goose Inn today offers Authentic Pudding Pies for dessert – which, like its more famous neighbour, the Bakewell Pudding, is made with a secret recipe! Meanwhile, a former landlord was Len Badger, a legendary Sheffield United full-back who made 457 appearances for the club before finishing his career at nearby Chesterfield.

There are two hamlets called **Woodside** in Derbyshire. A signpost at Horsley Woodhouse directs you southwards down Wood Lane towards the Sitwell Arms and ultimately the settlement at the bottom of Cloves Hill (*above centre*), where the road is also known as Woodside. The other Woodside is in the north-east of the county, and lies on a similar latitude to Wigley but the other side of Chesterfield.

Meanwhile, **Woodville** is a village and civil parish in South Derbyshire. In the 19th century, the fireclay deposits in the area proved an ideal raw material for the manufacture of sanitary wares and salt-glazed drainpipes in coal-fired kilns. The arrival of the railways saw Woodville become a major centre for the industry between 1875 and 1914, which was complemented by the village's acclaimed Bretby Art Pottery founded in 1882. Today, a large community of houses is being developed to the south of Woodville on the former site of Woodville Pipe Works and incorporates the planting of new trees on this former fire clay pit as part of the National Forest scheme. As for the place-name, Woodville is actually quite modern, dating from 1845. Up until then, it had been known as *Wooden-Box*, named after the wooden toll booth on the toll road there, but as the population around it expanded, it eventually became known as Woodville. That said, the area where the toll booth stood, is today represented by a busy roundabout, known as Tollgate, while Box House (founded 1881) and Box Close can be found either side of Tollgate as a reminder of its former resident.

Fox & Goose Inn on Pudding Pie Hill, Wigley.

Wigley Primary School and the view towards Chesterfield.

The Nelson Inn, Woodville.

NAME & STATUS:	**WOOLLEY** (Submerged Village);
	WOOLLEY MOOR (Replacement Village)
POPULATION:	c.200
DISTRICT:	North East Derbyshire
FIRST RECORDED:	Unknown
MEANING:	Wood or clearing frequented by wolves
DERIVATION	From the Old English words *wulf* (wolf) and *lēah* (wood, woodland clearing or glade)

Woolley Pub: The White Horse

The White Horse is located in Woolley Moor on Badger Lane (see *Quirk Alert* for more) and is now Woolley Moor's only pub since the demise of The New Napoleon. The latter was also the successor to Napoleon's Home – which went to a watery grave in 1958 (see *Historic Trivia*).

Woolley Church: St Mark's

St Mark's church (*above left*) is located between Woolley Moor and the hamlet of Handley, and at the top of the appropriately named Temperance Hill. The church building used to be the local village school and it still holds "grape and wafer" services with the children and parents of the local Church of England primary school.

Woolley Historic Trivia: Elevation and Inundation

Alas, little remains of the village of Woolley today, since most of it was submerged during the construction of Ogston Reservoir in 1958, including the Woolley House Hydro, the village store, the blacksmiths, the joiners, the laundry, the sheep-dip and the local pub that was known as Napoleon's Home. Also submerged was extensive farmland, roads and part of the Ashover Light Railway. As for Woolley itself, the only exceptions to the submerging were a couple of now-isolated houses further up the hillside and Woolley Methodist chapel which was recently beautifully restored (*above right*). However, the villagers of Woolley were relocated into council houses built in another elevated hamlet a mile or so to the north of the reservoir. Over time, the community became known as the village of Woolley on the Moor, before completing its transformation into the Woolley Moor of today. Of course, without the drowning of Woolley and the creation of Ogston Reservoir, Derbyshire may not have been home to Britain's most famous yachtswoman, as the reservoir is where Dame Ellen MacArthur quite literally learned the ropes.

Woolley Quirk Alert: Badgers and Wolves

When the inhabitants of Woolley were relocated to the hamlet further up the hillside to the north, that hamlet was known as Badger Lane – named after the road that ran through the hamlet. Of course, given the lupine origin of Woolley, one wonders if the wolves of Woolley used to prey on the poor badgers of Badger Lane!

The part of Ogston Reservoir under which the former village of Woolley was submerged in 1958.

NAME (STATUS):	**WYE** (River)
DISTRICT:	High Peak, Derbyshire Dales, South Derbyshire
MEANING:	Wye is an ancient pre-English river-name of unknown origin and meaning

River Wye Geographic and Historic Trivia

The River Wye rises just west of Buxton on Axe Edge Moor but then disappears underground before re-emerging in Poole's Cavern. This two-million-year-old, natural limestone cave was named after an outlaw who allegedly used the cave as a base from which to rob 15th century travellers. The Wye then flows out of the cavern and into the town centre of Buxton via the Pavilion Gardens. That said, the river is little more than a stream at this point – an unusual state of affairs for a river passing through an important town, you might think, but more logical when you consider that Buxton is England's highest town standing at over 1,000 feet. Nevertheless, the Wye's insignificance at this point also explains why the 5th Duke of Devonshire culverted the river to pass beneath his famous Crescent that he built in the 1780s, while more recently it was culverted again to pass beneath the Spring Gardens shopping centre, too. Emerging eastwards from Buxton, the Wye begins to swell into a sizeable river as it flows through a series of spectacular gorges, such as Ashwood Dale, Wye Dale and Cheedale. After flowing through the village of Millers Dale, the Wye passes the historic mills of Litton Mill and Cressbrook Mill before turning south-eastwards at Cressbrook. From here it enters the stunning Monsal Dale where the valley widens out, and which is dominated by the spectacular 19th century viaduct that emerges from Monsal Head and which was once part of the London to Manchester route. The line was opened in

1863 to widespread criticism from those who felt it destroyed the beauty of the Wye valley. Ironically today, it is seen as an object of great beauty, and in 2006, it was voted one of the Seven Man-Made Wonders of the East Midlands.

A mile or so to the south of Monsal Dale, the Wye flows under the ancient Sheepwash Bridge at pictur-esque Ashford-in-the-Water. Originally a medieval packhorse bridge, the structure got its name as a result of farmers placing the lambs in pens on one side of the river here, and then deliberately placing the ewes at the other side. Maternal instinct would then take over and the ewes would swim across the river to get to their offspring, thus giving their fleeces a good clean prior to shearing. From Ashford, the Wye then flows south-east-wards and into the town of Bakewell, first passing under another packhorse bridge known as Holme Bridge and then under its famous 13th century, five-arched bridge. We've already covered the latter on pages 22, 63 and 64, but the former was built in 1664 to connect Holme Hall with the road from Bakewell to Buxton. The bridge was only wide enough for horses and pedestrians, but crossing the river here also had the advantage of not having to pay tolls on the other, older bridge, further south, and which later became part of the turnpike route from Bakewell to Chesterfield. It was also just up the river from Holme Bridge that Sir Richard Arkwright built his third water-powered cotton-spinning mill, Lumford Mill, in 1777. Never far

The Wye flows down through Upperdale (also shown top left) and then turns west to pass through the spectacular viaduct at Monsal Dale.

The Wye then cuts through Monsal Dale and around the base of Fin Cop.

away from controversy, when Arkwright built the mill he deprived Bakewell's ancient corn mill of its water supply, although a solution was eventually reached after a long dispute.

After Bakewell, the Wye flows through a broad valley, passing Haddon Hall and the mouth of the River Lathkill, before it finally joins the River Derwent at Rowsley.

Understandably, the main attraction of the River Wye is tourism, and the beauty of the countryside through which it flows, draws in thousands of walkers, cyclists and tourists every year. It is possible to walk alongside the majority of the river, with the most popular part being along the Monsal Trail which follows the former Bakewell to Buxton railway including spectacular features such as the viaduct over Monsal Dale at Monsal Head. This was also the structure that so enraged John Ruskin when it was built in the 19th century, and prompted his famous rant: *"There was a rocky valley between Buxton and Bakewell, once upon a time, divine as the Vale of Tempe... You Enterprised a Railroad through the valley – you blasted its rocks away, heaped thousands of tons of shale into its lovely stream. The valley is gone, and the Gods with it; and now, every fool in Buxton can be in Bakewell in half an hour, and every fool in Bakewell at Buxton; which you think a lucrative process of exchange – you Fools everywhere"*. It is somewhat ironic, therefore, that the Monsal Viaduct is so iconic today, and pulls in so many tourists, particularly at Monsal Head with its spectacular views over the dale.

From a naturalistic perspective, the Wye is a limestone river, and its alkalinity provides a rich source of nutrients that leads to an abundance of insects, invertebrates and thus fish, making it very popular with anglers. Meanwhile, historically, the Wye divided the Neolithic people of Derbyshire into those who worshipped at either Arbor Low, or at the Bull Ring at Dove Holes. Centuries later, and the limestone plateaux on either side of the Wye contributed to the district's wealth courtesy of lead mining, while 17th to 19th century soughs drained lead mines of water and emptied their contents into the river. Throughout the same period, the southern-most end of the Wye was home to an important mill – initially a corn and fulling mill during the

The Wye in Monsal Dale.

reign of Elizabeth I. But then in 1874, John Caudwell took a lease from the Duke of Rutland and built a large mill to grind flour and animal feed and which was powered by two water wheels – but which were replaced in late 1880s by a water turbine while roller mills replaced the millstones. The mill eventually closed in 1978, but was soon re-opened and operated by the Caudwell's Mill Trust as the only complete Victorian roller mill powered by a water turbine in the country.

The Wye at Bakewell looking towards the 13th century bridge.

Caudwell's Mill at Rowsley. The Wye flows into the River Derwent a few yards downstream of here.

The famous Sheepwash Bridge at Ashford-in-the-Water.

NAME (STATUS):	**YOULGREAVE/YOULGRAVE** (Village)
POPULATION:	1,165
DISTRICT:	Derbyshire Dales
EARLIEST RECORD:	*Giolgrave*, 1086 *(Domesday Book)*; *Hyolegrave*, 1208; *Yolegrave*, 1259; *Yolgreue*, 1285
MEANING:	Place at the yellow grove or pit
DERIVATION:	From the Old English words *geolu* (yellow), and either *græf* (pit or trench) or *græfe* (grove or copse)

Youlgreave Pub: The Bulls Head Hotel

The Bulls Head Hotel is an old coaching inn that dates from 1675 and which today, is Grade II listed. The building sits opposite Fountain Square in the centre of Youlgreave, and shares the village with The George Hotel to the east and The Farmyard Inn to the west.

Youlgreave Church: All Saints

All Saints' church owns a rather striking 15th century tower with stepped buttresses rising to an embattled parapet; indeed, with its eight crocketed pinnacles and its twin-belfry windows, it is one of the finest churches in Derbyshire and the second largest in the Peak District. Many parts of the church date back to Norman times, including the fine south arcade of three bays with its 12th century pillars,

Youlgreave's unused 12th century Norman font.

capitals and round Norman arches. The church also has a very unusual 12th century font that originated from All Saints' church at Elton. Alas when the latter's steeple was destroyed in 1805 due to weakened foundations its priceless Norman font was cast out into the church garden during the building of the replacement steeple. Twenty years later, it found its way into the vicarage grounds at Youlgreave, where a wise old vicar recognised its value and installed it as the official Youlgreave font. When the folk of Elton realised their mistake, their squire requested its return but to no avail; instead, Elton had to make do with a replica. The font's strange design includes an additional small stoup fashioned out of the same block of stone – perhaps meant as a holy water receptacle – and which appears to be held in the mouth of a dragon or a salamander which is carved upside-down on the bowl of the font. Equally unusual are its central column and four stone shafts which make it resemble some kind of silicon-based creature!

Youlgreave Historic Trivia: Fountains and Fatalities

In tandem with so many other Derbyshire villages in the Peak District, the population of Youlgreave rose by 123% between 1563 and 1670, thanks to the growth of

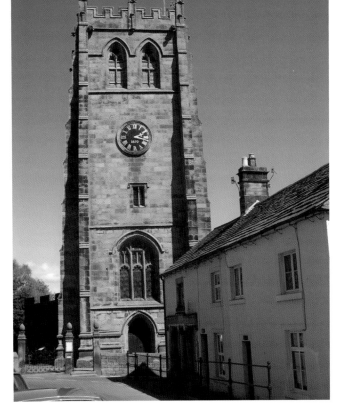

Youlgreave All Saints, one of the finest churches in Derbyshire.

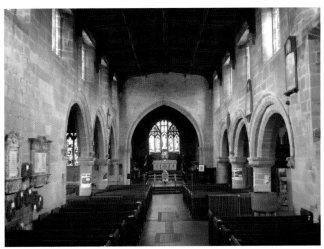

The nave of Youlgreave All Saints' including the south arcades (to the right) which are late Norman.

the lead mining industry. Conversely, when the industry declined in the 19th century, the censuses of 1841 and 1901 reveal a population fall from 1,230 to 1,077. That said, the local Mawstone Mine reopened after the First World War due to further demand, but closed in 1932 – which was also the year that an explosion killed five of the six miners working underground, while three of the rescue party also died of carbon-monoxide poisoning.

The 19th century also saw the creation of what is known as "Youlgreave Fountain". Located right in the centre of the village, the "fountain" is a gritstone conduit head storing water piped from a spring across the valley and which was built to supply the village with water in 1829, initially at an annual charge of 6d. It was built following a campaign by the Friendly Society of Women, who demanded a cleaner, healthier and more efficient supply of water following the deaths of a number of children over the years through the drinking of contaminated water. At a given time every day, the "waterkeeper" would unlock the tap and allow water to be drawn into the waiting pails of the villagers. The arrival of piped water in 1829 also stimulated the commencement of well dressings in Youlgreave, a custom that had been suppressed in Derbyshire as a "Popish superstition" at the Reformation, but which took off again throughout the county in the early 19th century. Of course, the annual custom of designing pictures from petals and other vegetation into soft clay spread on boards still survives today, and five wells are dressed annually to a high standard on the Saturday nearest St John the Baptist's day, in June.

Youlgreave Quirk Alert: Thimble Hall

Youlgreave is also the location of the Grade II-listed Thimble Hall, thought to be the smallest hall in the country and possibly in the world. It is a "one up, one down" affair, with each room measuring 8ft 1in by 7ft 1in and connected by a ladder. Built in the 18th century, Thimble Hall is also in the *Guinness Book of Records* as the smallest detached house in the world – and yet *eight* people once lived in it at one time in the 19th century. Throughout its life, it has also been a butcher's, a cobbler's and an antique shop, but was last used as a home in the 1930s. After that, Thimble Hall fell into a state of disrepair, eventually being classified as a "building at risk", in 1996 before being put up for sale in 1999 with a suggested guide price of £5,000 to £15,000. Astonishingly, though – and surely testimony to its quirkiness – Thimble Hall sold for £39,500, which basically made its price per square foot comparable with properties in Mayfair and Knightsbridge. Psychic Uri Geller was among the bidders, while others came in from as far afield as Athens, Hong Kong and New York. However, all were outbid by the Chesterfield ice-cream company, Fredericks – a firm who have a startling history of their own, having been set up by an Italian who in 1875 came to seek his fortune in England by walking the 1,000 miles from Parma to Sheffield!

A final piece of quirky trivia for Youlgreave is that the village is also home to the oldest newlyweds in the county, they being Eric Roome (ninety-five) and Sheila Mather (ninety) who married in October 2009. They tied the knot in style too, doing so at the splendid Hassop Hall that is located 3 miles north of Bakewell!

Youlgreave Fountain, founded in 1829 to supply the village with piped spring water.

Youlgreave cottages.

Thimble Hall, the smallest "hall" in the country.

Bibliography

The Arkwright Society, *Cromford Mills Guide* (Arkwright Mills Society, 2011)

Bryan Cleary, *Haddon Hall* (Heritage House Group, 2009)

Crich Tramway Museum, *Crich Tramway Museum* (Crich Tramway Museum, 2012)

Dennis Eardley, *Villages of the Peak District* (Amberley, 2009)

David Fearnehough, *Derbyshire Extremes* (Amberley, 2010)

Mark Girouard, *Hardwick Hall* (National Trust, 2009)

English Heritage, *Bolsover Castle* (English Heritage, 2000)

David Hey, *Derbyshire: a history* (Carnegie, 2008)

Simon Kirwan, *Beautiful Peak District* (Myriad, 2010)

Arthur Mee, *The King's England: Derbyshire* (Hodder & Stoughton, 1937)

Arthur Mee, *The King's England: Arthur Mee's Derbyshire* (King's England Press, 1990)

A.D. Mills, *Oxford Dictionary of British Place Names* (Oxford University Press, 1991)

Gerald Mortimer, *Derby County: The Complete Record* (Breedon Books, 2006)

Anthony Poulton-Smith, *Derbyshire Place-Names* (Sutton, 2005)

Richard Stone, *Exploring History in and around Derbyshire* (Breedon Books, 2009)